TEACHER-RESEARCHERS AT WORK

MARION S. MACLEAN   ◆   MARIAN M. MOHR

THE NATIONAL WRITING PROJECT

BERKELEY, CALIFORNIA

1999

Please direct reprinting requests and book orders to:

National Writing Project
2105 Bancroft Way #1042
Berkeley, CA 94720-1042

Telephone 510-642-0963
Fax 510-642-4545

Design and Layout: Paul Molinelli
Cover Design: William Peterson
Cover photo: Elizabeth Crews
Editor: Art Peterson

Library of Congress Cataloging-in-Publication Data

MacLean, Marion S.
    Teacher-researchers at work / by marion s. macLean adn marian m. Mohr.
        p. cm.
    Rev. ed. of: working together / marian m. Mohr. c1987.
    Includes bibliographical references (p.) and index.
    ISBN 1-883920-14-0
    1. Action research in education. 2. Teachers. 3. Cooperation. 4. Group work in
education. I. Mohr, Marian M. II. Mohr, Marian M. Working together. III. National
Writing Project (U.S.) IV. Title.

LB1028.24 .M64 1999
370'.7'2--dc21
                                                        99-051530

TEACHER-RESEARCHERS AT WORK

Acknowledgments

We gratefully acknowledge our teacher-researcher colleagues who generously contributed to this book by allowing us to use their research, log writings, data, and reflections on their research processes.

Randi Adleberg
Sally Bryan
Peg Culley
Pam Curtis
Barbara Falcone
Julie Fisher
Sharon Gerow
Bernadette Glaze
Leslie Gray
Roger Green
Alberta Grossman
Lisa Gruenhagen
Judy Grumbacher
Carin Hauser
Bob Ingalls
Gloria Johnson
Rita Johnson
Martha Kestermeier
Doina Le Compte
Shannon McClain
Theresa Manchey
Honora Mara
Jan Milkovich
Frances Nelson

Eve Newsome
Mary Ann Nocerino
Lisa Oram
Diane Painter
Carolyn Perry
Damali Pittman
Bill Plitt
Gretchen Portwood
Mary K. Prioletti
Courtney Rogers
Betsy Sanford
Valerie Sayre
Mary Schulman
Ann Sharp
Lynn Shafer
Lin McKay Spence
Sherry Tabachik
Tony Tendero
Trudy Todd
Elly Uehling
Veronica Washington
Patti Sue Williams
Anne Miller Wotring

Preface

This book had its beginning as *Working Together: A Guide for Teacher-Researchers*, first published in 1987 through the National Council of Teachers of English. Since 1980 we had been leading teacher-researcher seminars, sharing teachers' research articles with colleagues, and talking and writing about our work in various workshops and writing projects. Colleagues who were interested in setting up teacher research groups had suggested that we write about our experience with the teacher-researcher seminar.

We wrote *Working Together* — as we have this book — on weekends, in the evening, and during summer breaks from school. We wondered at the time if it was an "outline of a book that is not ready to be written." We did not want to have research processes reduced to products only, or to have the experiences of some teachers codified as a process that all should follow.

We had wanted to add our voices to the professional discourse, to remind our colleagues that teacher-researchers deserve a place in the educational community as people who make informed decisions based on their research about the conduct, content, and practice of the profession. We hoped that others would join us in a discussion of teacher research, and that has happened. Our colleagues' valuable work and our added experience were encouragements to us to accept the opportunity to reexamine and rethink — to write a revised edition.

OVERVIEW

In *Teacher-Researchers at Work* we describe what are for us the essential components of any teacher-researcher group, but we also describe an experience, a process, that we think aids a teacher-researcher in completing a study (Part I). We reexamine the issues and questions surrounding teacher research, as they have both shifted and steadied over the years (Part II).

A vital part of both the original book and this revision consists of research articles written by teacher-researchers (Part III). The articles we include — like the many references to our experiences — reflect our Northern Virginia background and context.

The last part of the book (Part IV) is full of resources that are now available to teacher-researchers, everything from e-mail addresses to worksheets to help you start and sustain a teacher research group.

We have added much new material to all parts of the book. The biggest change in the field of teacher research has been the increasing number of teachers worldwide who have recognized the opportunity teacher research gives them to understand their work and are contributing to the ideas and literature of their profession. Because of this expansion of the field, we have also needed to re-examine our assumptions, challenge our beliefs, and clarify our ideas — tasks that are as important in writing about teacher research as they are in a teacher research group.

We have repeatedly asked ourselves, "Who are we and why are we doing this?" and "What do we already think and why?" Our beliefs, assumptions, and ideas appear in statements throughout the book as well as in its organization and presentation. One of our assumptions, for example, is that teachers are thinkers and inquirers with knowledge about teaching and learning. Based on this assumption, we write and talk about questions we already have about teaching and learning at the initial gathering of a teacher research group. We don't "prepare" or "train" teachers to ask the "right" questions in the "right" way. Similarly, we begin this book with a chapter entitled "Choice and the Research Question: What do you want to know?"

Voice

The voice that speaks to you comes from two high school English teachers who have had varied careers and who care passionately about public school education. We speak colleague to colleague. Teacher-researcher to teacher-researcher. Our "you" addresses our readers, and most of the writing is in that voice. Our "they" speaks of teacher-researchers in general. Our "we" is our combined voice coming from our combined experience. We are not reporting on research, but are describing experience and practice.

Definition

The rather unwieldy term "teacher-researcher" is an important one to us. The combining of the two words and activities strikes some as unlikely, as if to do both, teachers must neglect one or the other. That is not the case. To understand the term it is necessary to look again at traditional ideas of both teaching and researching, for as teachers begin to think of themselves as researchers, they redefine their roles as teachers.

Traditionally teachers plan, prepare, and give lessons following an authorized curriculum; manage and motivate student behavior; grade students' work and evaluate their performance; and report to parents and administrators. They are considered subjective insiders involved in classroom interaction. Traditionally researchers develop questions and design studies around them; evaluate methodology and examine assumptions; collect, analyze, and interpret data; and report findings and implications to colleagues. They are considered objective outside observers of classroom interaction.

When teachers become teacher-researchers, the traditional descriptions of both teachers and researchers change. Teacher-researchers raise questions about what they think and observe about their teaching and their students' learning. They collect student work in order to evaluate performance, but they also see student work as data to analyze in order to examine the teaching and learning that produced it. To plan and prepare lessons for their students — lessons that address the needs assessed in their work — teacher-researchers also assess their own interpretations of the reasons for the students' performance.

They design a classroom curriculum that allows them to check out their interpretations with students. They monitor the behavior of their students, but they also write observations of that behavior to aid them in understanding what is happening. They discuss their research with their students and receive their students' helpful insights on teaching and learning. They use any of a variety of research methods to help uncover principles of teaching and to further students' understanding of what they are learning. They both teach and observe their teaching and their students' responses. As one teacher-researcher commented, "We are intending to struggle on the middle ground."

So what is teacher research? It is research conducted by teachers as they go about their daily work. It is enmeshed in the context of the classroom. It is designed so as not to expose students to harm in any way but rather to include them as participants in the process through which they and their teacher learn about learning. It offers students the model of an adult learner at work. It is an open inquiry, not a hidden agenda. It is based on teacher and student knowledge and thinking as a source of information.

So far our definition has stayed within the classroom, but a comprehensive definition of teacher research extends further. Teacher research is, for example, professional development that respects the knowledge and experience of the teachers involved. It is also a form of curriculum development, school planning and program evaluation, teacher preparation, and school reform. What connects these different definitions of teacher research is their reliance on knowledge generated in the classroom. It is this knowledge that gives substance and direction to those outside the classroom whose purpose is to support teaching and learning.

WORK

In one day of teaching it is possible to have many intense emotional and intellectual exchanges with students, to experience a wider range of thought and emotion than people outside the profession can imagine, and yet to feel separate and isolated with little control over the factors that make the work so demanding. The needs for learning and for emotional support that teachers respond to daily, needs of up to 150 young people, can also leave them shrinking from more human interaction. The emotional exhaustion and the need to pull away conflict directly with the corresponding need for more contact with colleagues for friendly support and professional discourse.

When teachers attempt to change their situation by working together to support each other and to improve their teaching, that in itself is a remarkable effort. Teacher-researchers go a step further. They assume the professional responsibility of documenting, analyzing, and writing about their work for other teachers. They extend their days and broaden their commitment to other teachers, and they do this in order to improve their teaching and to inform their profession. We honor this effort by titling our revised edition: *Teacher-Researchers at Work*.

— ◆ —

Note on references and citations: Several of the articles we reference have not been published other than as "deadline drafts" in class or school booklets for in-house use only. Copies are sometimes available from the authors, but they are otherwise not published in books or professional journals. Their citations in our reference lists are different from the published works in that they include the name of a school or a writing project, but do not include a publisher or page numbers. The unpublished articles are referenced at the ends of chapters only. The articles in the bibliography at the end of the book are all available in journals or books.

PART I

A TEACHER RESEARCH PROCESS

Beginning

What do you need?

To begin teacher research you need a question, a place to record your thoughts, and some colleagues to work with you.

You need a question about how teaching and learning occur in your classroom. Usually the questions come from your curiosity about how things happen. Why do so many of my students fail this part of the course? Why was this lesson so successful? What can I do to motivate my students to learn? You develop your own question from your thinking about your work.

You need a research log — a place to keep the record of your search for answers. You may carry it around with you or keep it in your computer, but it is the place where you enter the inquiry. Your thoughts and observations — personal, emotional, reflective — are part of your research. You have expertise about your classroom. You are a participant in it along with your students, and you are its observer and evaluator as well.

You also need a colleague or two to work with you. As a teacher-researcher, you are part of a learning community, not a lone adult behind a closed classroom door. You need the support of colleagues as you look closely at your teaching. They ask questions about your observations and assist in validating your interpretations of your data. You, in turn, accept the responsibility of doing the same for them.

The following three chapters discuss each of these topics in depth, giving suggestions of various ways to gather together what you need and describing the experiences of other teacher-researchers as they began their research.

CHOICE AND THE RESEARCH QUESTION
What do you want to know?

The first and most essential decision you will make is whether or not to conduct research. Your decision should be voluntary. Looking closely at your own practice offers great rewards but places unusual demands even on willing participants. It is equally essential to choose freely the focus and shape of your investigations. Choice matters throughout your research study, but especially in determining your research question.

In some research situations, you might have limited choice or none at all about your question. An instructor in a research course might give you a specific topic to investigate. In a large study, researchers may be told which different pieces of a puzzle they will examine. But conducting research on your own teaching allows you to develop your questions from your own thinking about your work.

Your development of a question often requires writing, discussion, and time, a process that extends throughout your research project. Alberta Grossman's research log entry illustrates one teacher-researcher's early thinking about her choice of research question and her efforts to see her research as having enough value to pursue. In the following log entry, she sorts through the ideas of others in her field to understand where her ideas fit.

EXCERPT FROM THE RESEARCH LOG OF ALBERTA GROSSMAN,
HIGH SCHOOL TEACHER OF LEARNING DISABLED STUDENTS:

> *9/22 — My husband says [Ken Macrorie's] I-Search is a phony idea. I don't think so. What I want to know is — can I get students who can write adequately to write more adequately and/or to feel more competent when they are writing about information and ideas. (I suspect that information and ideas are not the same — that is, do not present the same writing problem.) Something happens to stop the words from coming out of the pen — under certain circumstances for some people — Like me, for instance, back in college, when I used to sit for hours unable to produce a single word —*

or when I would get down a few nice phrases and nothing else. The problem is — "nothing to say" — no thoughts about something because no experience (?) — or what — this doesn't seem to be going too far. Is it better to keep writing — producing junk — than to produce nothing at all?

The first thoughts about the thinking/writing connections came from my own experience at [college].

But little glimmers of light have been shed on the problem since last summer in the writing project.

Fact one: Bernie Glaze [another teacher-researcher] told how well her students did in non-essay responses to social studies topics and how relatively poorly they did on essay test responses.

Question: were her standards lower or different?

– Did good literary quality cover up lack of information or thought?
    (I, from my own experience, would say probably "yes.")

– Or was it possible to accept "inferred" information/ideas in non-essay type writing?

More glimmers of light from Peter Elbow — when ideas are conflicting or confusing, writing stops —

More from Bernie — I-search better than Research — papers more interesting, more coherent, more believable when students wrote about what they were interested in (knew about/already had questions about).

There is research in reading that shows that people who read actively (with a question) do better (learn more) than people who don't.

Britton says writing (good writing?) arises from the expressive need (?) (I need to look that up) so having something to say or ask is paramount.

This is begging the question (?)

What about Lunsford's student who would always say, "I'll do it the easy way" and then start with an I-centered story?

According to Piaget (and Bruner and others), all learning begins as I-centered and thing-centered (concrete).

Grossman knew the subject of her inquiry from the start — How can I get my students to write more competently about information and ideas? Like Grossman, you might focus on the same question throughout your study. But if you are uncertain at the beginning, think of your uncertainty as an invitation to take a broad look at teaching and learning in your classroom, to write frequently about what you see happening, and to notice your recurring interests — what intrigues you most. Talk with colleagues about your ideas. Take student work that puzzles or surprises you to read with your research group. Let them help you identify — or select — your areas of interest, which question you might start with, and how you can continue to find out what you want to know. Even when you focus on the same question throughout your study, a large part of the work within your research group is the refinement of the question over time — its boundaries, its complexity, and its significance for you.

Here are some general questions to help you focus your inquiry:

- What are you curious about in your classroom?
- What puzzles you about your students' learning?
- What seems most successful about your teaching?
- What problem would you like to solve in your classroom? In your teaching?
- What would you like to try differently in your teaching?
- What have you read about in the professional literature that strikes you as true and potentially workable?
- What have you read about in the professional literature that strikes you as arguable?
- What is a problem in your school about which you have some ideas?

When you have identified a subject to explore, try phrasing research questions in the following three ways:

> *What happens when…?*
> *How…?*
> *What is…?*

"What happens when…?" and *"How…?"* both suggest observation and description. When Mohr wanted to study her high school students'

revision of their writing, she asked, *"What happens when* my students revise their writing?"* Posed in this way, the question suggests observation and description of her students' revision practices over time — and in the context of her classroom, curriculum, and school. Asking *"How do high school students revise their writing?"* also requires description, but suggests a need for looking closely at the specific practices of individual students.

The *"What is...?"* question suggests reexamination — looking at definitions that already exist and challenging previous definitions. Mohr's question about her high school students' revision could be phrased, *"What is* revision?" This question probes theory. If you are doing your research with a group of "Learning Disabled" students, for instance, you need to ask what that term means — professionally, in your school, and to your students and their teachers.

Forming questions in this way isn't intended to be prescriptive, and some of the questions work better than others within a specific situation. You may ask "How?" and "Why?" in combination or ask only "What is?" Brainstorm and write down all the related questions you can.

As the school year continues and your questions take shape, explore the relationship between the questions and the methods you might use to answer them. Some questions suggest specific kinds of methods. Some may, for instance, lead you to an examination of a single student work as a beginning, while another calls for careful observations of a class. Treat questions that seem to demand "proof" with caution, as they suggest the need for experimental design. A question that started out as, "How can I prove that the way I teach phonics helps students learn to read?" would become "How does my teaching of phonics connect with my students' learning to read?" Keep your focus on what happens in your own classroom with your students and your work with them. Here are some ways to think about your emerging question:

- ◆ Are there links between any of your questions? Are there underlying issues that several of them address? Could you, therefore, really be wondering about...? Alberta Grossman's log writing helped her uncover her questions about teach-

ing writing as well as her questions about her students'
behavior. She eventually combined them in a case study
of one student and his year-long efforts to improve his
informational writing as well as her year-long efforts to
teach him.

- ◆ How would you answer your question right now — what
  are your assumptions? Doina LeCompte, a middle school
  teacher whose work is described below, knew that her teaching of vocabulary *worked*. It was through repeatedly asking
  herself, "What are my assumptions about how my teaching
  of vocabulary works and how my students are learning?"
  that she was able to discover the connections between her
  teaching and their learning.

- ◆ If your question suggests a need for a "control group," try
  restating the question. "Does giving students choice about
  their reading increase their motivation to read?" might become "What happens when I give my students choices about
  their reading?"

- ◆ If your question implies a value judgment, try restating the
  question. "How can I get my students to listen to each other
  better?" might become "What is 'listening' according to the
  students in my classroom?"

At her research group's first meeting, Doina LeCompte said firmly,
"I need to *know* this." She wanted to prove that her highly respected
methods of teaching vocabulary worked. She herself is a person for whom
English is a second language. To her, "Vocabulary is life!" In subsequent
weeks, as she continued to talk with her group, she reported, "We are
still looking for ways to enter the questions that obsess us." Her own
question began to change as she gathered her data and continued to
talk with her group. She described her vocabulary teaching as bound to
all her teaching methods, calling it "an oversized spider web" in which
she herself — "the weaver" — was trapped. Her rueful image helped
her revise her question from an initial focus on proving that a method
worked to a focus on student learning and eventually to a focus on how
the learning and the teaching intersected — a web indeed.

As you consider the questions that are important to you, you might wonder if your research is so specific to your own classroom context that no one else will be interested. Keep reminding yourself that classroom context is missing from a lot of published research. Think of the studies you have read, scrubbed clean of the myriad variables that make your life as a teacher so interesting, and accept the task of describing those variables for yourself and other teachers. It is precisely your own rich, context-specific description and analysis that your classroom research has to offer to the research community.

You might worry about whether someone has "already done" the research you hope to pursue. If this is your concern, remind yourself of the value your research has for you and your students. Because your teaching and your students' learning matter to you, the questions you raise are ones that matter. You are an inquiring professional with knowledge that you bring to bear on questions about teaching and learning. As Grossman and LeCompte did, trust the significance of your own experience, the meaning of your own questions and insights, and your students' and colleagues' challenges to your assumptions and interpretations.

Even if you choose a research question related to a school-wide issue — your school's test scores, for instance — your primary responsibility is to your students and yourself. This was the case with middle school teacher-researcher Rita Johnson, who was teaching a new subject in her science classroom — DNA. The topic had been added to her curriculum in response to statewide tests being given to students to measure their knowledge of science. She had just taken a course in DNA herself and was working from a new textbook. She set about designing a way for her students to learn about DNA using writing as they worked their way through the new textbook. Her decision to do the research and her choices of research question and methodology were her own. Her findings served not only her students but also became part of the knowledge base at her school.

Bob Ingalls, a high school English department chair, along with his department, developed a study that had school-wide implications. They designed and conducted a four-year longitudinal study to document what happened to students' writing during their four years of high school

English. He wrote, "Living with a question can be hard, but it's easier than living with someone else's answers." He took the department's plan to the principal and other department chairs and garnered support for the research by having the study become part of the school's improvement plan. The research became a rich source of information for his department as well as a staff development opportunity. One of Ingalls's articles about conducting the study appears in "Part III: Teacher-Researchers' Articles."

Ingalls and Johnson both initiated their studies from questions they had about teaching and learning in their own classrooms and schools. Their independence in choosing their questions and their methods improved their chances of having an impact both in their own classrooms and in their schools.

Reworking your research question is a process that continues throughout your study as you make choices about your data and your teaching, as you voice your thinking, and as you listen to your students and research colleagues. Shifts may be radical or minute, but the process allows your data and your research questions to shape each other. The following excerpts from Mary Schulman's questioning process show the evolution beginning about halfway through her study as she restates her question. She knew she was working with her first grade students' writing and with her strong interest in how to confer with them about their writing. She also was interested in how they saw their writing in relation to the writing of the basal texts that were part of their instruction.

Research log entries from Mary Schulman:

12/7 — Maybe I need to ask the children these questions, look at the responses, and go from there. I may see something in the responses. I do still feel like I'm groping in the dark. I hope that's not abnormal for a researcher — especially at this stage of the game. I keep thinking I should know where I'm going, but I don't. I'm thinking I should have more data — I have my journal writings and writing samples — I'm going to go with the questions — then maybe some taping of conferences.

Why conferences?

Let's see — something impt. — I'm interested in the conference.

It's a valuable tool in helping children learn to write and to improve their writing.

But what facet would be worthwhile exploring?

Good question.

1/17 — I was driving home from school today and seemingly out of nowhere a question did occur. I wondered what would happen if a group of my second graders conferenced with a group of my first graders about their writing(s)? What kinds of questions will my second graders ask? Will my first graders revise their writings? Will their writing improve? How? Will the conferencing the second graders do with the first graders influence or affect how they conference with their own group? Will their conferencing techniques improve? Will their writing improve? What revisions will they make on their own writing(s)?

FROM AN EARLY DRAFT OF SCHULMAN'S RESEARCH ARTICLE:

When I began this study, I knew that I was interested in learning more about how beginning writers write and the actual use of conferences with beginning writers in the process of writing. This includes the types of questions I asked during the prewriting, composing, and rewriting stages of the writing process. My question became:

What types of conference responses or questions does a teacher make or ask beginning writers?

FROM SCHULMAN'S FINAL PAPER:

It was out of these questions and concerns that my research grew. My question became "What happens when young writers question and respond to the basal text?"

Schulman's final question at first seems unrelated to her earlier ones. But it was through her interest in the questions of the writing conference, both hers and those her students asked, that she was able to see a way not only to help her students manage their questions about the basals but also to keep her teaching and their understanding of writing theoretically consistent. In her conclusion she says of her students: "Responding to and questioning their own writing, each others' writing, and that of professional writers have developed their ability to make critical judgments."

As happened with Schulman, it is often not until the writing of the final report that we "know" what the question is we have been asking, even though we usually start with a basic question or area of concern. Classroom surprises, student performance, and spontaneous lesson changes often become turning points in the research, just as log writing, challenges to our assumptions, and data analysis become turning points in our teaching. When MacLean wrote in her research report, "I had not intended on that day in January to have my students comment on their own writing; we did, after all, have *Hamlet* to discuss," she described one of those spontaneous moments — well prepared for by months of thinking and deliberating — that became a turning point in her research on student evaluation of writing. Schools had closed early because of a snowstorm, and she read their comments that afternoon. As she read, she realized that she had just collected the data she needed to help her understand the relationships between their revision and their evaluation of their writing. Her question shifted from her earlier emphasis on her evaluation of their writing to her students' evaluation.

Because your questions and methods have to allow for these surprises and changes, the choice to conduct research needs to be yours. It is also important for you to be in control of your research in order to accept your own observing gaze. Looking closely at your teaching places you in a vulnerable position. The safety that makes such vulnerability productive comes, in large part, from the nonjudgmental, observing, and analytical stance that is crucial to this work — and from having that stance affirmed by other members of your research group.

Middle school English teacher Ann Sharp made the following comment as she was finishing the deadline draft of her research report:

> *You'll be glad to know that I finally framed a question: What happens when a teacher fragments an integrated program? You said no one was ever questionless, but I didn't believe you. And my question appeared in the final hour. The research fairy lives!*

Not all teacher-researchers admit to waiting so long for the questions to take shape, but we all begin with questions and end with questions for further study.

REFERENCES

Grossman, A. (1987). What happens when Mickey writes? Reading between the lines. In M. M. Mohr and M. S. MacLean, *Working together: A guide for teacher-researchers* (pp. 77-94). Urbana, IL: National Council of Teachers of English.

MacLean, M. S. (1983). Voices within: The audience speaks. *English Journal, 72* (7), 62-66.

Mohr, M. M. (1984). *Revision: The rhythm of meaning.* Westport, CT: Heinemann-Boynton/Cook.

Schulman, M. (1987). Reading for meaning: Trying to get past first basal. In M. M. Mohr and M. S. MacLean, *Working together: A guide for teacher-researchers* (pp. 111-120). Urbana, IL: National Council of Teachers of English.

Sharp, A. (1989). The importance of sandbags to hot air balloons and to teaching. *Language and learning: Reports from a teacher-researcher seminar.* Fairfax, VA: Northern Virginia Writing Project, George Mason University.

THE RESEARCH LOG
How do you record what you see and think?

As a teacher-researcher, you keep a research log. The physical log is, of course, not as important as what you put in it. One of MacLean's tenth grade students pointed out this distinction in referring to her reading log of J. D. Salinger's *The Catcher in the Rye*. MacLean was interviewing her in relation to research on reading and understanding literature. "It's not the log that's important. The log is just a basket you carry around with you to collect your thoughts. It's the thoughts that count."

What does seem to matter about the basket of choice is its convenience for use in and out of the classroom. Many teacher-researchers use spiral notebooks or speckled composition books; others write on notebook paper attached to clipboards or in tablets which they gather and eventually store in a loose-leaf binder. Some accumulate Post-its during the day and enter them in a notebook or computer later. If you have a computer close at hand, try keeping an electronic log, adding to it directly or from scraps of paper written elsewhere. It helps if your log, or some part of it, is portable enough to be carried in and out of the classroom, to meetings, and home. It should be inviting, not intimidating.

If you are accustomed to journal keeping or to writing informal notes about puzzling things that happen in your classroom, you'll find that your research log will be similar, but probably more systematic and organized. It will include dates and times, careful quoting, observations, and reflections; your entries will be field notes focused on a question that is emerging from your classroom experiences. Mohr keeps her log entries on the right-hand page of a composition book and leaves the left side for personal notes and outbursts, reminders, and ideas. She also numbers the pages and keeps track on the inside cover of the location of important ideas. You may find yourself using arrows, stars, sketches, diagrams, or any of a number of different connecting and organizing methods.

From the beginning of the research, teachers write, although there is great variety in how and where they do it. We describe the kind of writing we do in our logs as "think writing" after the work of our colleague, teacher-researcher Anne Wotring. Wotring enrolled in a high school chemistry course and did a study of herself and her fellow students writing as they learned about chemistry. Think writing is talking to yourself in writing, thinking as you write. The log entries of Mary Schulman and Alberta Grossman quoted in the previous chapter show the use of think writing to figure things out, raise questions, and pinpoint issues of concern.

Using the same strategies as Schulman and Grossman, Pam Curtis wrote the following log entry before the first meeting of her research group. She recorded her first thoughts and questions about a possible focus for her research.

> *9/22 — One thing I'd like to know is about parent involvement in the writing process. I have required my students to send papers through an adult (parent) editor for the past year, and I think it was of some benefit. I came up with the idea last Back-to-School night and I'm not sure whether I see a benefit because I'm defending an idea I liked or whether the adult editor really contributes something worthwhile to the writing process.*
>
> *How can I find out? What questions can I ask? How can I observe a parent responding to his or her offspring's paper? — go to their house? Ask them to come to school? Involve parents in the classroom process?*
>
> *Perhaps I'll find the whole requirement is counter-productive — so what.*
>
> *I've already sent out and gotten back parent questionnaires about their own involvement with & attitudes toward writing. Could I do something with those other than just tabulate them and forget it? What about the writing autobiographies my kids are doing?*
>
> *Typical scattered beginning!*

Teacher-researchers write in their logs as often as possible, but never as often as they might wish. Take advantage of any opportunity to write. Start looking for small portions of time to write in your log — between classes, during a few minutes of break, during a hall duty assignment, for a few minutes after school, or when announcements for the day come over the public address system. Even a few words can help you remember enough to write more fully later.

Also try to write about what is happening as you are teaching. When students are working together on group projects or at individual tasks, plan to observe and write down what you notice in your log. If you decide to ask the whole class a question about how they came up with a particular strategy, have your research log and pen in hand, writing down what they say as they comment. Keep your log dated and open on your desk and you will be able to grab it when you need it.

Often teacher-researchers meeting as a group start by taking some time to write about the teaching day and about their research. You may write about something that seems unrelated but is of immediate concern — the classroom you just left, a task that needs to be done, a promise you made, or other pressing matters on your mind. Your busy life and mixed attention, recorded in your log, become concrete documentation of the context of your work. By writing down even the interruptions, you'll free yourself to focus more fully and more reflectively on your research.

Log writings are data from your teaching life that you will take to your research group to read and discuss. It helps the group if you take copies for them to follow as you read.

To demonstrate different kinds of log entries, we provide below examples from English teacher Theresa Manchey's logs. She was conducting a study of the use of drawing to help her tenth grade students see concepts and read closely. She uses "blank books," many given to her as gifts, for most of her own classroom writing, but she also keeps notes in a computer log. Her finished article appears in Part III. Like Manchey's, your log will consist mostly of the following kinds of entries.

DESCRIPTIONS OF EVENTS AND INTERACTIONS THAT OCCUR IN THE CLASSROOM.

We worked with vocabulary cards 1st period. Kind of interesting. Most did find the drawings had helped them remember the words, a couple indicated it was because they did the drawing. "Someone else's drawing would not have helped."

BITS OF CONVERSATION, PHRASES OVERHEARD FROM STUDENTS OR OTHER PEOPLE AND JOTTED DOWN QUICKLY EITHER DURING OR AFTER CLASS.

In talking with one of our best English teachers about block scheduling, I found that she still really dislikes the idea. She told me she felt she got more accomplished in her single periods. She said the time she spent with those students was intense and productive while time spent with her other classes was often taken up with activities that were "nice" but really didn't mean anything — drawing and stuff like that. Can all that activity based "stuff" be just filler? Is nothing gained through drawing, charting, discussing, journaling?

* * *

V. [another English teacher who is also in the research group] came into the office about a week ago to tell me the drawings had some impact. She said she asked the kids in Honors 11 English what a hero is. One girl remembered the drawing they had done [last year] of a metaphor for the hero's journey. As she talked about it, V. said it was like a wave across the room, "Oh yeah. . ."

SURPRISES, PUZZLING THINGS THAT ARE UNEXPECTED OR CONFOUNDING.

[During a drawing session] *Student: How can we draw corruption without black?"*

* * *

I'm just baffled and puzzled by that article F. gave me where the guy claimed length of classes as the major predictor of student success. Doesn't what we do during that 90 minutes matter?

REFLECTIONS ON WHAT YOU SEE HAPPENING, SPECULATIVE WRITINGS, QUESTIONS, AND TENTATIVE HYPOTHESES ABOUT WHY CERTAIN THINGS MIGHT BE OCCURRING.

My latest and greatest questions:
  • *What happens when I ask kids to draw in response to their reading?*

- *Is drawing a relevant activity in English class?*
- *Will drawing help kids visualize what they read?*
- *How does time pass in English class?*
- *How can you tell when learning is taking place?*

Now I need to finish the interviews. For Friday: Ask 1 and 3 if they used their drawing for any of their projects on John Knowles's A Separate Peace. *The paper? The visual? It occurs to me tonight that I should perhaps have done the visual thing first. I'll ask them.*

PERIODIC DESCRIPTIONS OF YOUR ASSUMPTIONS AND PRECONCEPTIONS ABOUT YOUR QUESTION.

List of assumptions about my research question:
- *Many students find classrooms confining*
- *Sustained periods of time on task are better than fragmented periods of time on task*
- *There's no way to get every student to settle into a task immediately*
- *What I do in a classroom matters*
- *Worksheets are crap!*
- *Students need to be engaged to learn*
I still cannot believe it doesn't matter what we do in that 90 minutes.

THOUGHTS AND REACTIONS TO THE RESEARCH PROCESS ITSELF, TO WHAT YOU ARE NOTICING IN YOURSELF.

These days I'm really feeling the complexity of my task as teacher. One thing I'm hoping to gain from our [teacher research] seminar is the ability to bring some ORDER to this constant searching. I can accept the complexity, even kind of embrace it, but I just need ways to isolate and examine some parts of it.

* * *

Last night I felt pretty good about my research. Today I feel it's kind of lame. It will be interesting to know how this drawing thing works. But… will that get me any closer to the heart of my question: What activities really help kids learn and which are indeed "just filler"?

* * *

What I've learned about teacher research
- *Keep good logs*
- *Ask the right questions*
- *Organize your data*
- *Test findings and implications on lots of other people (and you're still insecure)*
- *Involve the kids*
- *Save everything*

TEACHING IDEAS THAT COME OUT OF YOUR RESEARCH AND DESCRIPTIONS OF WHAT HAPPENS WHEN YOU TRY OUT THE IDEAS.

I'm thinking tonight there are 2 things I want to get from A Separate Peace: *1. How symbols occur and function in a novel and 2. Vocabulary building. So here's what I think I'll ask them to do as they read — (1) Draw a picture or design to represent each chapter. (2)Write whatever kind of entry you've found helpful so far. (3) Make a list of unfamiliar words found with page numbers.*

* * *

Most people worked well today… J. wanted to know if we could see another movie. C. said the class seemed really short today. (Yea!!) The posters and stories aren't that great. I'm still looking for that one thing they'll want to put their best effort into…

Manchey's log entries cross over the classifications, of course, as will yours. The log entries are data from various sources; they are also part of the process of analysis. Throughout the rest of this book you will see references to many ways to use your log to further your research. It is central to your work, for, as Ann Berthoff reminds us, "Meanings don't just happen: we make them; we find and form them" (p. 69). The log is a place to record questions, observations, reflections; it is a place to think, plan, observe, reflect, read, reread, rethink, analyze, and, occasionally, celebrate.

REFERENCES

Berthoff, A. (1981). *The making of meaning.* Westport, CT: Heinemann-Boynton/Cook.

Curtis, P. (1982). What happens when tenth graders use an adult editor? *Research in writing: Reports from a teacher-researcher seminar.* Fairfax, VA: Northern Virginia Writing Project, George Mason University.

Wotring, A. and Tierney, R. (1981). *Two studies of writing in high school science.* Berkeley, CA: Bay Area Writing Project, University of California.

RESEARCH GROUPS
Who will support you? Who will work with you?

V alerie Sayre, an elementary music teacher, reflected on her research
group as the research process came to a close:

> *4/27 — This has been a true eye-opener into the world of re-
> search. I discovered quickly that I was not alone in my frustration,
> my feeling of total loss for a subject, my worries. It took me a while
> to feel at ease with my peers because I had to keep telling myself
> that, yes, these "strangers from another subject" were really my peers,
> and I had something to offer the group.*

Different disciplines, grade levels, and physical space separate teachers
from each other. Research groups cut across these distinctions and provide collegial balance to the individual work that occupies the teacher-
researcher in his or her classroom. Some teacher-researchers do conduct
research in isolation, but not usually by choice. Mutual support is important to both the researcher and the research.

The importance of groups in supporting teachers' research is clear
to us from our own experiences and also from the work of our colleague
Sharon Gerow, a teacher-researcher who has studied learning in small
groups for many years. Gerow began her research in 1984 as a middle
school social studies teacher. She formed her first research questions
around her interest in how small cooperative groups worked in her team-
taught English and social studies classes. Her interest in group work
persisted as she became the leader of the teacher-researcher group at her
school. She later entered a doctoral program, taught in a university
teacher research masters program, and conducted her dissertation research on teacher research groups. Gerow currently serves as chair of
the English department at a Virginia high school and continues to work
with the university teacher research program as well. You will find references to her research throughout this chapter as we describe the collaborative nature of teacher research.

A teacher research group typically consists of three to five teachers, at least one of whom has had experience in a research group and has conducted research in his or her own classroom. Your group may consist of teachers within your school or teachers from schools in the same geographic area. You might decide to meet because of a shared interest in examining one subject or issue (underachievement of "minority" students was the focus at Gerow's school) — or you might find several people who have different questions and interests. One of the teachers in Gerow's study noted:

> *I remember thinking that I didn't know if I could listen to my teammates' talk about their research. I was very sure it had nothing to do with me because we teach in different subjects and on different grade levels. The truth is, it had everything to do with me. The more we grappled with our research, the more we all saw connections between our classrooms. That's when it became very exciting, and I realized none of us was really alone (pp. 105-106).*

You will want your research group to meet every two or three weeks to sustain your research throughout the school year. Some of the group's talking and listening may be by phone or e-mail, but plan also to meet in person. Smaller groups with fewer schedules to juggle can make more frequent meetings possible and can also allow you more time to respond to each other's work.

As a practical matter, the group needs one member who will take responsibility for the group's management — send out timely reminders of group meetings, publish a list of phone numbers and e-mail addresses to the rest of the group, locate a regular meeting place sufficiently apart from the hectic crunch of the school setting, and rotate the responsibilities for bringing refreshments to group meetings.

Some group leadership responsibilities require experience with conducting teacher research and leading research groups, matters such as determining when, how often, and for how long you will meet and what you need to do during the group meeting time.

At the group's initial meetings, for example, the leader should be alert to seeing the daily stuff of classrooms as data and should be able to help pinpoint ways in which teaching practices and research methods connect. Another teacher in Gerow's study reflected on this phenomenon:

> *The more I asked them questions, the more they really began to consider how they learned. Before, they would say, "Mrs. Smith, I learned a new word." Now they say, "Mrs. Smith, I learned a new word. I remembered the picture on the poster and then I remembered that big letter with it, and then I saw it on this store, and my Daddy said..." It showed up in show and tell, stories from home, visits with grandparents, parent conferences... I will never look at my students the same way. Now I need them as much as they need me. (p. 97)*

When a teacher-researcher in a group tells a story like this, it helps to have someone who has been through similar research experiences to draw the group's attention to the connection between teaching and research. Conducting research on your own teaching helps you anticipate what others will need to know or what they may experience. If you become the leader of your group, check out the section called "What happens when I lead a teacher research group?" in "Part II: Questions and Issues."

What usually happens when small groups meet is that teachers read and discuss their research logs, data, attempts at analysis and findings, and drafts of articles. The group challenges each other's assumptions, proposes alternative interpretations, offers suggestions about research methodology, responds to drafts, and often lends personal as well as professional support. The group also validates the members' research data and analysis by questioning and offering a variety of interpretations in addition to those of the researcher. Honora Mara, a high school English teacher, summed up her experience in her research group in the following way: "Without the research group, I would have gone crazy. They kept after me to get beyond fussing at myself and the kids — and to figure out what was going on."

Research groups support the process of analysis — keeping the focus on figuring out what's going on — and the support is mutual. Bernie Glaze, Mary Ann Nocerino, and Courtney Rogers conducted research on a teacher research seminar led by Marion MacLean in 1988-89. They examined the role the groups played in supporting and challenging teacher-researchers' work and looked closely at several exchanges that occurred during small group meetings. In the excerpt from their research report below, they describe Bob Ingalls's strategy of not answering Randi Adleberg's questions but instead helping her "examine her own hypotheses, identify a focus, clarify what she wanted to pursue." The authors note that Ingalls's questions and responses assisted Adleberg, but they also highlight Ingalls's reporting of the mutual benefit.

> **Bob (to Randi):** *So you could interview them* [her students].
> **Randi:** *I could ask them, "Why did you write this piece?"*

> *In the small group, the teacher-researcher is both a researcher and audience for research. The going back and forth as researcher and audience supports the research process.*

> **Bob to Randi:** *Tell me what the kids did when they were learning in groups. You don't have to prove that this* [strategy] *is better. Describe what is happening. Tell me your theory.*

> *Bob commented later that he needed to hear himself say this for himself, illustrating the dual role he plays in the small group.*

> **Bob:** *You know that's why I need this group... by telling Randi, I reminded myself. It's like going from audience to researcher to audience and back... I needed to hear myself say that, too.*

When several small groups join together, the mixture of teachers from different schools (as in the seminar) provides a broader kind of support and a new context for familiar questions. A small group might discuss concerns about finding time for log-writing, for instance, and then discover that almost everyone in the large group shares the same concerns. In addition, the large group provides a wider audience and can confirm for each of you that your study seems interesting or valuable. The small groups also combine for discussions of readings and presentations by guest researchers. And, of course, your refreshment break allows you time to seek out and talk further with those who are not part of your small group.

In school-based teacher-researcher groups, teachers often make time to talk with each other — when paired up on hall or cafeteria duty, for instance, or waiting in line to use the photocopier. A school-based group can foster cross-disciplinary discussion, support, and collaboration rather than competition and "turf" jealousy.

The research group's supportive atmosphere makes it possible for teachers to be honest about what goes on in their classes, about both the problems and the successes, which seem equally hard for them to discuss openly. Valerie Sayre wrote the following comments in a teacher-researcher seminar in response to MacLean's request for reflections on how the research was going.

> *11/10 — I am so glad to have such a supportive group, and I appreciate the extra time you gave us tonight to talk things through. My colleagues have suggested extra questions to include in my questionnaire that I did not think of, and they were very relevant questions. One suggested that I ask the questions a section at a time so as not to bombard my students or tax their thinking. Another suggested that I add another category to find out more about the individual rather than the musician, and thus discover why maybe it is difficult for some students to be creative. All these points are well taken and I'm getting a clearer focus on how to begin my questioning.*

The reciprocal nature of the group is mirrored in the idea that we learn not only by being helped but from helping others.

The benefits move beyond the individual and even beyond a group. Summing up the overall experience within a teacher-researcher group, one teacher-researcher in Gerow's study remarked:

> *At first, I thought [my research study] was very individual. Why did I need a team for that? That was a silly thought. They were 2/3 responsible for the course of action my study took. They helped me make decisions, see things in a different way... things I*

would not have seen on my own. Somehow we must figure out how to work this way in our schools. (p. 130)

So far we have discussed teacher-researcher groups as useful to teachers' research in their classrooms and in their schools. Such groups can also change the ways that schools operate. We agree with Gerow who finds that by working in collaborative teams, teacher-researchers

> *...began to question the location and wisdom of power and authority within their school and county practices and structures. For sure, they gave up waiting for someone else to find the answers because now they knew they were capable of doing so themselves. Professionalism became evident in the quality of their practice and continued to grow and deepen in meaning and expand in vision (pp. 140-141).*

REFERENCES

Gerow, S. (1997). Teacher researchers in school-based collaborative teams: One approach to school reform. Unpublished doctoral dissertation. Fairfax, VA: Institute for Educational Transformation, George Mason University.

Glaze, B., Nocerino, M. A., and Rogers, C. (1989) Learning to lead among peers: The teacher-researcher seminar. *Language and learning: Reports from a teacher-researcher seminar.* Fairfax, VA: Northern Virginia Writing Project, George Mason University.

Sayre, V. (1989). Musically gifted children: Unwrapping the gift. *Language and learning: Reports from a teacher researcher seminar.* Fairfax, VA: Northern Virginia Writing Project, George Mason University.

TIMING

How does the research look during a school year?

Now that you have drafted a question, started recording your thoughts in a research log, and met with your research group, it will help to have an overview of the year's work. The chart below suggests research activities for each month of the school year and questions to explore as you move through those activities. This overview, of course, does not fit everyone's research process and certain months are stretched more than others, but it is offered for anticipation and planning in the same way a teacher might hand out a course description or syllabus at the beginning of a course.

TENTATIVE RESEARCH PLANS AND TIMELINE	
September Begin Research Log	What is research? What is teacher research? What are the expectations for this project? Where do research questions come from? What is my research question?
October Begin Data Collection	How do I find out more about what interests me? How do I look at what I'm curious about? What is data? What does it tell me? How do I revise my research question?
November Data Collection	Where does the data lead me? What else do I want to know?
December ...and Analysis	What questions are emerging from the data? What is my research question now? What does the data mean?
January Complete Major Data Collection	Looking at my data as a whole, what is my research question now and what do I think I've learned?

February Begin Draft Writing	
March **April**	As I write, what am I learning? How can I best show what I have learned? Where are there gaps in my research?
May Deadline Draft of Research Report	What can I say, at this point, I've learned? What questions do I want to study further?

OBSERVATION AND REFLECTION

What do you see?
What do you think about what you see?

As teachers, we observe our students constantly and reflect often. The difference for teacher-researchers is the regular recording of those observations and reflections in writing, systematically, over time. As you read the next few paragraphs describing the way one teacher-researcher teaches, consider how she is both teaching and researching.

> With her log open on her desk, a teacher-researcher starts the day's work with her students on *Romeo and Juliet*, expecting to take students through some contemporary near-examples of tragic heroes and extract from those examples some character traits. Later in the period, they will consider Romeo and Juliet as tragic heroes. One of the many goals this teacher-researcher has for the class session on this day is the participation of as many students as possible through their comments, ideas, and questions. She has planned several class activities to promote participation, among them writing, talking in pairs, and small group brainstorming.
>
> The teacher-researcher is also interested in what participation is for high school students as they study literature. She is on alert. Her log remains open. As the small-group class activity begins, she looks around the room and jots down some brief notes — whatever catches her attention. She may observe from a constant vantage point or move around the room with her log in hand. As she observes, she writes what she notices, perhaps writing down a sentence or two directly from the students' conversation. She observes their posture and expressions, their use of books or writing, their topics of conversation, and their progress in completing the activity.

This description shows classroom observation in action. As the teacher observes, she is writing down what she sees and hears, noting all that's relevant to her research question, but she is also alert to other occurrences. She may interrupt her observations to assist students in getting back "on task" or to make a clarification. But mostly she listens carefully and asks questions about *how* the students are learning as well as *what* they are learning. She watches and waits to see what the students will do rather than acting on the assumption that she knows what they should do.

When you observe and take notes as you teach, you are teaching and researching at the same time. Observations are not complete, however, without reflection. After you have observed your students at work, review your notes for missing details. If your students are busy at a different task later during the lesson — or if you have a few minutes before your next group of students arrives — seize the opportunity to fill in details about what you observed. Record as many of your immediate impressions, reactions, and thoughts as you have time for and can remember.

As soon as possible, whether later that day or over the next day or two, take time to reread what you have written. As you reread, fill in more of the details as you remember what happened. Then write reflectively on what you think about what you saw and explore understandings that the observation gives you. You may also find it helpful to write about the process of observing how you look at your students and how you feel as you do the writing.

After writing the following observations of her high school students, Veronica Washington reread her entries and wrote reflectively about what they meant to her, the questions they raised, and the contributions the observations made to her thinking about her research.

10/14 — The students are writing a timed essay. They have been allowed to use their reading logs, so many of them are flipping through their notes, pausing occasionally to ponder a point/idea. One minute lapses — everyone is now writing. Pens are moving quickly across the page. They're hovering over their papers, intently pushing pens rapidly across their papers. One boy scratches his head, pauses, then begins to write again. One girl is turning pages, mouth-

ing the words she is reading. She begins to write, moving her head very close to the paper. Everyone has at least one arm on the table, many have both, with their heads resting on a curved arm.

I remember that I was always told to sit up straight, with my back against the back of the chair, feet flat on the floor, and my left hand in my lap. I remember many spasmodic movements in elementary school, when I tried to get comfortable while sitting like a statue. This is a new day. Several students pause, their heads on their arms, or hands, concentrating. Then begin to write again. One student keeps shaking his right leg as he frantically writes with his left hand. His right foot is propped against the table leg.

Interrupted: "How do you spell con*?" I point to the dictionary. Student rushes over to get dictionary, frustration evident as he sighs loudly.*

Interrupted again: "How do you spell innocent*?" I write it on a scrap of paper. Student returns to her seat, starts writing.*

Student is still shaking his leg, now starts to tap his left foot, stops writing and puts pen in his mouth. Starts to write again — shakes right leg.

Interrupted again: Student comes in late. I explain he has to make up assignment.

Many students are starting to proofread their papers, revising, crossing out. No one talks. One student flexes his fingers. Now students start bringing their papers up to the desk. Time is up. Still no talking. (Student shaking his leg wrote one-half page.)

10/21 Reflection on 10/14 Observation:

This is my first observation of an 11-12 class and the first time I've observed students writing under pressure. I didn't observe that the students were tense or nervous; they've done this type of assignment two previous times in this class. What comes to my mind is the ease, or ability to adapt to a comfortable position for writing. For me, it's important to have a certain type of "space" in order to be comfortable — to feel somewhat alone or distanced from the crowd. In fact, during my observations I sit at a relatively uncluttered and often empty table.

The students, however, seem very comfortable in creating/adapting to their own "space." Somewhere I read that students in formal/school incorporated writing classes aren't given an opportunity to experience writing in solitude. The writer suggested that the students' inability to experience writing in a quiet, solitary environment causes them to compose poorly, and also to develop poor attitudes about writing. This is an interesting point for me.

(1) About half of my students said they enjoyed/required *quiet when asked to describe how they write.*

(2) Whenever I've told students to spread out, make themselves comfortable, and write, they have selected various niches in the room — corners, under tables, behind chairs and dividers, etc.

(3) This particular class seemed to establish barriers by positioning themselves in certain ways — arms on tables, heads resting on curved arms, bodies hovering close to their papers.

(4) The students sitting at the table with the boy who alternates between shaking his left and right leg and writing with his left hand don't appear to notice his movement — it was driving me crazy! I could just imagine the table vibrating.

Spelling *surfaces again! I wonder if the students realized my different treatment and reaction to the two students who asked how to spell words. I'm sure the boy I told to get a dictionary noticed! I remember thinking how I wanted to be sure to record accurately his frustration and the way he approached using the dictionary to look up his word. However, in the midst of this thought, I was interrupted by another problem speller. By the time I finished scribbling the words the first student had looked up his word, and resumed writing! Now* I *was frustrated!!*

This October log entry was Washington's first try at observing this class. In the midst of the observation, she recalls what it was like when she was in elementary school, then goes back to observing her students. This kind of interruption by your own mind, as opposed to a student question, is frequent and the best thing to do is simply write it down quickly. Although it is not part of the observation, it may help when you reflect later. In her reflection, Washington also notices immediately what happened when students requested spelling help. This kind of reflection on your interventions as a teacher is one of the reasons that observing and reflecting assist both your research and your teaching.

As you become more experienced with writing observations and reflections to collect data, you may find the following suggestions helpful.

- ◆ Observe small single events (such as a math test) or an ongoing series of related events (such as learning math facts in the first grade).
- ◆ Explain to your students ahead of time that you will be observing and writing as they work. Your observation offers the opportunity to explain ahead of time to students about your research and gives you their comments afterward for clarification and depth of understanding.
- ◆ Check the validity of your observations immediately, if time permits. Show or read your students and/or your research group the tapes or notes of your observation and your reflection. Use their responses to help you interpret what you have seen and plan your next observation.
- ◆ Don't worry if your question changes in later months and your observations relate to a different subject. All of the data you collect — even the data that precedes the change in your question — serves a useful function. Reexamine the old data in light of your new question.
- ◆ Observe yourself as you practice observing your students. You may notice a shift in your behavior from automatically intervening in students' work to holding back in order to observe. Sometimes this holding back allows you to listen in a different way to students and to question your interventions. Whatever happens for you, note the changes carefully both as you observe and as you reflect.

The following excerpts from two teacher-researchers' logs illustrate the effect of their observations on these teachers' thinking about their students — and on their thinking about their research questions as well.

EXCERPT FROM ALBERTA GROSSMAN'S RESEARCH LOG:

Many of the problems the students are experiencing finding information and getting started I attribute to me. I feel as if I ought to have been organizing and prearranging more for them — on the other hand it's not easy in our school with our librarians — there is not a sense of being welcomed.

But maybe organizing is actually contra-indicated. After all the thesis of I-Search is that the interest in the quest facilitates the quest. (But let us not kid ourselves, the research itself is often an anxiety-producing drag. Witness some of my own feelings while researching the evaluation of writing — even though there was basic curiosity and much satisfaction.)

What if the teacher's own need for closure forces kids to take the path of least resistance?

EXCERPT FROM COURTNEY ROGERS'S RESEARCH LOG:

9/29 Reflection on 9/21 Observation:

I have probably waited too long to do this reflection but rereading it takes me back fairly well.

I wonder about the physical act (acts? action?) of writing. Some of the individuals look totally engaged, absorbed, at times, but I wonder how it differs for each. I think about occasions when I have been mentally engaged in the writing, mainly so that the physical act of getting the words down seems really secondary, and even a hindrance. I can't write fast enough. On other occasions I recall focusing more on the physical act of writing and watching my pen move across the page, the thoughts temporarily at least taking a back seat to the forming of letters and words on the page. I wonder what the relationship of these two is for myself or for them. (Is this what I'm supposed to be doing in this reflection or am I getting too far off base?)

I described Lynn and Gina very similarly in the physical act of writing, yet knowing what I do about their apparent abilities, I wonder if the same thing is going on for both of them. Both appear ex-

tremely engrossed in what they are doing, yet I find myself wondering if
Lynn is more mentally engaged and Gina more physically engaged in
the act of writing. Thinking about that, my question seems ill-placed.
My suspicion is that both happen for all writers, I guess.

How did Elizabeth get started considering she didn't feel cre-
ative (interpret that as not in the mood to be mentally engaged.)
Could the physical act of writing stimulate the mental activity? I
think or know (I think!) that that has happened to me.

Both Grossman and Rogers reflect in their writing about what they
have noticed about themselves as well as their students. Their discoveries were not anticipated, but lead them toward new ideas for data collection as well as new ideas for their teaching. Reflections on observations and the new ideas that come from them become the first attempts
at analysis. Teacher-researchers' log entries, as ongoing documents of
classroom life, point in a gradual way toward the findings and interpretations that eventually result. In later rereadings of your log, an early
hunch or clue becomes a full-blown finding.

Sometimes the idea of collecting data through observing and reflecting seems difficult to teachers not because of the classroom stance
it requires but because of the writing itself. Teacher-researchers come to
writing from varied backgrounds and experiences — and with a variety
of expectations, assumptions, and (at times) apprehensions. Both of us
have many years of experience as writers, as teachers of writing, and as
Writing Project teacher-consultants. Our work with teacher-researchers regardless of their experience has confirmed for us the value of reflective writing for anyone who does it, and that it is possible for any
teacher to do it with encouragement and practice.

Strategies that support writing and reflection appear throughout
this book, as do references to the work of others who have studied teachers' reflective writing. Teacher-researcher Betsy Sanford studied her own
log writing and the writing in other teachers' logs. Her classroom research in recent years has centered on how students learn mathematics.
In her article "Teacher Research and Writing," she remarks on the analytical purpose that the log writing serves:

One of the big surprises of this year's research has been seeing the frequency with which major developments in my understanding are predated by "glimmers" of connections in my log writing. For instance, in December, as I began to narrow my research focus to how first graders learn number facts, I wrote, "the whole issue with the math facts is that I want to move kids from procedural performance to strategic performance." At the time I could sense the importance of a strategic approach to number fact learning, but it would be a long time before I fully grasped that conceptual knowledge lies at the heart of a strategic approach. While writing helps me make big connections — ones that are apparent even at the time of the writing — this quote shows how it also helps me make little ones that pop up and then recede, perhaps with a cumulative effect, as they help me hammer out understanding.

Sanford is a journal and log writer of long standing, but she understands that for many teacher-researchers writing is a double-edged sword. She ends her research report with a statement from one of her colleagues, Sally Bryan: "I find writing very painful… I wonder why? And yet, when I have 'seen the light' and know what I want to say, I feel so satisfied. If I had never tried teacher research, I would never have known this aspect of teaching and learning which I now consider very important, very special." If you are apprehensive about the writing involved, we want you to know that many other teacher-researchers have felt the same way initially and have persevered to their own and their students' benefit.

REFERENCES

Bryan, S. (1997). The role of technology resource teacher: A catalyst for change. *Lemon Road Elementary School Teacher-Researcher Project.* Fairfax County, VA: Fairfax County Public Schools.

Grossman, A. (1987). What happens when Mickey writes? In M. M. Mohr & M. S. MacLean, *Working together: A guide for teacher-researchers* (pp. 77-94). Urbana, IL: National Council of Teachers of English.

Rogers, C. (1987). A teacher-researcher writes about learning. In M. M. Mohr & M. S. MacLean, *Working together: A guide for teacher researchers* (pp. 94-102). Urbana, IL: National Council of Teachers of English.

Sanford, B. (1997). Teacher research and writing. *Lemon Road Elementary School Teacher-Researcher Project.* Fairfax County, VA: Fairfax County Public Schools.

Washington, V. (1983). Dispelling myths about the writing process. *Research in writing: Reports from a teacher-researcher seminar.* Fairfax, VA: Northern Virginia Writing Project, George Mason University.

DATA COLLECTION

How can you find out what you want to know?

Classrooms are full of data, although what happens there is not often thought of as research. You collect data whenever you grade students' papers or listen carefully as a student struggles to talk through a problem. You are also collecting data when you write in your research log — recording field notes, classroom observations, and reflections — and when you write and revise your research question. You will probably, in the midst of your research, recognize happily that everything is data about something. You are surrounded, immersed, inundated.

How do you know what to collect? While we suggest that you plan what, how, and when you will collect, data may appear unexpectedly as you talk with a student or suddenly realize the depth of a class discussion and its relevance to your study. Many teacher-researchers begin with an informal survey related to their research topic, asking students the questions that are on their minds. Looking over the survey results helps point the way to the next data needed. Research groups are a help, too. Together, researcher and colleagues match up the proposed question with possible data sources for answers. If the researcher is asking a question about how computer use affects students' learning, for example, the data collected has to be related to the computer and show evidence of students' learning.

Although question and data seemed coordinated, what results is not always what the researcher expects. When you are disappointed in what your data seems to show, it is not really the data's fault; data is just data. It may lead in new directions or clarify previous ones, but whichever happens, collecting more data will help.

Whenever you have data in your hands, get in the habit of quickly recording the date, time, and other identifying details in your research log or on the data itself. Those details are additional data and will help you sort accurately later. Reviewing what, how, and when to collect will show you opportunities for data collection in your day-to-day teaching.

DATA SOURCES

Consider the following possibilities:

Student talk. There are many ways to capture student talk.

- Have your log at hand to write down single-sentence quotes from your students that seem noteworthy. Some students eventually get to the point of saying, "You better write this down."
- Take notes and/or tape record as you listen to a small or large group discussion.
- Interview with prepared questions.
- Ask a question and have students write out their answers and then discuss the results.
- Ask students to think aloud to you while performing a task or immediately afterward.
- Conduct a retrospective interview immediately after a lesson or when even more time has elapsed. In the latter kind of interview, you can stimulate their recall by asking the students questions to help them remember.

Products written and made by students in your classes, such as completed assignments and tests and the plans and drafts that created them. Interesting data can come from a class in which the students themselves write the questions, plan and evaluate the test, or even teach the lesson. Their posters, presentations, charts, drawings, booklets, and other work hanging around in your room are data that you can discuss with them and observe over a period of time.

Quick Surveys of student thinking on a particular subject. Give one or two-question surveys with open-ended answers or longer surveys with answer selections provided. Compile survey results and present them to your students. Record their answers to follow-up questions to help clarify the results and add additional data. If the results puzzle you, you can ask about them, as in, "Why did you think that this was an important cause of the Diaspora?"

Tests or a series of tests on material students are learning. Ask an additional question at the end of the test about how the students completed their answers. ("Which question was the hardest to answer and why?" "What do you wish I had asked you about?")

Notes, formal and informal, to and from students, colleagues, or yourself. Set up a system in your classroom for notes to the teacher — a folder and some blank paper or Post-its work. Remind students of the opportunity and from time to time respond to them as individuals or to the class as a whole when it seems appropriate. All these scraps of paper are, of course, data.

Classroom records such as grades and absentee reports, lesson plans, and daily agendas. General classroom data can give you a baseline, an additional viewpoint, and a sense of the class as a whole. One difficulty with this broad kind of data is that sometimes it is hard to connect to your specific question. For example: Are the students not getting the math facts because of absenteeism or for some other reason? And every teacher knows that lesson plans don't do their lessons justice.

Short oral answers to informal questions you ask on the spur of the moment when you think the information will be helpful. ("What preparation helped you the most as you performed your *Hamlet* roles today?") You jot down the questions and the students' answers in your research log.

Comments (make copies) that you make to students either orally or in writing about what they are doing and writing. If they write back to you, save that, too.

Memories recalled in tranquillity. These may help you clarify your other data. Sometimes it helps — after you find some tranquillity — to sit with your log and ask yourself, "What's going on here?" Write your answer letting your mind wander over the various facets of your research and your classroom. New and helpful ideas often come from such writing.

Folders or portfolios of students' work over a period of time. These are gold mines of data, especially when the students have done some evaluation themselves.

Video or audiotapes as students give presentations, hold discussions, or do other activities related to your research question.

Charts or graphs of categories or lists of learning problems solved by students or new learning acquired. These can be kept by you or your students or over a period of time as knowledge accumulates. Sometimes they may be displayed on a classroom poster and added to or revised from time to time.

Time sequences important to learning such as number of times or lapse of time needed for learning to take place.

Field notes taken by someone else in your classroom — a fellow teacher or a student — during an activity related to your research.

The data collection possibilities discussed above will sound familiar to you since you are already collecting data in the day-to-day work of teaching. Discussing your data collection with your research group helps make clearer the connection between data collecting and teaching. When your group meets, take a look at the following questions and try them out on each other.

How would your students answer your research question?
How can you plan your data collection to give you several points of view?
How will your research log observations and reflections contribute to your data?
What would happen if you asked your students for data collection suggestions?
How will you collect data over time?
How can you summarize survey results and use them (or other data) in a lesson?
What follow-up data would clarify the results of earlier data?

Each of you will answer the questions differently according to your research topic, and your group's suggestions will enrich the possibilities for all of you.

DATA IN ACTION

Data is not difficult to find — the problem is keeping track of it and managing it so as to assist you in analyzing it. In this section we discuss data in action with detailed examples from teacher-researchers at work. Some kinds of data help you see other kinds of data. Classroom observations recorded in your research log, questionnaires and surveys, student comments about their learning, interviews, and student work — all are useful in reflecting back to you what you are researching.

Observation data from your research log. Your log provides many different kinds of data. Rereading it as you go, even highlighting significant passages, helps you see the direction your data is pointing. Sherry Tabachik, a middle school physical education teacher, studied the relationship between leadership and achievement in her classes. Her brief observations of student behavior, recorded regularly in a very few minutes after class, helped her to see how leadership developed. The following is one of these entries:

> *11/11 — First day of football. S.'s response to my comment that we must "learn the skills before we play" was "That sucks! I already know how to play!"*
>
> *I started class by asking who knew how to throw a football. S. raised his hand. I then asked who would like to show us and explain the process. Apparently S. did not hear me say "to explain." He quickly raised his hand and I just as quickly called on him. S. came up front and started to throw the football.*
>
> *When I said, "Now, explain what you did," he said, "I can't do that," and immediately sat down. I asked for another volunteer who proceeded to explain. S. realized that he could have explained and [~~blurted out~~] finished the other student's sentence. I requested that he let the other student finish and then said, "S., I knew you could explain it; you just panicked."*
>
> *The next time I asked for a volunteer to explain what a pattern is, S. raised his hand and I, of course, called on him. His demonstration was on target and I praised him for it.*

Tabachik collected many of these observational log writings about several students. Her entries are brief, to the point, and frequent. By crossing out one description and trying a less judgmental one (from "blurted out" to "finished"), she shows her effort to limit her observational writing to descriptions of what happened.

She reread the entries as she progressed through the semester and was able to see certain patterns. The students needed both to be appreciated by the teacher and also to challenge her authority. Eventually she saw their challenges as part of their need for learning how to lead, and she developed ways to teach them how to be leaders in her classes.

Questionnaires. A survey or questionnaire gives you a broad base for understanding your students' ideas in regard to your research question, a profile out of which a more specific study may take shape. Peg Culley used a survey of her students' grammar history to begin her study on the teaching of grammar. Below is the survey and her log writing as one class was completing it.

9/84 Grammar History

I.   Write about your history as a student of grammar. Think back to your grade school years and beyond and describe your training in grammar to date. How did you learn grammar? What are your memories about learning grammar?

II. Describe in writing what you first think or feel when you hear the statement, "Now, we will begin our study of grammar."

III. Answer one of the following:

   IIIa. If you wrote all positive responses to question II, can you think of and record the negative responses to grammar that you may have?

   IIIb. If your response to question II was negative, can you think of and record your positive responses to the study of grammar?

IV. What do you enjoy most about learning grammar?

V.   What do you enjoy least about learning grammar?

VI. How do you see that the study of grammar has helped you develop as a writer?

Thank you for your help with this questionnaire.

Observation from Peg Culley's log, 9/84

I just did it. I handed out the questionnaire. All here but C. (19 in). Lights are out. One unit exploded and sparked and smelled as I sat eating my lunch. I expect a maintenance man any minute.

Students going up and down hall — noisy. I'll close the door, open windows.

I want to go back and talk more about how I started this out. I told students about the light problem and then told them that I wanted their help w/grammar. I explained that I will be trying something new re: teaching of grammar that I hope will help them learn more and remember more. And since I was trying something new out, I want to study what they did as I tried my new teaching methods out. So I was going to be a little like a scientist.

I told them first I wanted to know something about their relationship to grammar and so I was giving them a questionnaire relating to how they learned grammar. (C. is looking over at M.'s writing.) I asked if they had any questions. Y. asked — so we will tell you about how we learned grammar? I said, yes — and they didn't have to be writing them. I was going to give them a paper w/questions on it. (L. and P. are passing notes. C. and M. are talking. H. and K. are giggling, L. is red-faced.) P. said, — so we're your guinea pigs. I responded — I hope not because guinea pigs don't really interact w/researcher. And I need your responses and your awareness in this.

Culley is careful to record the details of the context of her classroom situation, not prejudging their value or significance. She records her way of introducing the survey as well, a log entry that helped her later in understanding the students' responses.

Survey data can show you the scope of your question and tune you in to the general understandings of your students. In a study of how teacher-researchers teach, Mohr asked students in first through twelfth grades in three different schools one question: "If you were going to teach somebody something, how would you do it?" After they wrote their answers, she conducted class interviews to gather further information and clarify what they had written. The survey information helped illuminate the classroom observation data that followed and grounded Mohr's interpretations in student thinking about teaching.

Survey results can be compiled in a variety of ways, sometimes by counting only certain answers, sometimes by looking for recurring ideas or statements, and sometimes holistically, as a basis for further questions of the class or individual students. The advantage you have is that you return to the takers of the survey every day and can find out what the students meant by their answers.

Written comments by students about their work. Frequently teacher-researchers ask students to reflect on what they think may be happening in their work, to write (admittedly with hindsight) about how they did something, or to keep track of a process as they go through it. This data adds another point of view of the student work and contributes to an expanded, broader-based analysis.

Washington, whose observation and reflection you read earlier, asked her students to describe how they wrote and how they had changed as writers, if they thought they had. One student wrote the following:

> *Mostly when I write I think an awful lot. Because to me thinking is the best form of writing. How do I think thinking is a form of writing? Well, if it wasn't for thinking there would be few things written. But I also like to imagine. You know, to really go all the way, to make things more dramatic, or even to make a fairy tale so real that you start believing it.*
>
> *I'm not sure if I see any changes in the way I write. To be honest I didn't know I had the ability to write the things I do. In other words, I didn't realize that I had such a talent. Well, I'm not sure how to write down what I'm thinking at this point. I suppose that I have made a tremendous change in writing, or maybe I just never noticed. My eighth grade English teacher didn't write how good our paper was, or how well we had written them. He would just tell us our mistakes and give us our grade.*
>
> *I'm not sure that it is my writing that has changed. I believe that it is my attitude towards writing, and my mind itself. My writing itself has always been there, but, this class brought it out, or showed it to me.*

From this complex response from just one student, Washington was able to find themes that reverberated in her other students' writings, themes that eventually led her to describe "myths" about writing that students believe.

Honora Mara did a study of student motivation in her ninth-grade classes. She asked the question: "How can I get my students to produce more and better work?" Through the year she periodically asked students to comment on questions relating to her developing ideas about what motivated them. The question that brought out the most from her students was, "Thinking back through all the time you've been in school (K-9) what were the times you really looked forward to going to school (class activities, not just seeing friends)?"

She included the following responses to that question in her research report as she delved more deeply into student-teacher relationships as a key to motivation.

- *I look forward to getting back tests to see if I got a good grade. In a way it's sort of suspenseful.*
- *When I was in 4th, 5th, 6th grade I always looked forward to going to chorus because it was the time to learn fun, nice songs... We got to go to churches and sing for the old people and they really looked forward to us coming.*
- *I enjoyed the last few days of 8th grade. In class we didn't have to worry about work or deadlines. The teachers didn't seem like teachers. They seemed like real, actually cool people (well only about 3 or so. Maybe more)...*
- *Working hard all night on a project and looking forward to presenting the project.*
- *I don't like the way they force you to go. You have no choice but to go. You have to go! You have to do the work! You have to do whatever they say! It does not really encourage you to do anything. In preschool to 3rd grade I loved to go to school and learn. I would pay attention like my ears were glued to her words... From 3rd to 6th grade it started getting annoying having to do whatever the teacher says.*
- *I look forward to coming. It's not because of killing time, it's using the time to pay off in the future.*
- *I have had 3 teachers in my life mean something to me but now I don't know where they are.*

- *The Planetarium, for example, is a place to learn about constellations and the solar system, but the best thing is that it's a comfortable and relaxing atmosphere.*
- *In 1st grade my teacher was more like a friend rather than a teacher. I knew I could talk to her about anything. And I think that was good for me being so young to know that I have someone who's willing to help and listen other than my mother.*
- *Basically I want to talk about stuff that matters, how people see it, and then you can make it easier on yourself when having a disagreement with someone. It helps you to be more open minded... you don't end up wasting your time trying to figure out why people dress, act, or think the way they do.*

Based on these responses and many others throughout the year, Mara developed ten conclusions about attitudes and motivation in ninth graders which she then discussed in relation to her teaching.

Interviews. In contrast to questionnaires and surveys, interviews offer a highly specific case which can shed light on your research as a whole. Interviews with single students may require the student's willingness to meet with the teacher before or after school or during lunch. We think it is important to let students know that their teachers are interested in recording their comments — and to let them know why — always respecting any reservations a student might have.

Teacher-researchers are conscious of the fact that students may try to please them by saying what they think the teacher wants to hear, or that students may wish to do the opposite — express their anger against the classroom and the teacher. As a teacher-researcher you have several advantages that allow you to determine the validity of your students' comments to you. You see your students regularly, often, and over an extended period of time. Assuming a research stance allows you to hold judgments in suspension as the complexity of their comments and their learning unfolds. In addition, your own reflective writings about student data and your solicitation of comments from your research group help you determine what rings true. With this kind of scrutiny, your understandings move beyond broad generalizations such as "they like it" or "they don't like it."

Students are often very helpful and honest in interviews, if they believe that you are able to listen and to, occasionally, hear a difficult message. MacLean interviewed one of her high school students during her study of reader response writing. Earlier in the interview MacLean asked the student for permission to use her response log on *The Catcher in the Rye* by J. D. Salinger in a presentation on the use of writing to understanding literature.

> **K.:** *I think… That would be great… except for… I think that they have to understand one thing — that a reading log… When you ask your student to do a reading log, you can't expect anything of it.*
>
> **M.:** *What do you mean by that?*
>
> **K.:** *Well… the first fifty pages of this book is contained in the first half page of my reading log. That about sums it up. And… I think they can… I had to* make *myself write that much. I really did. And something… Then something happened in the book and it's like I'm making this mad dash to write down everything I can remember and I'm skipping paragraphs and putting "made" instead of "mad" and all this stuff down and just misspelling words, but I'm scrambling to get it all in 'cause I don't want to lose those thoughts. So when you use a reading log, I think you really need to… I think that you have to understand that it's different things for each person, that you can't expect every night to have a page on, you know, the book or even for there to be any consistency in it. It's totally up to the person who's writing it.*
>
> **M.:** *What do you think made it possible for you not to worry about your reading log and to go ahead and write what you were coming to understand about Holden? What was the point at which that happened for you, because it* seems *to have happened. Did it?*
>
> **K.:** *I think… Yes, it* did. *I think it was the fact that I finally understood this person and nobody else in the class did, and I was so proud of myself. And I just wanted to scribble everything down as fast as I could. And I think… I think the fear never actually left. I think it was just kind of overridden.*

M.: Overridden by... by what?

K.: Excitement. I mean, just, ummm... by realizing Holden's gift I think I overcame... I overcame my fear of... to write this. And that sounds sort of stupid. "Yes, I have readinglogophobia."

By expressing interest in and acceptance of this student's frustrated reaction to the reading log assignment, MacLean was able to learn more about how reading logs function in student learning about literature.

Student Work. Student papers, drafts, portfolios, and projects — the artifacts of the classroom — may be collected over the period of a semester or longer, or may be used as a single example of an assignment you are studying. You collect student work as a matter of course, but don't ordinarily look at it as data to be analyzed, although you do something similar when you evaluate the papers and the lesson from which they originated. Student work may be the centerpiece of your data, helping you to understand and interpret all the rest.

Mary Schulman used the data on the following pages in her study of first grade writing. She combined interview data with an analysis of student work. In her interview Schulman treats her student's writing as seriously as the text of a Nobel Prize winner. It was through many such interviews of students about their writing, that she developed her classroom curriculum for teaching writing to beginning writers. She also learned a lot about beginning readers.

QUANTITATIVE DATA

The data collection suggestions we have offered rely on qualitative data because of what it offers to an in-depth study of teaching and learning in the context of a classroom. In our experience, most teacher-researchers use qualitative data because it fits naturally into their work as teachers, not because of a bias against experimental design or statistics. They see teaching experimental and control groups differently or attempting to control the variables in a classroom as incompatible with teaching and resulting in a distorted view of learning.

You do, however, pay attention to statistical information. Standardized test results and other scores pile up in students' records. Your record books reflect grade distributions for student assignments. You calculate

SCHULMAN: STUDENT WORK SAMPLE AND INTERVIEW

Kimberly: *Look,... want me to read it?*
Teacher: *Oh, yes!*
Kimberly: *I want to go on a swing. [Kimberly reads text aloud.]*
Text: *I   wk   t   A   s*
Kimberly: *I   want   togoon   a   swing.*
           [Kimberly points, trying to make the talk and graphics match.]
Teacher: *Oh...*
Kimberly: *That's me [points to figure on right]. Those are the swings at Kings Dominion [an amusement park]. My mom took us there.*
Teacher: *You got to ride the swings at Kings Dominion? Who went with you and your mom?*

Kimberly: My sister.
Teacher: I bet you had fun.
Kimberly: We went on lots of rides... but I like the swings the most.
Teacher: Why?
Kimberly: 'Cause they go high and fast.
Teacher: Wow... they go high and fast. Will you add that?
Kimberly: No, I don't want to.
Teacher: Tell me,... why did you cross out here... and here? [I pointed to the first two lines.]
Kimberly: 'Cause you do that when you write.
Teacher: Oh,... I see. This is a good try writing "I want to go on a swing." I want to show you something.

[Lightly in pencil, I wrote "I want to go on a swing." under Kimberly's writing. I said, "Look how close you are." I pointed to Kimberly's written text and then to my text, and began: "Look, you have the word "I"... you left a space after the word "I"... you have the "w" in the word "want"... the "t" in "to"... and the "s" in "swing." You know, you have most of the beginning letters in the words you wrote! Kimberly smiled.]

percentages of students who receive various grades and use the information to help you evaluate teaching and learning. But as a teacher-researcher, you interpret those statistics with knowledge of the context of your classroom and with vital information from your students about their learning and performance on the assignments, the kind of information you get from qualitative data. Statistical information is part of a classroom context, but fails to tell the whole story.

Experimental designs, controlled variables and statistical frequencies are critical when medical researchers, for example, measure the effects of quantifiable substances under controlled circumstances. Teachers, however, know that no two groups of students are sufficiently the same to set up comparison groups, that no classroom's variables can be completely identified much less controlled, and that teaching and learning are too

complex to be accurately quantified. Teacher-researchers understand
Lawrence Stenhouse's comment: "Predictions based upon statistical levels
of confidence are applicable to action only when the same treatment
must be given throughout the entire population. This condition does
not apply to education." (Ruddick, J. & Hopkins, D., 1985, p.12)

Lisa Oram's work on a survey she gave to 91 students about how
they regarded different kinds of lessons shows a teacher-researcher counting and comparing amounts. But ultimately she uses the data to help
her interpret what her students think and how their preferences are
related to what she believes they need to learn. In the survey she asked
the students to rate certain kinds of lessons with a "3" (usually satisfied), "2" (sometimes satisfied), or "1" (not satisfied). She compiled the
numbers in various ways and then wrote:

> *There are a couple of results I can mention that are surprising
> or seem most interesting to me. I was more surprised with "mini
> lessons" and "group day." Group day is most problematic because I
> don't really want to change it or know how to change it. If I'm going
> to be true to the survey, I need to go and see what activities got rated
> best and use that as a guide. But, I have the fewest ideas for change
> in the group day category, and also really want to keep that day to
> serve issues of importance to me, rather than the kids.*
>
> *I don't know exactly, but I feel resistant to following the lead that
> the information about group day presents. Maybe I will come back to
> it. It also involves a lot more calculation, which at the moment is very
> unappealing. As I was tabulating, I felt myself hoping that the group
> day numbers would stop growing, but they didn't. I guess that's the risky
> part about research or about giving your kids a voice. You have to be
> willing to respond to what you learn. You have to be open to finding out
> things that you didn't really want to know.*
>
> *The other interesting thing to me about looking at the results of
> the survey is how it makes me feel about my teaching. Last year it
> probably would have been devastating to realize that not every kid
> rated every category a 3. My expectation would have been across the
> board perfection. This year, I feel OK with the results. Only one kid
> wrote all 1s, and 5 wrote all 3s. 22 kids wrote a majority of 3s. As*

I counted the 1s I thought to myself it's good that most of the kids are only dissatisfied with one part of the class. I can't expect to be all things to all people... I notice a difference in my reaction and I feel it's positive. I also feel a need to accept it with caution. When you give up the goal of perfection, there are a lot of degrees of variation below that. I fear when I lose my intensity, yet I know on some levels I need to, and clearly, I have.

Oram uses a numerical analysis of her survey to understand something about herself as a teacher as well as to understand her students' reactions to various parts of her classroom curriculum. Her next data collection was an attempt to find out why the students thought as they did about the various elements of her classroom curriculum and which assignments helped them learn.

In teacher research both quantitative and qualitative data are used to develop interpretations and understandings of the complex interactions of teachers' teaching and students' learning, but neither kind of data alone is enough, especially for findings that are meant to go beyond classrooms to school districts as a whole. As teacher research contributes more widely to evaluations of achievement and programs at the school level, we believe that a combination of qualitative and quantitative data will enable schools and districts to make decisions that are data driven and informed by local research.

MacLean, leader of a teacher research project at her high school, recently worked with colleagues to conduct a schoolwide survey on block scheduling, which was being implemented that year. The change to block scheduling had been controversial among some members of the faculty, and there was a need to discover the range of responses across the school. The survey was designed to yield both statistical and qualitative information; some questions called for answers on a graduated attitude scale, some open-ended questions called for written responses, and some questions yielded both. Problematic issues, such as how to handle attendance and makeup work when students absent for one day actually missed two periods of the same class, were the subject of both kinds of questions.

As the survey committee compiled the data, they grouped the answers and calculated the frequency of different responses. The results — both quantitative and qualitative — were compiled and distributed to the faculty, who were then asked to attend a meeting where the results would be discussed in small groups, using the following questions as guidelines:

What conclusions can we draw from the data?
What conclusions can't we draw?
What should we research further?
What are some important areas of intervention for which the faculty should devise a work plan to address?

With the data in their hands, the faculty were able to look at the survey results as researchers themselves, see the initial responses comprehensively, and organize committees to deal with some of the problems (such as attendance and makeup work).

We have reported this instance of teacher research in some detail even though it was not done with students in a classroom. MacLean and other teacher-researchers have begun to use their research skills to assist their schools in decision-making. We think that one direction of teacher research in schools is toward more teacher participation in school-based decision making that includes both qualitative and quantitative data and is responsive to the context of individual classrooms and the school as a whole.

Whether your question is school or classroom based, your need four or five sources of data from various points of view to compare and contrast as you begin to look for valid interpretations. As a teacher-researcher, you have the advantage of ongoing analysis — reflecting on the data you are gathering as you gather it and then planning what more you need to collect as you see your students daily. You also have the helpful responses of your research group to question your interpretations and suggest different ones as needed.

SYSTEMS FOR DATA COLLECTION

Even closely watched data has a tendency to grow and multiply, or so it sometimes appears. A data-collection plan can be very useful, especially if it gives the researcher a feeling of being organized. We have written, revised, and rewritten many such plans. Your data-collection plan should include times to re-examine what you have and re-assess the plans. Research is intentional and systematic, but it is not rigid and unyielding in the face of reality. You may find it helpful to use some of the following strategies as ways to get data under control.

Process tracing. Follow a behavior or assignment through time (a class research project, for example) showing its evolution. The record of your thinking and choices at the beginning will help you and others understand the learning and production process as it unfolds.

Case study of a class. Collect a variety of data from one class, describe as many variables as possible, then interpret class behavior as it relates to your question. It is not necessary to analyze the data from all your students even when you are collecting the same information from them all. You may look at how a whole class learns a new subject in your curriculum, as Rita Johnson did with DNA in her middle school science class, and look for the progress in their learning as a group.

Focus groups. Use a smaller group from the class to respond to a tightly focused issue that has come from your broader baseline data. It will give you a closer look at the issue and more in-depth responses from students. If you are studying a class research project, for example, a small focus group of students in the class might provide answers to questions about the dependability of internet sources for research. You might even hold the focus group as a panel for the rest of the class. The focus group discussion can help you understand the data from the class as a whole.

Recurring themes. Identify recurring themes about student learning that appear in your data. For example, you might discover repeated comments by students in your social studies class that they need to study less for tests if they have kept a learning log of written responses to the important questions in the unit. Use the themes you discover to guide your subsequent data collection. If you collect data that doesn't fit the theme, if, for example, a small group of students do not seem to benefit from the learning log writing, revise or expand your categories as your understanding grows. You are looking for an inclusive system, not an airtight one.

Data reviews are helpful periodically during the process of collecting. After quickly looking through your data, ask yourself or the members of your research group the following questions:

What do you think about what you've collected?
Do you have any existing additional data? (observations, student papers, or remarks that you haven't "collected" but that cast light on your research questions.)
What do you notice from your review of your data?
What do you believe you need to do next?

Quotation data. If you don't have time to fully describe something significant that happens while you are teaching, write down a brief statement by one of the students, since it may become a theme or motif that helps you put together other parts of your data. A single quote might not sound like much of an organizing plan, but even if said in the midst of a tumultuous class discussion, it can reverberate through the rest of your study, helping to explain many other comments and data.

From data to question to data, etc. If your data seems frequently to veer away from your original research question, consider changing the question rather than rejecting the data. Your data may be trying to tell you something. It is not unusual for a teacher-researcher to open the meeting of a research group with the comment: "Well, I have a new research question. Again." The group will then need to discuss how the data changed the question and what new data the teacher-researcher can collect that will shed light on the new path. Slowly the focus becomes clearer, and findings and interpretations begin to connect with the question and the data.

Simple lists. Data typically makes your question more complex rather than simplifying it. If the complexity seems to be getting out of control, try listing what you know in a reduced and uncomplicated — simple phrases — manner. Simple lists can help you because, for the time being, they put aside the question of how things are related to each other.

In addition to various ways to structure and control data, we also use a variety of filing systems, boxes, notebooks, folders, clipboards, color coded slips of paper, pencils and pens, to say nothing of computer disks and programs. We suggest that you buy some new highlighting pens or dedicate some new computer disks in your favorite color to your research. Do anything you can to make living with your data agreeable.

REFERENCES

Culley, P. (1987). What students tell me about grammar and writing. *Research in writing: Reports from a teacher-researcher seminar.* Fairfax, VA: Northern Virginia Writing Project, George Mason University.

Mara, H. (1995). "Give me a Z+": Inquisitiveness and creativity go both ways. *Falls Church High School Teacher-Researcher Project.* Fairfax County, VA: Fairfax County Public Schools.

MacLean, M. (1997). Not entirely by design: Connections between teacher research and school planning at Falls Church High School. *Falls Church High School Teacher-Researcher Project.* Fairfax County, VA: Fairfax County Public Schools.

Oram, L. (1990). Using student input: How a second year teacher makes decisions. *Research in language and learning: Reports from a teacher-researcher seminar.* Fairfax, Va: Northern Virginia Writing project, George Mason University.

Ruddick, J. & Hopkins, D. (1985). *Research as a basis for teaching: Readings from the work of Lawrence Stenhouse.* Westport, CT: Heinemann-Boynton/Cook.

Schulman, M. (1982). The novice writer. *Research in writing: Reports from a teacher-researcher seminar.* Fairfax, VA: Northern Virginia Writing Project, George Mason University.

Tabachik, S. (1987). Raising Achievement Through Developing Leadership Skills. *Teacher research on student learning.* Fairfax County, VA: Fairfax County Public Schools.

Washington, V.(1983). Dispelling myths about the writing process. *Research in writing: Reports from a teacher-researcher seminar.* Fairfax, VA: Northern Virginia Writing Project, George Mason University.

DATA ANALYSIS

What are you finding out? What does it mean?

I t is difficult to believe that a collection of data will eventually make some kind of sense and to trust that patterns will emerge. What you will need is the patience to reread your data and to write about what you see as you reread, noticing what ideas and questions occur to you in the process. Imagine what preliminary data analysis might look like for one group of teacher-researchers:

On a February afternoon, the group gathers after school in an area of the library. One of them parks her canvas bag of data near her chair, sits down, opens her research log, and begins to write before rereading her previous log entries. A second teacher looks carefully through a collection of his students' math projects, reviewing the final products and the students' assessments of their own work. A third has arrived with stacks of student work — a set of tests with a companion set of the test-takers' comments about how the test worked to capture their learning and folders of selected students' other work. She has also brought her own notes from class discussions, notes from a brief interview with one student, her grade book, and of course, her research log. She reaches into her bag for a collection of colored pens, sits down, opens her log, and begins to reread. Around the tables, other teachers in the group are busy with their own data.

After an hour or so, the group gathers together. "How did it go?" the group leader asks.

One teacher, eager to talk, begins, "I don't know how many times I've looked at that group of essay tests. This is the group of essays I set up with the choice of two out of five questions. As I was sorting the answers by their choices, I noticed that almost all the students in one class chose the same questions to answer. In fact,…"

She continues briefly before a different teacher takes his turn. "I thought my research question was about what happened when learning-disabled students were mainstreamed with their teacher in my regular social studies classes. But now I'm wondering if my question isn't really about how *any* student connects with ancient civilizations."

Another, this time the group leader, presents a puzzle: "I don't know what to make of this. They've been doing great work with the personal writing. They have lots of honest, compelling accounts of their own experiences. And we went through a process of their choosing which ones they would turn into essays. They just turned in their drafts of the essays early this week. I was shocked! They're *nothing* like the exploratory writing they've done. All their detailed, thoughtful writing had turned into dry, distant prose. How did that happen?"

A member of the group asks, "Have you asked them?"

"Not yet, but I plan to tomorrow." The group continues to talk through the possible reasons for the unexpected shift in the students' writing as the teacher wonders how best to pose the question to her students. Before they leave, the teacher-researchers take a few minutes to write about their meeting.

— ◆ —

The group described above met for the purpose of data analysis, but they were also at work on their teaching and their students' learning. Throughout the research process, their research and teaching have intertwined through their systematic and intentional efforts to interpret their data.

Teacher-researchers do not collect data for very long without stopping to reflect, analyze, and reset their sights. When you use your data and analysis to figure out your next steps, you create an incremental understanding that provides structure for your research. Although data analysis and the writing of the research report occur intensively in the second half of the school year, analysis also involves an ongoing effort to make sense of the observations and data as they are being collected, right from the start.

Throughout the research, data analysis performs important functions — not always in a predictable sequence. Below we list some of those functions along with an illustration of each in a teacher's voice.

- **To establish the context and scope of the research:** My question, "How do my students revise their own writing?" might shift. It might become a question about how my students revise a particular kind of writing or about the revisions of only one small group of students.

- **To sift out the research question or issue:** I started with a focus on students' learning in groups but keep getting data on their understanding of social studies. Is my data telling me to change my focus?
- **To determine next steps in data collection:** Maybe I will ask my students why they think this happened in their writing. Maybe I will ask one student. Maybe I will videotape them the next time they write.
- **To probe and focus:** I have one student who is astonishingly accurate in solving math problems but seems at a complete loss when I ask him to explain how he arrived at some of his answers. I'm going to brainstorm all the possible reasons that those two behaviors could coexist logically and then collect data to figure out more.
- **To challenge assumptions and interpretations:** Am I assuming that choice is always a positive factor? Have my students actually failed to learn this material or has my assessment failed in some way to capture their learning? Or is there something else at work?
- **To confirm and validate:** I knew my seniors were more active thinkers than they appeared to be, and my research identifies the topics they think about actively and the conditions they need in order to do so.

The ongoing process of shifting back and forth between tight focus and broad view also supports the building of theory, leads to the discovery of findings, and projects ahead into the implications that theory and findings have for your teaching.

The rest of this chapter is divided into four parts: strategies for data analysis, data analysis and writing, findings, and implications. In all these sections, data analysis is the constant as the research moves from data and log writing to the multiple drafts of a research article. The drafting and revision of a final article often intensifies and supports the final data analysis.

STRATEGIES FOR DATA ANALYSIS

Although data analysis starts with the first collection of data, the analytical work that begins about halfway through the year's process involves a new effort to see the research so far as a whole. The following strategies are designed to help you move in and out of your data, from discrete parts to whole views.

Identify and acknowledge assumptions. Writing about what you expect to have happen — or what you expect to find out — can help you and others see ways to check out those assumptions and question them throughout your data analysis. Identifying assumptions may help you reframe your research question and identify your theories.

Carolyn Perry included in her 1997 research article, "Huh? A Teacher Looks at Students' Listening and Learns Some Lessons About Teaching," a description of uncovering her assumptions as a high school journalism and English teacher-researcher. After a data analysis session like the one described at the opening of this chapter, Perry reported that her colleagues had helped her see the many different assumptions she had had from the start. In her article, she listed those assumptions, then wrote the following:

> *The process of identifying these assumptions was exciting.... I returned to my students' responses with new insight. I now realized that I did not know how these students defined listening.*

Later, after Perry asked her students about "listening responsibility," both that of the teacher and the students, she received some information that she found irritating — that the students saw the teacher as being at least partially responsible for the listening that occurred in the classroom. Perry herself acknowledged:

> *Now, I had long believed that part of my job as a teacher is to find ways to make sure the students find some interest in and usefulness for my messages. And sometimes I'd found some pretty good ways to do that. When I finally sat down... with my small group partners..., I realized that my original emotional reaction reflected*

an assumption I hadn't acknowledged: that the listener (student) is fully responsible for his or her ability to pay attention and listen to a speaker (teacher). Yet, during that second glance, I noticed that most of the kids wrote thoughtful things about the sharing of that responsibility.

One student wrote in response to the question of who is more responsible, "Me, mostly. The teacher also. Teachers are so important. A good teacher can make the difference between liking and hating a subject."

And I do believe this is true. I was ignoring my sixth assumption which stated, "Listening is a relational activity and therefore can only truly be understood when all participants in the communication interaction are considered."

I wasn't supposed to be looking at only the students' roles in this process. I, as a teacher, had a part in this, too!

But it took the small group meeting — where I had to face my response to the responsibility question — to jolt me into the next phase of understanding: Teacher research must be relational in nature because teaching is. If a teacher does not acknowledge the information received from his or her students, then it is not really knowledge.

Perry's discovery of her assumptions throughout her research gave her opportunities to probe even more deeply for the insights that, in the end, made a difference both to her study and to her teaching.

Speculate. Identify your hunches about what your data means. Make an educated guess and see if your data supports your hunch. Look for ways to challenge and test your own assumptions in this way.

Categorize and sort. Having read through all of your data so far, decide on several categories that help you see what you have. Try grouping your categories in different ways — as an outline, Venn diagram, web, list, or chart. How much can you fit into your categories? Consider what both the categories and the "left out" parts tell you about your data as a whole.

Make up your own charts, pictures, lists, and systems since the frameworks offer information about the context. A physics teacher, for example, might seek to understand what happens in learning logs in terms of problem solving. If you have used the taxonomies of other researchers, notice the ways in which they can help clarify your understandings as you frame your own.

Physically move your data around. Use floor, table, or wall space to group and sort the data differently so that you can try out new ways of putting it together again.

Order. Decide on an order, a logical progression, for your data and try it out. You might organize chronologically, by chain of effects, by frequency of occurrence, or by degrees of importance.

Compare constantly. As you examine your data, keep comparing what you are looking at to the data you have looked at previously. If you have examined students' writing for speculative language, for instance, develop some categories, collect more data, and then compare the new data to the previously categorized data to see how your categories hold up, revising where needed.

Shift your bases for comparison. For example, if you have been examining the purposes of students' talking to learn during small group work using audiotape recordings, examine the same students' purposes in writing to learn. How do purposes for talk and writing compare? Use your comparison to help you focus and refine your questions.

Pay attention to surprises and unexpected results. Look for what doesn't fit your assumptions, expectations, or theories — or the theories of other researchers.

When you come upon data or events that contradict what you expect, probe to uncover the underlying principle that makes the occurrence of two seemingly contradictory events happen. For example, if most competent revisers in an English class revise large-scale issues in their pieces before smaller questions of mechanics, but one student (also a competent reviser) always corrects spelling mistakes first, what is the underlying principle that unites the two seemingly contradictory approaches?

Triangulate. Check out the same data from three different angles. This strategy is designed to challenge assumptions and to validate your research. In a study of one student's writing, Bob Ingalls noted a strong sense of purpose, voice, and clarity in the informal notes that the student wrote to his peers as compared to writings for English class. Ingalls's observations of the student's interactions with others in the class, his subsequent interviews with the student, and his investigation of the student's standardized test scores uncovered issues of power, authority, and identity that played critical roles for that student in the classroom. When you collect and compare different kinds of data on your question from a variety of sources, as Ingalls did, you are triangulating.

Talk with others about your research. Describe your data and interpretations to your colleagues. Listen to what *you* say — and see if they can see what you see. Listen to them openly to clarify, broaden, and otherwise validate your findings. During data analysis, the research group becomes a critical questioning and response group that challenges and provides essential help in seeing patterns, a developing focus, and organizing principles of the research.

Ask your students what they think. As you interpret your data and draft your final report, your students may act as an additional research and revision group for you. They may listen to your drafts and validate or question findings. They may return with new ideas about their own learning, for they have recognized that how they learn is important information to you. They may become co-researchers, a relationship that both simplifies and intensifies the problem of confidentiality in the research.

Alberta Grossman wrote in her research log about the experience of reading to her students a draft of her research report, "What Happens When Mickey Writes?"

> I read my students my report of what we had just done. Good response. The first thing they said before I began was, "You're not going to use our names, are you?" They were pleased that I had changed their names. "Mickey" made a little fuss — "That means I have big ears" — but then he decided he liked it. He also responded to, "People don't learn from absorbing. They learn from mucking around and finding out for themselves." He said, "See, you finally learned it."

Restate. Periodically, rewrite your question. Change your question when necessary to fit new directions in your data. Expect the question to become more global at times and at times more focused. Mary

Schulman's log entries about her first graders' reading (quoted in "Choice and the Research Question") show the evolution of her question from the beginning of the research to the final draft.

Abstract and distill. State the essence of your findings as if you had to explain what you had discovered in 50 words or less. Write as if you have been invited to speak extemporaneously at a conference or as if conference planners have asked you to FAX an abstract of your research to them the next day. Following is a form we've used.

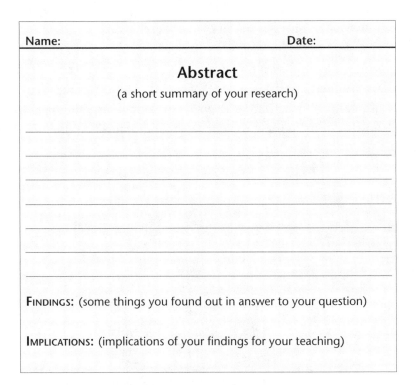

Name: Date:

Abstract
(a short summary of your research)

FINDINGS: (some things you found out in answer to your question)

IMPLICATIONS: (implications of your findings for your teaching)

Take a break. Remember that periods of distance and separation — in addition to (the elusive) uninterrupted periods of concentration — can further the attempt to understand what your data reveal. If work or life events (a winter holiday, for instance) cause you to set your research aside for a time, try to make the break a clean and clearly defined one. Your mind will keep working for you.

Visualize. Create a visual representation of your data. Sketch the metaphors that come to your mind when you think of your data and what it means. Use colors, shapes, and placement on the page to show different ideas and groupings. Frances Nelson describes the fruits of such labor.

> *My moment of awakening came when I had to draw my data and I discovered a bunch of crap going in forty-seven directions with no connections. That was scary and I knew I had to come up with some kind of question. I can't really remember when the idea of writing about the reading logs came forth, but I know it never would have if I was not in this [research group].*

Spend some time with the two visuals below. They were created by Patti Sue Williams and Gretchen Portwood. The meanings that you derive from your visualization depend on your interpretations, often after showing your "poster" to your research group for comments.

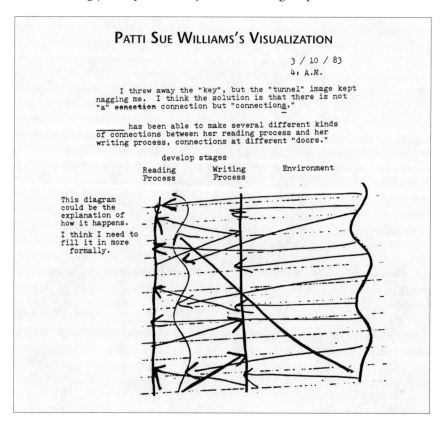

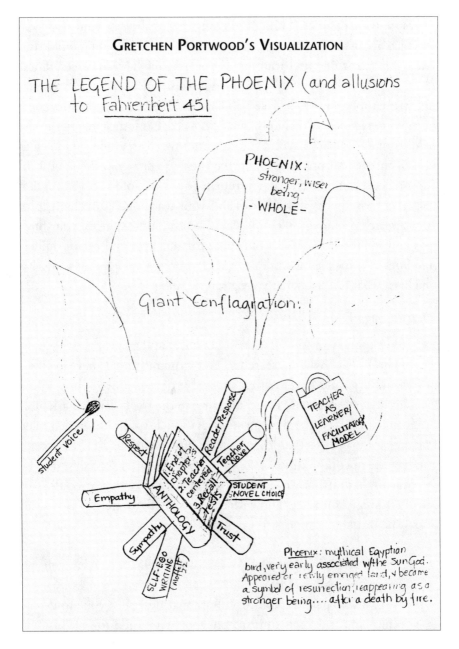

GRETCHEN PORTWOOD'S VISUALIZATION

THE LEGEND OF THE PHOENIX (and allusions to Fahrenheit 451

PHOENIX:
stronger, wiser
being
- WHOLE -

Giant Conflagration:

Phoenix: mythical Egyptian bird, very early associated w/the Sun God. Appeared or rarely enraged land, & became a symbol of resurrection; reappearing as a stronger being..... after a death by fire.

Use what works for you — what ordinarily helps you organize, sort, synthesize, and interpret. If you tend to make lists, lists may help you look at your data; if you work well with folders, try filing systems. Use your favorite utensils and strategies.

State your theories. Through the ongoing analysis of your data, you articulate the assumptions basic to your teaching and revise and build your ideas about teaching and learning as you try out new strategies. These ideas — your theories — are grounded in your practice, even if you have not written them down or talked about them before. Your theories come from your experience, including your knowledge of other theories in the field. Your data analysis allows you to work toward an articulated integration of theory and practice. Often the process shows you theoretical inconsistencies that, like errors in a student paper, are informative data that help you revise both your theories and your teaching. With the help of your research group and plentiful data from multiple sources, your findings and interpretations will contribute to your own and others' understandings of principles at work in your classroom — not "what works" as much as "what is *at* work" in your given situation.

WRITING AND DATA ANALYSIS

To the many strategies that help us collect and analyze data, we add writing itself. Even when researchers know their findings, have outlines of their reports, and have written short abstracts, writing a final report gives additional shape and understanding to the work. Particularly useful during analysis is the drafting and revision at this point which may, in fact, be the analysis that leads to your understanding of the research you have been conducting.

Starting a draft, however, is not always easy. We have used the following strategies ourselves and with other teacher-researchers as ways to overcome initial roadblocks to getting started:

- After rereading your data, write to yourself about what you think you are seeing.
- Try a one-page exploratory draft that describes your findings so far. It is helpful to set your data aside for a while before you do this.
- Meet with a few colleagues and agree to write for a set amount of time (20 minutes, for instance); then stop and read what you have written to the rest of the group.

- Plunge into an exploratory draft as if you had already finished analyzing.
- Concentrating on your data as a whole, write quickly as if you were talking to someone about your research.
- Write as if you were talking or writing a letter to someone you know, telling the story of your research.
- Although this is research, you are a teacher. Write about what has happened to your teaching as you've been conducting research. What methods have you used, developed, discarded? What have you learned that might help other teachers? What does your research imply about methods of teaching?
- Using the web below, start at a place that seems easy or possible to you and write about that first, moving on when you are ready. Develop your own headings.

Once the drafting has started, we have used many of the following questions and suggestions to help us and other teacher-researchers support each other's work.

During data analysis and early drafting:
- Organize your data chronologically or see if organization by topic works better.
- Try different pieces of data in different categories. Treat the categories — whether they are yours or someone else's — flexibly. Revise categories, as needed.
- Display the relationships of parts of your data. What would a chart show? A diagram? A map?

- Select the data that you will include to support your findings. Challenge your findings and your data again as you do.
- Draft possible implications for your teaching from your findings.
- Take the data (or finding) back to your students to see how they interpret it.
- Think about how you might teach based on your implications. How will your reasons for teaching something in a particular way be different?
- Make distinctions between findings and implications.

During drafting and revision:
- See what happens when you divide the paper into chapters or subheadings under different topics.
- Try showing students' behavior with data alone — leaving out value judgments.
- Choose a variety of kinds of data to support findings and to show how you arrived at them.
- Deliberately sort your feelings from your interpretations of data (as Perry does earlier in this chapter).
- Decide how much of your research process your reader needs to know.
- Identify your intended readers and the voice you will use in writing to them.
- Show your draft to your students and see what they say.
- If your question and your findings don't seem to fit together, try restating your question. So, your question is… and your findings are… How do they fit together?

As difficult as the analysis and writing can be, the writing itself helps us know what we know. Even with the best of suggestions, however, this part of the research is challenging, and we suspect that you will recognize the reactions Mary K. Prioletti describes below. Prioletti and her research group met one weekend to respond to each other's drafts as they were finishing the writing of their final research articles.

As I sat with my group on Sunday evening, we came to the conclusion that, if there is a God, waiting at home for each of us was a message from Marion stating that the major objective of this course was the research process *and the product was in fact, not necessary. Relax — forget the paper. We all agreed that the research process has been a great learning experience — and the paper more than a bit frustrating. However, only four days later I can say, besides that I'm glad to have the paper done, that I never could (or would) have looked inside my teaching for "why's" had it not been for this final paper…. This paper brought it all together — 3 years of teaching — but it was the actual writing of it that made* me *aware….*

FINDINGS

Although we treat findings and implications separately here, they both refer to the end result of your analysis, an interpretive task that allows you to see and know what you think to be true based on your study. Teacher-researchers often describe their learning as finding or discovering something. We believe, however, that there is also a sense in which what you find is already there and what you are really doing is interpreting what exists.

Some teacher-researchers call their research results "conclusions," showing how their original assumptions have been challenged or revised into new theories which they propose at the completion of their studies. Whatever they are labeled, your findings are statements you know you can make about your own teaching and your students' learning *because* your analysis of your data led you to the statements. The analysis lets you know what you know; the findings are the statement of what you know.

Findings usually appear near the end of a teacher research report, often stated in a list form and numbered or underlined and elaborated. MacLean, in her first teacher research study on how her students made revisions and editing decisions, introduced her findings at the very end of her paper.

My students have helped me to understand the following:
- *Students not only can but do make judgments when they write.*

- *Most of those judgments ordinarily lie beneath the surface of awareness.*
- *Commenting on their own writing brought to the surface three voices among the many that speak to us and with us from within when we write.*
- *Those three voices are the voice of the imagined external audience, the voice of the student as writer, and the voice of the student as his or her own audience.*
- *The voice of the imagined external audience usually inhibits; the voices of the student as writer and audience usually help the student make choices.*
- *Commenting on their own writing helped students not only become aware of those voices but also set up a dialogue with the writing teacher.*
- *In making comments on their writing, students worked toward becoming masters of their own work, not masters of a teacher's writing, yet they learned willingly from the teacher as a consultant.*
- *The internal audience probably operates in shaping a writing throughout the course of the writing's development; listening to the internal audience may help students gain confidence, trust themselves, take responsibility for their writing and free them to take risks.*

Teacher-researchers usually present these findings, as MacLean does above, in an order that shows how they are related to each other. Jan Milkovich, a third-grade teacher, studied structured and unstructured talk among her students during a "buddy" reading and writing program with kindergarten students. She presents her conclusions as a discussion at the end of her report:

> *In observing unstructured and structured student talk in my classroom this year, I have reached a few conclusions. Student talk serves many purposes in every lesson, activity, or time of the school day. The more we ask students to work cooperatively and make decisions, the more conversations will become a part of learning. The classroom envi-*

ronment is a social one where students need to learn to get along with each other by holding conversations, expressing their feelings and thoughts, asking questions, and responding to each other and to the teacher. Young children are using their language to solve problems, to learn from each other, and to make friends. Through whole language learning activities in the classroom, students are getting to know and evaluate each other as learners.

In addition to the ways MacLean and Milkovich treat their findings, you will find others in the teacher-researcher articles in Part III.

Implications for Practice

As a result of the meanings you constructed from your data — your findings — you now know that you have reason to teach in a particular way. Your ideas about how you might teach are the implications of your findings for your practice.

After Milkovich wrote about what she found out, she noted that her findings had led her to reexamine her own teaching. She identified her reexaminations as implications for her teaching and summarized them in the following way:

> *This leads me to examine my own teaching. I am more aware that I both lead and direct the language of the learning in whole group discussions. Implications for my teaching from this quest are the following:*

- *I will continue to have students write their thoughts from a given prompt because students learn more when they think about the content.*
- *I will try to encourage small group discussions, so more students may become engaged in the talk.*
- *I will continue to observe and provide feedback to my students as a way of identifying appropriate learning behavior.*
- *I will continue buddy lessons as these are rich in talk and learning.*
- *I would like to let students have more control in group discussions as I take on more of a facilitator role to the discussion groups.*

These implications for my teaching have a domino effect. They lead to future research questions to achieve these goals. What is the role of a teacher-facilitator in the changing classroom? How does the teacher-facilitator encourage increased student language? How does the social nature of the classroom have an impact on the role of the teacher-facilitator?

Notice the inclusion at the end of Milkovich's report of questions for further study. You will often realize that you cannot present a finding on what you know is an important element of your question. Possibly an implication of your current study suggests something new you would like to investigate. Keep a list of the unanswered questions that have to wait for another year, another research project, and add them to your report as direction for further study. They help give your report boundaries at the same time that they offer additional ways of looking at your findings and implications.

We do not mean to suggest that implications for practice apply only at the end of a study. On the contrary, you are acting on what your data implies throughout your research. Ordinarily you might try a lesson, notice how it goes, decide whether or not it works, and then either discard or file it for future use. When conducting research, however, you keep track of the teaching process and the students' reactions, collect and analyze this data, organize it into findings, and then consider the implications. Your research makes daily lessons part of a much larger picture and enables you to develop interrelated practices and theories that take many variables into account.

The following log entries from Leslie Gray, a high school social studies teacher, illustrate the immediate effects or implications of her research for her teaching. She is also using her research log to plan lessons.

9/13, in class

I'm curious about concept development and how that can be enhanced by writing…. I'm also curious about their current events logs. What happens when they write for an audience in the future about how they see their world today? Will they see the past differently if they are writing a "primary source?" Will they care about the present more?

9/14, in my classroom/free period

It's changing the way I teach — the Current Events log — I'm using it to introduce the unit of Labor Unions. I'm going to have them look at that picture on 273 of the coal-mining boys — what questions would you ask them? What would you want to know about their jobs? their lives? the way their jobs impacted on their lives? For this log they will write about their jobs for a future audience. Will they care more about those boys? Will they think more about work and its place in American society? About its priority and place in their lives.

I think I'll have them hand in a piece of historical evidence w/ this one — a pay slip…. They'll come to learn about how to be object literate & document literate by gathering evidence from around them and deciding why it is significant. I will encourage them to find a picture of the personality they wrote about last week — this log needs to come to life — maybe that will bring some voices into their writing.

After 3rd period class

We listed on the board questions they would ask the boys in the picture if they could. That was the prewriting for this log. These prewriting sessions on the log are worth looking at. Instead of taking time from instruction they have become instruction….

What are we doing here? What happened in my class today?

1. *Motivation — They are now interested in the plight of the working class in the late 19th century.*
2. *They are becoming document literate. By attaching some "thing" from their workplace to their entry, they are seeing how historians can use documents to study the past.*
3. *They are relating past to present — sensing similarities and differences.*
4. *They are relating present to future — seeing their lives & jobs as being historical fodder for the future (alliteration?).*

Gray's teaching and her research worked together. The results of her teaching became the questions of her research, and her tentative answers became the implications for her teaching.

The following log-writing excerpt was written by Judy Grumbacher, a high school physics teacher-researcher, during her study of using writing to learn physics.

> *Oct. 31, 11 A.M.: I was having trouble explaining to a kid how forces act through a hinged joint. I knew I had to do a better job than I'd done — simply saying "forces can act in any direction through a hinge" didn't help the kid. I suspect that others in class wondered about this also, but didn't want to ask. Many of my GT kids just write down everything I put on the board and assume it's right — A bad assumption since I've been making mistakes right and left recently when I solve problems on the board.*
>
> *Back to the hinges — so I sat down yesterday during 6ᵗʰ period — while the class was taking a quiz — and wrote about what I needed to clear up in class today. As I was writing I thought of a bunch of examples to use about how force acts through a hinge. I think those examples will help. Now it all seems clear — how to present the hinge problem — I need to start by talking about — demonstrating's even better — the handle on a lawn mower. As the angle changes, so does the effective force — this is an example more kids are familiar with than the boom crane I started with. Writing to learn how to teach!*
>
> *(I'm sorry now I didn't write all that stuff about hinges and cranes in my log… I'm getting as careless as my students…)*

Integrating their teaching and research, both Grumbacher and Gray use the ongoing implications of their research, first to revise their plans for their next lessons, and second to develop and revise their theories about learning.

Theresa Manchey suggests a third use of the implications of teachers' research — one that applies beyond the individual classroom. In the final paragraphs of her report on a study of the use of drawing in a ninth-grade English class, she quotes her students' advice and then gives some of her own:

In the future I will continue to use drawings and I will not feel they are a "filler." Still, I will continue to observe my students' responses to these assignments. I will heed Mary's caution to impose more of a time limit on such activities, but I will also remember Jane's needs:

> *The poster or project lets you put all your ideas and feelings into one. They all come together. I think the visual helps me understand the story a little better.*

I believe school offers little opportunity for students like Jane to exercise their strength. Maybe further studies in this area will help to change the current balance of time in our classrooms.

REFERENCES

Gray, L. (1987). "I think it has something to do with our minds": Using synectics to learn about history. In M. M. Mohr and M. S. MacLean *Working together* (pp. 67-77). Urbana, IL: National Council of Teachers of English.

Grumbacher, J. (1988). How writing helps physics students become better problem solvers. In T. Fulwiler (Ed.), *The journal book*, (pp. 323-329). Westport, CT: Heinemann-Boynton/Cook.

Ingalls, R. (1989). Finding a balance. *Language and learning: Reports from a teacher- researcher seminar.* Fairfax, VA: Northern Virginia Writing Project, George Mason University.

MacLean, M. S. (1983). Voices within: The audience speaks. *English Journal, 72*, 62 – 66.

Milkovich, J. (1994). Social encounters of the learning kind. *Language and learning: Reports from a teacher-researcher seminar.* Fairfax, VA: Northern Virginia Writing Project, George Mason University.

Nelson, F. (1989). Reading logs? But this is a writing class! *Language and learning: Reports from a teacher-researcher seminar.* Fairfax, VA: Northern Virginia Writing Project, George Mason University.

Perry, C. D. (1997). Huh? A teacher looks at students listening and learns some lessons about teaching. *Falls Church High School Teacher Researcher Project.* Fairfax County, VA: Fairfax County Public Schools.

Portwood, G. (1989). Is there literature out there everywhere? *Language and learning: Reports from a teacher-researcher seminar*. Fairfax, VA: Northern Virginia Writing Project, George Mason University.

Prioletti, M. K. (1989). Evolution of a primary teacher. *Language and learning: Reports from a teacher-researcher seminar*. Fairfax, VA: Northern Virginia Writing Project, George Mason University.

Williams, P. S. (1983). Back and forth: One student's reading-writing connections. *Research in writing: Reports from a teacher-researcher seminar*. Fairfax, VA: Northern Virginia Writing Project, George Mason University.

READING

What and when do you read in the research process?

Reading the work of others can give you a starting point and push you in a new direction but should not limit your thinking. Bernadette Glaze did her first teacher research study on writing-to-learn in history in 1981-82. She had learned from studying the work of James Britton, and his terminology had helped her understand what she was noticing in her students' work. But there was not an easy fit between her data and the writing classifications Britton had developed from his research. She worked and reworked her data and worried that the lack of fit suggested problems with her research. In fact, however, Glaze and Britton were creating together a better understanding of how writing-to-learn works. It was the "together" part that she found hard to accept. Her own sense of authority was not as developed as her acknowledgment of a recognized authority.

After several more studies of writing-to-learn with her students, Glaze looked back at her experiences of learning to question authorities as peers. She wrote: "Once I had the power to ask questions and the self-confidence to find the answers to those questions — it was at that point that I became a professional… a professional who made decisions about teaching and learning based on research I had done and also on research that others had done."

As Glaze did, give yourself theoretical authority in your classroom research. Trust in your own honesty and analysis, with the help of your colleagues. Read others' research with a critical eye. Design your own interpretations, charts, diagrams, and ways of interpreting your data. Compare, but don't try to make what you find fit into someone else's theory or diagram. Develop your own terminology and categories, your own ways of describing what happens.

Begin as if you were the first researcher to study your question. Take a fresh look at it. You are familiar with the work of other researchers from your professional reading over the years and your reading inspires and informs your teaching, but what you look at first, as a researcher, is your classroom. You do not have to begin a teacher research study with a period of reading through all the work of other researchers in your field. You have rich sources at hand — how your students learn, how you teach, and the interaction between the two.

It is possible to conduct a study skillfully and to state data interpretations accurately, not knowing that another researcher has preceded you and expressed thoughts similar to yours. You have probably had the experience at least once of reading an article in a professional journal and realizing that another teacher or researcher has been working on the same problem and come up with some of the same conclusions that you have. You may even have thought, "I could have written that article." Your article would have been different, however, because your way of teaching and your class of students create a different context for learning and teaching. Research knowledge grows through the contributions of many people over the years, and all researchers add to or chip away at the body of knowledge that is understood to exist.

To say all this is not to deny your connection to a professional community of theorists, researchers, and practitioners. You might derive your research question from professional reading or from the work of a colleague as it relates to your own practice. Often you know that the research or comments of another have influenced your thinking. If you have read and admired the work of Paulo Freire, for example, you may realize that the way you and your students worked out an assignment has something in common with his concept of dialogic curriculum and you want to figure out how it works in your classroom. If your research is on the responses your students make to their reading, you will read and study Nancie Atwell, Robert Probst, and Louise Rosenblatt as fellow researchers. If you are interested in how researchers like Matthew Miles and Michael Huberman or Yvonna Lincoln and Egon Guba describe research methodology, you bring to your reading your experience of teacher research methods.

The reading you do for your research is not necessarily limited to other research. Martha Kestermeier, a high school biology teacher-researcher, and her students investigated the effect of reading great science writing had on their ideas about science. They read from Lewis Thomas, Loren Eiseley, Rachel Carson, and others. Kestermeier reported how her own reading influenced her "science mind." "I can emphasize the big ideas and weave a better tapestry of biology, as I teach cells, anatomy, genetics, and ecology." Her classroom research was indebted to the science writing of others, and through her study she discovered new connections to that writing in her teaching.

Whatever you decide to read, give credit in your reference list to those you know have preceded you in the field and whose ideas you know have led you to discover your own. Such credit acknowledges the connectedness of the search for understanding common to all researchers. It is also courteous and fair. Acknowledge the influences that you know.

As you research more, write up your results, and move from one question to another, you become more involved with a wider professional community and see your work in a wider context of professional research. Not only will you read the work of others in your field, they will begin to read yours. The more research you do, the more you will become involved in the field, but remember that your groundedness in classroom interaction is the authority for all your work and your offering to the field of educational research.

The amount of reading you do as part of your research process varies from study to study and is based on the decisions you make about what you need to know. You will usually combine reading about research with readings of research, especially readings of other teacher-researchers.

A suggested chronology for reading that will support you in the research process follows.

1. **Begin with reading to get acquainted with the ideas of qualitative, descriptive, interpretive research in comparison to experimental or quantitative research.** It helps to have an understanding of the broad range of methods available and their philosophical underpinnings. You might read from Miles and Huberman's discussion of qualitative and quantitative research as complementary (p. 40-43) or study the chart in *Inside/Outside* by Marilyn Cochran-Smith and Susan Lytle (p.12-13)

that compares research on teaching with teacher research. If you are reading in a book on qualitative or ethnographic research methodology that does not cover teacher research, it will be helpful for you and your research group to discuss how the situations described are like and different from yours as teacher-researchers.

2. **Next, you might spend some time on readings that address the role of the teacher as researcher and at the same time begin to look at research as a process.** An article we often use is Nancie Atwell's "Wonderings to Pursue" or Bernadette Glaze's "A Teacher Speaks out About Research." Also look at articles that define teacher research such as Glenda Bissex's "What Is a Teacher-Researcher?"

3. **Next, select readings to highlight the process of research.** We read about the emergent nature of research findings, researchers' comments on their research processes, and the purpose of different activities during different times of the research. Look for chapters on interviewing or writing field notes in some of the research texts such as Lincoln and Guba's *Naturalistic Inquiry* and compare their suggestions with your own situation. You probably will not use their filing systems, interview questions, or methods of analysis directly, but you can adapt them and get ideas for your own methods. Various teacher research articles themselves are useful at this point, especially when they discuss the research process. Reading from Ruth Hubbard and Brenda Power's *The Art of Classroom Inquiry: A Handbook for Teacher Researchers* and other books written directly about the process of teacher research will also be helpful at this time.

4. **After you have collected and begun to analyze your data, the next kind of reading that is useful is that which raises questions about assumptions** — assumptions underlying particular theories as well as those that underlie different kinds of classroom research. Two articles that have always generated a lot of discussion in our groups are Janet Emig's "Non-Magical Thinking" and Magdalene Lampert's "How Do Teachers Manage to Teach?"

5. **During the second part of the year, when you are beginning to write up your research, you will want to read reports that other teacher-researchers have written,** not as direct models but to see what final drafts look like. Our research groups discuss the content of the research

and its implications, as well as the process. How did the teacher select a final area of focus? What data might have been set aside? How did the context of the study become part of the final report? How did the final report itself incorporate data, methodology, findings, interpretations, and implications? Any articles in Part III would be appropriate for this kind of analysis.

6. **As you work toward your final draft, you may read articles about writing up research, articles that challenge your ideas of what research must look and sound like.** In addition to an understanding of Ken Macrorie's "I-Search" process, many find Don Murray's "Write Research to Be Read" helpful. We also suggest Harry Wolcott's "Writing up Qualitative Research."

7. **At the very end of the process, you may want to look ahead to your future life as a teacher-researcher.** Articles such as Rita Johnson's "Where Can Teacher Research Lead? One Teacher's Daydream" or Mohr's "Wild Dreams and Sober Cautions: The Future of Teacher Research" offer the opportunity to think about how teacher research can continue to be a part of your professional life.

Reading is an integral part of your life as a teacher-researcher and many choices are available. If you become interested in the bases of teacher research, the bibliography of suggested readings at the end of the book is a place to start. There we include works from a variety of fields that describe the history of teacher research and its theoretical underpinnings as well as research ideas from sociology and anthropology. Of course, there is always one book or article that is missing from all the bibliographies and all the catalogs — the one that you are getting ready to write.

REFERENCES

Atwell, N. (1990). Wonderings to pursue: The writing teacher as researcher. In B. M. Power & R. Hubbard (Eds.), *Literacy in process* (pp. 315-331). Westport, CT: Heinemann-Boynton/Cook.

Bissex, G. (1987). What is a teacher researcher? In G. Bissex & Bullock, R. (Eds.), *Seeing for ourselves: Case study research by teachers of writing* (pp. 3-5). Westport, CT: Heinemann-Boynton/Cook.

Cochran-Smith, M. & Lytle, S. L. (1993). *Inside/Outside: Teacher research and knowledge.* New York: Teachers College Press.

Emig, J. (1983). *The web of meaning*. Westport, CT: Heinemann-Boynton/Cook.

Glaze, B. (1987). A teacher speaks out about research. In *Plain Talk About Learning and Writing Across the Curriculum* (pp. 87-99). Richmond, VA: Virginia Department of Education.

Johnson, R. (1993). Where can teacher research lead? One teacher's daydream. *Educational Leadership, 51*(2), 66-88.

Kestermeier, M. (1989). You can make a biologist by writing alone. *Research in Language and Learning: Reports from a Teacher-Researcher Seminar*. Fairfax, VA: Northern Virginia Writing Project, George Mason University.

Lampert, M. (1985). How do teachers manage to teach? Perspectives on problems in practice. *Harvard Educational Review, 55* (2), 178-94.

Macrorie, K. (1980). *Searching writing*. Westport, CT: Heinemann-Boynton/Cook.

Miles, M. & Huberman, A. M. (1994). *Qualitative data analysis*. (2nd ed.). Beverly Hills, CA: Sage.

Mohr, M. (1996). Wild dreams and sober cautions: The future of teacher research. In Donoahue Z., Van Tassell, M. A., & Patterson, L. (Eds.), *Research in the classroom: Talk, texts, and inquiry* (pp. 117-123). Newark, DE: International Reading Association.

Murray, D. (1982). Write research to be read. In *Learning by teaching* (pp. 103-112). Westport, CT: Heinemann-Boynton/Cook.

Wolcott, H. F. (1990). Writing up qualitative research. *Qualitative Research Methods Series #20*. Newbury Park, CA: Sage.

DISSEMINATION

How do you go public with your research?

Going public with your research means explaining to professional colleagues what you did and what you found out. It is a vital part of the research process, whether you do it by talking with the teacher in the next classroom or publishing in a professional journal. Dissemination furthers the ongoing search for understanding of teaching and learning. Researchers question, criticize, and challenge each other about methods and results to make sure that trustworthy new research makes its way into professional knowledge. The knowledge derived from teacher research is of value beyond the classroom and school where it is conducted, and our professional discourse needs the participation of teacher-researchers.

Dissemination of your research that is meaningful and long lasting usually begins in **teacher-to-teacher talk** when professional issues are discussed. Just as your students ask you questions about your research, your colleagues will want to know why you are doing it and what you are finding out. When you respond, their comments and questions help you to develop and revise your ideas. You may not think of yourself as a staff developer, but when you talk to your colleagues about your research, you inform them not only about your research but also about research itself and, in the process, may contribute to a change in their thinking.

Although some argue that publication is not necessary for a teacher's research to be useful and valuable, we think it is important to bring a study to a conclusion in the form of a **written report**. This is true, regardless of how tentative the findings are and how clear it is that the study will continue. The research report at this time is a deadline draft, a description of where you are now in your research and in your thinking about your question. A deadline draft is important as a stopping point in the process of researching. Without these drafts you could go on collecting data in boxes in your dining room or under your desk without ever approaching analysis. Writing a deadline draft requires you to stop and say, "Here is where I am now, this is what I think now, and these are the questions I still have."

The teacher is rare who is able, without the pressure of colleagues and deadlines, to write and publish for his or her own satisfaction. Because teaching in grades K-12 does not encourage contemplation and writing, in our own research we have needed an agreed-upon deadline and the support of our research groups to get through drafting and revision. Final (or deadline) drafts are of lengths compatible with professional journals (usually 5-15 pages) and are seen as open to further revision for publication. When the teacher-researcher group is organized as a course, deadline drafts fit into the course organization. When the research group is school-based or across schools, the group itself agrees upon deadlines for their own informal publication. Deadlines which hover around the first week of May have been the most successful because they happen before the vigorous round of end-of-school activities begins.

Teacher research reports vary in content and form. In essence, the **content** includes some discussion of your research process and presents some of your discoveries about teaching and learning supported by appropriate selections from your data. Not all of your data will appear in your report and not all of your questions will be answered. Even though the broad outline of your research includes the teaching and learning of everyone in your classroom, including yourself, you may choose to describe only part of the study in your written report. Be explicit about the way you are focusing and limiting your report.

Examples of different ways of reporting on the content of your research follow.

+ Explain how you came to understand your teaching during your research.
+ Show your changes as a teacher in relation to changes in your students' learning.
+ Describe and analyze the usefulness of a particular way of teaching or a particular assignment as it unfolds in your classroom.
+ Write about a teaching idea you have developed, along with your observations, documentation, and analysis of what happens to the idea as you teach.

- Focus on classroom management and describe the interrelationship between curriculum and management.
- Show your students' learning in one specific area that interests you or in relation to a particular assignment or part of the curriculum.
- Document what the students have taught you as you looked at the classroom as a place to conduct research.
- Trace the learning of one student or a small group of students in a particular curriculum area.

Just as the content of teacher research reports varies, so does the **form**. Some possibilities are:

- A chronological narrative beginning with the story of your interest in your question, describing your research methods and what you found out.
- A more conventional exposition with sections on the background of the question, the research methodology, and your interpretations of the results.
- A proposal, using your current study to plan a larger project based on what you have discovered so far and your plans for the future.
- Scripts for various voices.
- A hypertext with links to your data, findings, implications, and other elements of your study.

The form used to report your research depends on your purpose and intended audience. Middle school science teacher-researcher Rita Johnson, for instance, has published her research in a variety of publications, adapting to varied audiences and purposes. A member of the American Association of University Women, Johnson offered to write a column on education for her chapter's newsletter while she was conducting research on gender equity in science learning. In each issue she wrote about part of her research, adjusting form and content appropriately for the readers of the newsletter.

A few years ago, Johnson lay in bed thinking about the effect of teacher research and its possibilities for the future when, at 4:00 A.M., she decided to wake up her husband to discuss her ideas. The article resulting from their conversation, "Where Can Teacher Research Lead? One Teacher's Daydream," was published in *Educational Leadership* in 1993. She continues to conduct and disseminate her research on middle school science teaching and learning — on gender equity, on topics related to the wetlands her school protects and cares for, and on preparing students for the new state achievement tests.

A research group at Robinson High School in Northern Virginia is planning to publish their articles on their school's web pages and to present the articles to their colleagues (along with refreshments) during their planning periods. Colleagues and researchers will meet in a room with several computers and get practice in finding articles they are interested in on the web as well as discuss teacher research in general.

In the final months of the school year, as publication deadlines approach, we suggest that you and the other members of your research group give each other five- to ten-minute **informal talks** about your research, tracing its progress and citing your findings and their implications. Your colleagues will probably ask you questions and express continuing interest in your work, often remarking on how your study connects to theirs and pointing out common questions or different findings. These oral reports serve to help synthesize the work and sometimes result in last-minute revisions of the written reports.

Another way to disseminate your research is through **common group findings**. We generally explore common findings only after the whole group has read all the reports. The group discusses and lists any similarities they find in their work and looks for findings they think are common to all. Group members are used to challenging each other at this point and are discriminating about what they will include as common to the group.

At the Langston Hughes Middle School in Fairfax County, Virginia, where Rita Johnson taught and began her teacher research, the school's teacher research project was generally focused on students who were not achieving up to their potential, especially those who were designated as belonging to a minority group. In May, as the publication was being readied, the group met to report on their work to each other. During the conversation they began to identify some common findings. Here are two examples of these findings as printed in their group publication:

- *Students need many role models of learners among the adults in their lives. Teachers cannot change a student's home life, although they listen to and learn from students' views of their problems. Teachers can change students' lives at school, however. Our role is that of adults who respect them, do not give up on them, and expect a lot of them.*

- *Situations in the classroom need to be arranged so underachieving students can feel more in control of their learning. They usually feel that their lives and their learning are not under their own control, that things just happen to them. These students need to "buy in" to their learning, to make choices about what they do, to participate in organizing their work, and generally to be given the opportunity to take responsibility for their learning. This responsibility makes them feel worthwhile.*

The teacher-researchers went on to identify teaching strategies that they had seen work successfully with their underachieving students. Those included using response writing, questionnaires, and learning logs; teaching with various kinds of group work; and raising expectations for underachievers through the use of teaching strategies from above-average and gifted classes.

If your group is school-based, the discussion of common and divergent findings has implications for the school as a whole. If you all have similar findings about student reading, this could be information of use to other members of your faculty. If your group has been working on questions related to the same topic — ninth graders' achievement, for example — your common findings are more generalizable than those of each individual report. If your group consists of teachers from different schools, you have a chance to see also how your interpretations and findings apply to broader contexts or how closely embedded they are in an individual context.

Disseminating your research within your own school works best, we think, in a voluntary, informal, colleague-to-colleague **presentation**. Some schools have small publication parties where the researchers are available at roundtables to discuss their work, and those who attend receive a copy of the collected deadline drafts. At other schools, individual researchers have made themselves available to teachers who are interested in their work and have offered brief after-school presentations with the promise of follow-up. In some cases teacher-researchers have been given time during the school day to work with other teachers in their building. At the middle school we have been highlighting, the faculty was invited to a cookies and punch meeting at which they received their copies of the publication and heard a few of the researchers speak briefly about their findings. Those who wished to stay longer participated in roundtable sessions with a teacher-researcher.

Dissemination beyond your school may take the form of presentation at a conference or publication in a professional journal — sometimes even before you give presentations on your work at your own school. It is sometimes the recognition of your work on a state or national scale that brings inquiries from school colleagues.

Attending and giving presentations at state and national conferences are valuable ways to disseminate your work and to become part of a larger network of teacher-researchers nationwide. It is exciting and helpful to speak with others and to see how your work fits into that of the larger research community. Conferences also offer information about grants and publishing opportunities for teacher-researchers.

Increasingly, teacher-researchers' articles are welcomed by educational publishers. In fact, teacher-researchers' lively documentation of classroom activity and conversation, plus their careful analysis, are sought by professional journals eager to publish teacher-researcher articles. If you are interested in publishing, start reading the "Calls for Manuscripts" printed in the professional journals you read. Look for similarities between what you have written with the subjects and themes they mention. It helps, sometimes, to broaden your interpretation of what they have called for in order to include the ideas in your research. Keep a file and calendar of this information along with the deadlines so that you can plan ahead to submit your work.

The journals in which teacher research is most often published are those of the various disciplines such as English or mathematics. Currently, two journals are especially hospitable to teacher research — The National Education Association's *Teaching and Change* and *The Journal of Teacher Research*, edited by Ruth Hubbard and Brenda Power. Recently teacher research articles have appeared in *The Harvard Educational Review, Research in the Teaching of English*, and *The Quarterly of the National Writing Project*. Online journals of teacher research are being established. Increasingly books that are collections of research articles include teacher research on the topic that is the focus of the book. Rarer are whole books such as Scott Christian's *Exchanging Lives: Middle School Writers Online* and Karen Gallas's *The Languages of Learning* based on their work as teacher-researchers.

As more teacher-researchers publish their work, teacher research makes its way into professional bibliographies. Bibliographic dissemination is vital for the health of the profession and for the inclusion of teacher research in the knowledge base of the profession.

REFERENCES

Christian, S. (1997). *Exchanging lives: Middle school writers online*. Urbana, IL: National Council of Teachers of English.

Gallas, K. (1994). *The languages of learning*. New York: Teachers College Press.

Johnson, R. (1993). Where can teacher research lead? One teacher's daydream. *Educational Leadership, 51* (2) 66-68.

Langston Hughes Middle School Collaborative Research Group. (1988). *Teacher research on student learning*. Fairfax County Public Schools, Fairfax County, VA.

Macrorie, K. (1980). *Searching writing*. Rochelle Park, NJ: Hayden Book Co.

TIMING IN RETROSPECT
What happened to two teacher-researchers?

B efore we close this section with Julie Fisher's article on her life as a teacher-researcher, we include the following detailed outlines by Marion MacLean and Carin Hauser to show you how two teacher-researchers saw their research — in retrospect — over a year of school time. Both MacLean and Hauser prepared the outlines after completing their research as a way to help themselves as well as others see how the year's work had come together as a whole.

— ◆ —

An Outline of a Teacher-Researcher's Process After the Fact
by Marion MacLean

The following outline is one I created only after I had completed "Voices Within," the article that resulted from the study outlined here. It represents what was clear to me in retrospect, and I caution readers against thinking that this kind of plan is possible at the start. Even as I reviewed this outline for publication, I couldn't help thinking how methodical, purposeful, and thorough the process looked. But during that research year, the process seemed haphazard, almost slipshod — guided only by the roughly intentional purposes of the unsettled problems I wanted to solve about evaluation and writing. I had to caution myself not to think I had done such a great job planning my research back then.

Having participated in the Northern Virginia Writing Project's Summer Institute during the summer of 1981, I started the following school year with many questions about my students' writing processes and about how to assess students' writing. As the year progressed, an important issue for me came to be that of evaluation: how do I evaluate my students' writing? how do my students evaluate their own writing?

An Outline of a Teacher-Researcher's Process
After the Fact
(M. MacLean)

Late August:	School starts. Teaching English 9 and AP12. Seniors start with tragedy — *Oedipus Rex*.
Thurs., Sept. 10:	In-class response writing to first half of *Oedipus Rex*.
Fri., Sept. 11:	In-class response writing to whole play.
Mon., Sept. 14:	Think-writings on articles I assigned students to read about *Oedipus Rex* reveal that many of my students are writing *to me*. We discuss audience and writing to ourselves.
Wed., Sept. 16:	I assign a think-writing on Artistotle's *Poetics* that I don't collect (on purpose).
Tues., Sept 29 to Fri., Oct. 2:	Conferences on *Oedipus* papers.
Wed., Sept 30:	**First teacher-researcher class meeting.**
Thurs., Oct. 8:	During the essay test on *Oedipus* I try a lengthy, detailed observation of one student. (Response to research class.)
Tues., Oct. 13:	After a couple of days of personal writing ("When I was a kid…"), I ask my seniors to write down their reactions to writing personally and any reasons for their not wanting me to read what they had written. (Some have expressed reservations in class.)
Wed., Oct. 14:	More personal writing in class after which I read aloud what I have written. **Research class meets.**
Thurs., Oct. 15:	I ask the seniors to write a description of the audience to whom they imagine they are writing their college application essays.
Mon., Oct. 19:	Taped interview with one student about his college application essay.

Marginal notes:

These early in-class writings reflect my interest in asking my students to use writing to think, learn, and explore — at the time a relatively unfamiliar strategy for me.

<— Major Data Source (Thurs., Oct. 15)

<— Major Data Source (Mon., Oct. 19)

Tues., Oct. 20:	Taped interview with Chris about his *Oedipus* and college essays.	<— **Major Data Source**
Wed., Oct. 28:	Research log entry on feeling that I can't grade papers any more. **Research class meets.**	
Fri., Oct. 30:	I ask my students (who are well into the writing of their college essays) to write out the story of writing that essay or to describe where they are at this point in shaping it into a final writing.	<— **Major Data Source**
Sat., Nov. 7:	I write in my research log a conference with myself about my research "question." Later I will see that I am listening to an internal dialogue similar to ones that show up in my own students' comments on their papers.	
Wed., Nov. 11:	I ask my students to write out evaluations of their work for the first quarter. **Research class meets.**	
Mon., Nov. 23:	My students meet in reading/writing groups for the first time. I write many observations of them and their subsequent R/W group meetings in my research log.	
Wed., Dec. 2:	**Research class meets.**	
Mon., Dec. 7:	I ask students at the end of the R/W group sessions to think about the criteria for evaluating writing: what criteria can we use to designate any writing as excellent?	
Wed., Dec. 9:	We discuss the criteria that they came up with. I then ask them to write their reactions to being evaluated by those criteria.	
Wed., Dec. 16:	**Research class meets.**	
Tues., Dec. 22:	I ask one of the AP classes to write evaluations of their work in the R/W groups.	
Wed., Jan. 6:	**Research class meets.** My log reflects that I feel awash, uncertain, overwhelmed.	

Thurs., Jan. 7:	Discussion of evaluation of papers (I'm behind in evaluating theirs.)	
Wed., Jan. 13:	Their critical analysis papers are due. I have them write their own comments on their papers. That afternoon I interview Chris again before school releases early because of snow.	<— **Major Data Source**
Wed., Jan. 20:	**Research class meets.** We attempt to write clearly limited research questions.	
Wed., Feb. 3:	I ask my students to write out evaluations of their work for 2nd quarter. **Research class meets.**	
Mon., Feb. 8:	I ask my students to write about the writing of their *Hamlet* papers.	
Wed., Feb. 10 & Thurs., Feb. 11:	I interview six students about the comments they wrote on their papers on January 13th and encourage them to talk about their writing.	<— **Major Data Source**
February – May:	Six more research class meetings. Much rereading of data, attempts at analysis, drafts, students' responses to drafts, revisions, pressure, publication. Research report due Wed., May 5th.	

The History of a Research Project

Carin Hauser created the following detailed description based on research she conducted on her students' revision practices during the span of one school year. She used her own experience as a basis for the recommendations and suggestions she offers other teacher-researchers in the right hand column. Hauser's article, "The Writer's Inside Story," was published in 1986 in *Language Arts, 63*, 153-59.

September — During the first seminar meeting, I reflected on what I was curious about in my writing program. What puzzled me? Intrigued me? Bothered me? My initial journal entry was: I am curious about young children revising. I'd like to know more about how they view revision and what reasons they have for doing it.

Our research group met every other Thursday for two semesters. During the September meetings, my fellow researchers and I discussed articles we had read pertaining to the history of writing research and to its methodology. Cindi, Elly, and I formed a small group; this was the start of a very special collaborative relationship.

In my own classroom, my students and I participated in a writers' workshop every day for almost an hour, as we did throughout the school year. I tried to record in my journal what I saw going on in our writers' workshops. I had a heightened awareness of the way children talked about their writing, and I tried to make notes on this "talk." Early in my study, I closely observed one child, Tara, while she wrote, and entered this information in my journal. I noted her pauses and rereading; all of these notes became helpful information later.

October — during our teacher-researcher meetings, we continued to read and discuss articles about the methodology of teacher research, noting especially the nature of context-dependent studies. In the small group, Cindi, Elly, and I read portions of our journals to each other and helped each other begin to clarify where we were going with our research and how we would collect data. We each had

Start with a question about your students' learning or your teaching — something you care about, something that you want to clarify or understand.

Meet with other teachers to discuss your research as you develop the study and collect your data.

Keep a log; record observations and reflections on those observations; record your reactions to the process of your research study; raise new questions pertinent to your data.

intuitions about our general directions, but we had not focused our questions clearly, yet. The seminar leaders, Marian and Marion, provided us with useful, challenging responses to our written queries and entries. Informal chats with these veteran researchers also helped us over stuck points, steered us towards more productive routes of inquiry, and just plain encouraged us.

Read the reports of other teacher-researchers. Study the methodology behind their findings.

In my classroom, I interviewed all of the students, asking them to find their best piece of writing and to tell me why they thought these were their "best so far." I recorded each child's answer, analyzed (examined, compared, categorized) their responses, and coded them. I was surprised and a little disappointed with the results of this informal inventory. However, this was the beginning of a wonderful partnership between my students and me. As they watched me write down their responses in my journal, some of them even giggled. They saw that I was interested in what they said about their writing. At this point, I thought I'd study the evolution of writers' talk in our classroom. I had in mind some kind of "before and after" comparisons.

Establish a broad base for the collection of data. Document as fully as possible the context of your study.

Follow your instincts.

During writers' workshop, students started talking about the changes they make on their drafts and about the problems they find and solve in their writing, as part of sharing time. I continued keeping "field notes" and started to tape some of the reading/writing group conferences as part of the data I would need to analyze the writers' talk going on in the class. I saved most of the students' drafts, along with any revisions, in their writing folders.

Keep up your log throughout the entire study; even when you start to write your report.

Use several different means of collecting data in order to confirm the results of your analysis. (triangulation of data)

November— Research seminar continued. In our small group, we shared journal entries and data we'd collected so far. We made attempts at refining our questions.

Clarify and refine your research question as you continue your study.

I started to focus my observations and note-making on Lindsay and Andrew, while noting the development and interactions of the other children. I examined closely the revisions Andrew and Lindsay made to their texts and taped a conference with Lindsay. Afterwards I made notes on her conference behaviors. In my journal, I started to question why Lindsay revised and to reexamine my own behaviors during the conference.

As non-judgmentally as possible, consider your behaviors

December — Our seminars focused on analyzing data; we discussed model studies. The Estabrook article "Talking About Writing: Developing Independent Writers," became an important article for me. In our small group, we attempted to clarify the contents of the "data packet" each of us was assembling. We made further attempts at clarification of our research questions. Each of us began to focus our attention on a smaller portion of our original student group.

I asked each child to answer a questionnaire: What makes you feel like a writer? What is your best piece of writing? And why? What would you like to change about the writers' workshop? In order to start the analysis of my project, I compiled a data packet, which included key drafts from Andrew and Lindsay, journal notes, and notes on the conferences. The journal notes already contained some analysis of the conference behaviors (both students and mine). In my journal, I tried to make sense of the observations I had recorded. I kept trying to focus my question.

January — I asked Andrew and Lindsay to choose their three best writings and to examine any changes they had made to their first drafts. In the margin of each story, they wrote about their reasons for the changes. I then taped interviews with Andrew and Lindsay about these three "best" pieces. I also taped a revision conference with each of them.

In an exploratory draft, I tried to write about Andrew's and Lindsay's development as revisers over the course of the first four months of school. I scrutinized their writings, the taped conferences, and the interviews, as well as my journal. I was surprised at what happens when you examine a small packet of data intensely. I began to suspect that I didn't have as much data on Andrew's development as I did on Lindsay's development as a reviser.

In analyzing the tapes and notes, I realized that Lindsay's behaviors during the conferences had changed, opening up a new avenue of thought. I found myself wondering about the structure of the conference and how that structure influenced revisions.

and interventions in the study.

Make an attempt to define a reasonable time frame for collection of data. Start serious analysis of what you have found. Share your tentative findings with other teachers. Ask for feedback.

If you are concentrating on a small portion of our class (such as in a case study), continue to note the interactions of the children in the larger group.

Continue to refine your question. Look for emerging patterns in your data.

Take a break from pondering the meaning of your research.

Ask yourself: what do you still need to know?

February - April

We had an unusual assignment. We were to draw a picture of our research. The purpose was to help us see the connections between the different parts of our research, to start to visualize our analysis. My picture resembled a web of ideas. The exercise forced me to see connections: revisions, conferences, writer's intuition. The workshop environment emerged as the key components of the study. We researchers then wrote our first drafts. During the writing, I realized that I did not have enough information about Andrew's process of writing. I decided to pursue only Lindsay's development and save the data on Andrew for another study.

The small groups were extremely helpful during the writing of many drafts and the difficult task of analyzing what was happening in the data. At different points during the writing of the research, Cindi and Elly urged me to go back to Lindsay and find out more information, to consider my role objectively, and to describe further what was going on in the rest of the class to make the picture more realistic. In early April, I conducted a follow-up interview with Lindsay. The findings surprise me, showing that her concept of revision was continuing to evolve as she became a more experienced writer and as she matured.

The writing of the report was a very messy event, resulting in two final drafts and about four distinct and very different in between drafts.

May

Group publication and dinner party.

After the exploratory draft, ask again, what do I still need to find out?

Analyze your data. What are the patterns you see reflected by the data? Strive for objectivity. (This is hard!)

Attempt to find new meanings as your write your report. Go back to your data.

Share your drafts of your report with other teachers. Share your drafts with your students, too.

Share your findings with other teachers. Pose new questions.

MY LIFE AS A TEACHER-RESEARCHER

or How One Thing Led to Another

BY JULIE FISHER

One of the difficulties of conveying a realistic sense of teacher research is that every teacher's experience is so individual. Although we have described the generalities — choosing your question, writing in a research log, forming a research group, observing and reflecting, collecting data, analyzing data, and writing about the results — we have also offered you the stories of individual teacher-researchers that provide a glimpse of how they saw their experiences. In "My Life as a Teacher-Researcher or How One Thing Led to Another," Julie Fisher introduces herself as a beginning teacher, and the reader then follows some of her experiences as she illustrates how she integrated teacher research into her teaching life as well as the life of her school.

When I think about my time as a teacher-researcher, I think of the Eveready commercial with the pink bunny and the expression "It keeps going and going and going...." I feel like that bunny. I was introduced to teacher research three years ago, and have not stopped since.

I was just starting my third year of full-time teaching. Although it was my second year at Langston Hughes Intermediate School, it felt like my first. I had spent the previous year teaching in a trailer and had felt pretty isolated. Now I was teaching in the building. I was eager to belong, to get involved in the school.

During the year I spent in my trailer, a team of teachers from Hughes received a grant to research their own education questions about minority students' achievement. I did not become aware of this until the end of the year when every teacher received a copy of their published work. I took it home over the summer and began to read it, more out of deference to my colleagues than anything else. Yet as I read I became really intrigued. The questions that the teachers studied provided practical ideas to use in the classroom. These were people I knew writing about students I had. And unlike many of the articles I found in research journals, these articles were interesting, readable, and understandable.

The next school year, the research team opened up to involve new members in several groups structured around their findings of the previous year. The groups were the Cooperative Learning Study Action Group, the Writing to Learn Study Action Group, and the Support Group for Underachieving Targeted Students.

MY FIRST YEAR AS A TEACHER-RESEARCHER: WRITING TO LEARN

I decided to join the Writing to Learn Study Action Group. I have always loved writing but felt that math and writing were incompatible. I have to admit that I was intimidated at the first meeting of the Writing to Learn group. I had not seriously used writing in my classroom in the past, and now I was supposed to share meaningful experiences with my coworkers. I did not even know how to introduce writing into my curriculum, let alone have a success story. I know that, if I had felt uncomfortable after that first meeting, I would not have gone back.

Fortunately, the members of my group were extremely supportive. The make-up of our group was an important factor. Not only did we have people from different subject areas, but we also had people already using writing in the classroom as well as novices like me. The experienced people were able to guide the rest of us, answering questions and reassuring us when something did not work. The teachers just beginning to use writing contributed an eagerness and new perspectives. I guess it was like when you have out of town guests and show them the sights; you see it anew when you see it through their eyes.

I began to experiment with writing in my math class. I required my students to keep math journals, and the results were exciting. The students' journal entries were wonderful! They were using math vocabulary, exploring their math concepts in new ways, and sharing more in class. The students who never volunteered to answer a problem were willing to share their written responses. From my work with the study action group and articles I had read, I was able to develop activities such as: "Write a conversation between a positive integer and a negative integer describing how they are alike and different" and "Pretend you are 7,000 in the problem '7,000 minus 19.' Describe what happens to you." I even put on a chef's hat and had the students write recipes for word problems.

As I shared these experiences with my Writing to Learn Study Action Group, I could see that my colleagues were as enthusiastic about my students' writings as I was. We would share different ideas, discuss why something worked or didn't work, offer suggestions on what could make it work better, and see how we could adapt each other's ideas to our own classrooms. The group helped me with a major concern — how would I evaluate the journals? I had already tried to read all the journals and I knew that I would not be able to do it two or three times a week. My group members suggested that I not try to read all of them all the time; rather, let the students share their writings orally, calling on different students each time to share. This strategy worked well. I was able to have a good overview of my students' writing and the progress they were making.

I kept a journal of my own, recording the student entries and my own reflections. The journal served two very important purposes. First, it enabled me to analyze what was going on in my teaching. Too often, due to all the demands of school, teachers simply "love it or leave it." That is, if it works we keep it and if it doesn't, we throw it out. We never really spend the time to look at why something was a success or failure. I learned that a good idea that didn't work might be saved if we gave it a closer look. I knew that I could just describe the lesson and then share it with my group. They would help me sort out the details. The second important purpose of the journal was that it gave *me* time to write. Before, I pushed writing aside as something that I didn't have the time for, but now I had a compelling reason to write.

I was becoming more and more involved in the writing, but I was also becoming more involved in the school. I formed some lasting friendships with my groupmates, and they were a support in other areas of the classroom. I'll be honest; we did not spend every minute of our meetings discussing writing to learn. Naturally we talked and learned about each other. I can't stress enough how supportive that was to a new teacher. I felt that I had set down roots, and that this was now my school.

The cohesiveness of the group made the research itself seem much less threatening When I heard that we were going to keep records of student achievement, I imagined test scores and graphs. I was nervous. However, when staff members of the research and evaluation office came to talk to us, I was surprised. We were doing qualitative research as well as quantitative research. As a group we decided how we wanted to describe as well as measure the impact of writing on our students. We then developed a data collection instrument to help us take a look at progress each quarter. We looked at students' grades, but we also looked at characteristics, such as sharing in class and completion of assignments, which often go unrecognized. For reporting purposes, we each chose several underachieving minority students to monitor.

Throughout the year, I followed the progress of these students using the data collection sheets we developed. I know that without those sheets, I would not have been as aware of the progress the students were making. I would have focused more on the scores and grades, and less on the other factors we monitored, such as willingness to write, willingness to share writing and participate in class, use of math vocabulary, and more. At first I felt uncertain about what we were doing. Was this research? Yet, as members of my group pointed out, we needed to see if the things which we hoped would ultimately influence students' grades and test scores were actually happening in our classrooms.

In the fall and in the spring, the three branches of the research group came together in meetings using funds for substitutes provided by the grant. It felt exciting to be part of this group of professionals studying what went on in their classrooms. At these meetings, each group shared ideas and results. These meetings served a staff development purpose as I got to hear from people that I would not have had the opportunity to hear from otherwise. It often seems that it is easier to go to a conference than to find the time to learn what other teachers are doing in your own school.

Day-to-day leadership of our project was provided by participating teachers. Our principal attended our large-group meetings, and this was the only time that he took an active role. He was very supportive in that he understood the importance of what we were doing and gave us free rein to explore. However, he maintained a low profile and learned with us from the results.

A fellow math teacher and I had always shared ideas. Now she was in the Cooperative Learning Study Action Group, and she introduced me to the idea of students working in groups in the math class. We began combining our two research studies and had the students do projects that involved writing and cooperative learning. During one journal activity, I asked the students to teach a math concept through a written skit. These turned out to be so wonderful that we had each group produce its skit, and then we videotaped them. A parent of one of my students, a math teacher at another school, came to watch the taping and then tried it with her Algebra students — and so the project spread even further.

At the end of the year, my group produced a poster that said "Branch Out — Use Writing to Learn." We drew a tree, and on the branches were our names and many of our ideas for writing. I was so proud of that poster I felt that I had gone from trying to get my act together, as new teachers do, to actually making a significant contribution to my school and other teachers.

Besides learning about myself, I learned many things about my students. I learned that many students, after the initial grumbling about writing in math, really do enjoy writing. I found that many of them realized that the writing helped them learn the material. On the end of the year evaluations I asked students to complete, I read comments such as "I like the journal writing very much. It helps you to not forget the material" and "It helps you learn more about what you're doing." I also read "Annoying, but it's better than a worksheet." I learned that you can't expect seventh-grade students to keep journals stacked neatly, by class, on a shelf. I had to purchase five laundry baskets to give them somewhere to aim!

We gave each faculty member a copy of the poster at an informal inservice held by the three branches of the project at the end of the year. We provided lunch, and during their lunch time, teachers, administrators, and counselors ate, listened to what each of the research groups had done, and gathered ideas. I even presented a mini-lesson that I had done with my students. It was hard for me to believe that in just one year, I had gone from someone who had never used writing to someone who could teach other teachers about writing.

We wanted the faculty to see the results that we gathered. We were excited by our findings and felt we were learning about teaching that really did make a difference with our students. However, our motives for sharing with the other teachers were not totally innocent. We wanted more faculty to join the project. We hoped that the research project would grow even further and we wanted as many teachers as possible to be involved.

My first year in the project gave me some wonderful experiences I am just now beginning to fully appreciate. The Writing to Learn Study Action Group was able to use some of its resources to work with Donald Graves. I now realize what an opportunity it was to see this guru of the writing process. I realized he was an interesting teacher with good ideas about writing; I had no idea that he was one of the people changing the way that writing was being taught. I was able to work with Marian Mohr who led us through the writing-to-learn process with velvet gloves, warning us of the pitfalls but letting us learn from our mistakes.

I was also able to see the school district Office of Research and Evaluation in action as it worked with us throughout the year. ORE staff members were there to answer questions and help us collect and interpret our information about student achievement. Mostly, they were there to support us, and by saying, "Wonderful! You're doing a great job," showed us that research doesn't have to be scary. It was crucial having ORE involved. They were our link to the grant and the "outside world." We became so involved in what we were doing that sometimes it seemed we forgot we were doing any research. ORE was a gentle reminder that we were collecting and reviewing data that would interest others outside our school as well as answer our own questions about improving student achievement.

REFLECTIONS

Now, after recording my experiences, the researcher in me wants to analyze and conclude. Looking back, I can see that there were some crucial points in my successful experiences as researcher.

I had individuals who were supportive and willing to share with me and learn from me. *This is extremely important.* That give-and-take was crucial; I had to feel that I was a contributing member. I also know that I was very lucky to have mentors. I had persons looking out for me, who let me know that they were willing to share their experience. My principal was quietly supportive, giving us the room we needed to mold the research to our and our students' needs.

I understand now how important the grant itself was. Not only was it the catalyst for the research, it provided many of the opportunities necessary for our success. The grant enabled us to meet during school by providing for substitutes. I don't know how many of us would have been able, or willing, to work and share during the weekend.

The Office of Research and Evaluation was instrumental in helping us understand that the world of research was not foreign to our classrooms; it was just waiting to be discovered. ORE showed me that I had a role, not just as a teacher, but as a researcher.

I hope I have not given the impression that being a teacher-researcher is easy. It is not. It involves work, and that is something that all teachers feel that they already have more than enough of. However, research can blend smoothly into the classroom. How many of us have looked at a lesson and asked, "Why didn't that work?" Or looked at a group of students and thought, "What can I do to make them learn better?"

I know that being a teacher-researcher gives me the confidence to look for these answers. It is no longer enough to know that something works; now I want to understand why. Maybe it doesn't work; that's okay. I'll talk about it with other teachers and find out what went wrong. The important things are to *observe, record your observations and reflections, and talk about what you see.* For only by learning about what goes on in our classrooms can we truly teach not only the students but ourselves.

PART II

QUESTIONS AND ISSUES

In this part of the book we discuss questions and issues that are frequently raised when we give presentations or just talk with other teachers about teacher research. Most of them are a part of any researcher's life — concerns about methods, validity and reliability, and ethics.

There is some overlap with the discussions of teacher research as a process in Part I. We also make reference to teacher research articles in Part III and to the resources in Part IV. Here are the questions to follow:

- ❑ *What happens when you teach and conduct research?*
- ❑ *What makes your research valid and reliable?*
- ❑ *What ethical principles guide teacher research?*
- ❑ *When do you find time to do teacher research?*
- ❑ *How do you lead a teacher research group?*
- ❑ *How do you explain teacher research to others?*
- ❑ *Of what use is teacher research?*

WHAT HAPPENS WHEN YOU TEACH AND CONDUCT RESEARCH?

E ven before you think of yourself as a researcher, there are moments in your teaching when you are aware of presenting a lesson or listening to a class discussion and *at the same time* observing yourself and your class learning together. This combination of teaching and learning in a classroom has a history in ethnographic and interpretive research methodology, where it is described as "participant observation." But it is also a development of teacher research itself, jokingly referred to as the "out-of-body" experience. As a teacher researcher, you welcome that double view and the insights it offers you.

An ethnographer might ask, "How can I interpret the meaning of these people's experience when I am an outsider in their culture?" Ethnographers — and other social science researchers — are trying to find out how a particular culture works or how a group of people interact. They assume that the people and the culture work according to principles the researcher must come to understand. Because they are new to and relatively separate from the situations they enter, distance is their starting point; their initial role is that of observer and outsider. Their challenges are gaining entry, establishing and maintaining trust, and then dealing with the role tensions that arise out of being both participant and observer. The management of these tensions can be tricky because of the relationships and responsibilities that are at stake. On one hand, researchers must form trusting relationships. On the other, they must report the findings from those relationships.

In a 1993 article, Shirley Brice Heath reviews a transcript from her study *Ways with Words* and reflects on evidence of the multiple roles she played in that study — woman, parent, teacher, academic, and ethnographer. She writes, "The ethnographer attempting to avoid 'taking sides' is right in there in the fishbowl of multiple and conflicting roles and values" (p. 261). As a teacher-researcher, you, too, are in a fishbowl of conflicting roles and values, but for you the starting point is one of participation, not observation — immersion, not distance. For you, distance is the ultimately unachievable condition, just as it is participation that is ultimately unachievable for an ethnographer. A teacher-researcher's problem arises, then, out of the effort to gain "exit" rather than "entry" — to learn and make use of the role of the nonjudgmental observer.

Imagine yourself as the teacher-researcher in this classroom situation: Your ninth graders are trying to write journal entries at the beginning of the class period. Jeff, a student who has been cutting up in class frequently enough to get on everyone's nerves, is staring at his paper and drumming his pen more and more loudly against the metal base of his desk. As a teacher-researcher, you are trying to observe, describe, and reflect on what is happening in the classroom: to question, not to make assumptions. In your research log, you write your observations of Jeff's behavior and make notes on reactions or the lack of reactions by the rest of the class. You jot down your own feelings and reactions, too. Finally, as a researcher, you make a note to ask Jeff a question later that will help you understand the function of his pen-tapping during that day's journal writing.

But you are also the teacher, and in that role you have a responsibility to make the classroom an environment in which everyone can work — assuming that a reduction in "noisy" distraction will help people work. As a teacher, you want Jeff to be quiet and to get his writing done even though you may wonder why he isn't writing. In this situation you experience a tension between your responsibilities as classroom manager and classroom researcher, but your examination of Jeff's writing practices adds insights to your teaching as well as data to your research. Sometimes classroom management and discipline become less problematic when you and your students examine the issues together.

You may also experience tension between your roles as teacher and researcher as you come to see your students' work differently. You receive a set of papers, for instance, and look through them that night, only to discover how little the students have done to live up to your expectations. You feel disappointed. As a researcher, though, you try to understand what these students' papers show about what has happened. Your students' papers become interesting and informative data, documents that lead to the discovery of principles and assumptions at work in your classroom. With the distance that the researcher's stance offers, both you and your students can look at work in progress to figure out what makes the most sense to do next. No matter what the performance or the quality of the work done, student errors become something of interest, not something that needs to be punished or hidden. They are the points of change, informative shifts, and important clues to the learning process.

These descriptions show the tugs and tensions among various roles in a classroom. Being a teacher-researcher requires that you explore the roles of teacher, researcher, and learner, questioning the authority of each. Some of what you do may initially seem contradictory. Why would you encourage students to examine your teaching and raise questions about how they are learning? Why would you listen to what students have to say when they seem to be questioning your authority? The following sections describe how this exploration and questioning can result in your achieving perspective on the fit between your teaching and your research.

EXPLORING THE ROLES OF TEACHER, RESEARCHER, AND LEARNER

As you enter the role of researcher, you have the opportunity to examine both your students' and your own assumptions about these roles. Lin McKay Spence, a high school English teacher-researcher, has looked at issues related to her role as both teacher and researcher in two studies conducted several years apart at different high schools. Spence made the examination of students' roles in teacher research the focus of her first study by looking at what happens when a teacher acknowledges her students as the sources of information that the teacher needs to know. The following is one of her log entries, followed by a few of the student samples.

Reflections

Since I'm tempted to try to write the story of what's happening now as I have begun the research in class, I'm interested in knowing what's happening to the kids as we embark together. Hence, the question I posed to them: "What happens to you when you're aware that I'm observing and recording the actions of the class as you all write?" I'm interested not only in the story of my question, "what happens when students make observations about their writing," but *also in the story of the research experience itself. I've received some interesting observations which I've attached.*

Students' comments:

- *When I'm writing and get observed, it doesn't really distract me but encourages me. It lets me know that I should be writing, nothing else. I feel better, for some reason, knowing that everyone else is doing the same thing.*

- *When Mrs. McKay [Spence] is watching me write, a question appears in my mind. "What am I doing to attract this attention?" It must be she likes young minds to think and express their ideas. I'm not afraid of this stare but I still wonder.*

- *I really don't really feel anything when you're observing us. I get involved in what I'm writing and I can't concentrate on two different things going on at the same time, so I just write and not worry about anything else.*

- *I really don't mind when you observe me writing. In fact, half the time I don't even notice and the other half I kind of like it because I hope you'll write down something about "Karen's unique ways of writing." I think it would be neat to be used in one of your seminar thingys, so no I don't mind it when you observe me, as long as you observe quietly!!*

- *When you observe us — this may sound stuck up — I feel like I need to put on a show. This probably doesn't do anything for your study but I can't help it. I feel like I really want to be part of something. Even a stupid survey.*

Most of these students are self-conscious yet seem pleased to be regarded as "young minds that think." Whatever they think, they write and participate in the research, providing Spence with what she needs to know.

In her most recent study, Spence started the school year with a new preparation — a course called "Scholastic Development" designed to teach learning strategies to a small group of ninth graders viewed as "underachievers." In her research article, she wrote that before school opened, she "imagined what I usually imagine before school starts: an idealistically successful year in which the students soar with enthusiasm and laughter and, together, we discover possibilities that make us a bunch of happy learning groupies!" When the students rejected her assignments — "Any assignment seemed the cause of their suffering" — she looked for ways to understand what was happening and chose to focus on this class for her research study.

Throughout the year, she questioned these students about how they could learn best and tried several different projects, insisting that they participate in the planning and evaluation of each. She wrote, however, that she listened with reservations: "I still wasn't sure whom to believe — my students or the academicians who had prescribed the alternative program for these students. I decided, for the time being, to keep an ear open to the students. Good thing. They were to become my greatest resources." In fact, in their final project — a poetry collaboration with the physically disabled students at a center within the high school — the ninth graders themselves became teachers both of their peers and of Spence. As a result of her persistent questioning, listening, and openness to reviewing her assumptions, Spence had assumed the role of learner and student. At the same time, of course, she retained her roles as researcher and teacher, developing principles of learning for and with her students. The title of her article highlights the importance of the shifting roles: "When Students Teach, Everyone Learns."

Questioning traditional roles can make both teacher and students a little uneasy, but it can also allow everyone to shift position occasionally to examine those roles. Students come to see themselves as important to the teacher's teaching and research, sometimes becoming co-researchers. The roles do not blur; instead, teachers and students assume different roles as needed to study together the teaching and learning in their classroom.

At first your students may react with surprise when you ask them questions you don't know the answers to, questions about their learning. Your students are your subjects — not in the sense of a kingdom, not even in the sense of a psychology laboratory, but in the sense that they are the subjects you go to school to learn about. When Peg Culley, a high school English teacher, was beginning to conduct her research on teaching writing and grammar, she explained to her students the part they would play in the study. One of her students laughingly commented, "So, we're your guinea pigs." Culley replied, "I hope not, because guinea pigs don't really interact with the researcher. And I need your responses and awareness in this!"

QUESTIONING AUTHORITY

When you conduct your classroom in ways that challenge the traditional roles of student and teacher, you are also setting the stage for examining issues of authority. As a teacher, your authority traditionally stems from your adult status, your preparation for your position as teacher, and the ethical fulfillment of your professional (and contractual) responsibilities. These sources of authority do not change when you conduct research in your classroom, but your research stance allows you to examine what you see and to question your students' and your own assumptions.

MacLean's first study of writing evaluation is a case in point. She had given her senior English students several writing prompts designed to help them write with conviction from their own experience. She then asked them to use the powerful writings that had resulted as the source of essays they might send with college applications. To her surprise, the essays were only pale reflections of the vivid originals. She had failed to account for the effect that the shift in audience might have on her students' revisions.

As she reconsidered her assumptions about the assignment and about teaching writing, she made an additional discovery. Her students attributed to her, too, the kind of harsh judgment they feared from college admissions officers. Despite MacLean's teaching strategies and methods of commenting on their writing, her students' negative assumptions about the teacher's role became evident as MacLean openly questioned them. As a researcher, she could express her interest in their assumptions and explore their thinking with them. Her analysis of the problematic data led her to examine her authority as a teacher of writing while at the same time providing her the means to establish her authority as a teacher-researcher.

Patti Sue Williams, a first grade teacher, reflected in her research log about the voice of authority that she could see in her own writing that had emerged as a result of her own research, something she had recognized first in one of her students.

My writing is more and more reflecting my voice and it's not a weak voice. I think there was a time when I delayed writing because I feared having a weak, non-authoritative voice.

I think Kim [the student in William's case study] discovered her voice before I did. I wonder if she is aware of it. How can I make her aware of it? I think my "specialty" is being able to look at children in their writing and discover each one's uniqueness, their own process, and see myself mirrored there.

Gloria Johnson, a high school English teacher, reports a similar shift in her view of herself as a teacher:

Finally, my increased awareness has altered my perception of my role as a teacher of writing. I feel more and more important in the directional process, not the evaluative process. Together, students and a teacher can discover and enjoy writing. While I observed my students beginning to own their writing, I began to own my teaching. What a marvelous feeling!

MacLean, Williams, and Johnson each questioned their authority as teachers differently. MacLean questioned her assumptions as she examined student data which surprised her, Williams questioned her writing voice as she learned from her student's example, and Johnson questioned her previous relationship with her students as they began to show ownership of their writing. In all three cases, the research stance allowed them to question their authority and to assert a different kind of authority as a teacher-researcher.

ACHIEVING PERSPECTIVE

Another role tension you might experience as a teacher-researcher comes from the tug between immersion in your students' learning and the need for distance from that immersion. The physical, emotional, and intellectual concentration required for teaching can be consuming. When you have even a short break, a three-day weekend, for example, it's easy to forget that intensity and to base hopeful plans on an imagined version of your classes, a version necessarily stripped of some of the details of reality. For your relaxation and health, not to mention your research, you *need* to forget and retreat.

Teacher research makes it harder to forget, but easier to live with the concentration by helping you to achieve perspective on your work. Barbara Falcone, a middle school teacher-researcher, reflected on this difficulty and on the role "retreating" had for her in the following log writing.

> *I feel like a yo-yo. High hopes one day — dashed down the next!*
>
> *Tues, 11/3 — 3rd period — So much for my high hopes — These kids really make it tough to be optimistic. Perhaps I take things too seriously — but I believe their doing well in school is serious business.*
>
> *After roll call I was not allowed to go over yesterday's classwork — they are so rude and disrespectful. I cannot tolerate it and it really hurts my feelings. I want so much — more than anything else in the world to teach them — and they won't let me.*
>
> ***
>
> *"A" keeps talking back to me — Infuriates me — Her whining.*
>
> ***
>
> *This class in Reading/Writing groups is a farce — Maybe I should drop it. They'll write "good," "nice," "great" on each other's papers — no matter how poorly or how well (a rarity) they are written.*
>
> *As a group, they've just not "caught on" to the PROCESS yet — but I'm determined to hang in there.*
>
> ***
>
> *I asked Leila what she was doing and she replied, "Nothing." I praised her honesty.*

This is honest writing by a teacher-researcher struggling to discover what will work as she teaches these students — her dashed hopes as well as her determination. Her research does not allow her to escape the realities of her situation. Instead, she writes about what she sees, even when it is difficult to acknowledge. What her research does allow — what it requires — her to do is to write about the realities, an act that in itself helps her step back. She presents the realities to her research group and engages in a discussion and analysis of what's going on. As a researcher, she will also check out her theories by examining other sources of data about her students' learning.

The research process, while it requires immersion in classroom tensions, helps Falcone gain some control and authority over her work from an involved distance. In her research article, she writes about the help a research stance gave her as a teacher:

> My daily log of observations and reflections proved to be most beneficial because it offered me an opportunity to study the psychological interaction of teacher, student, and environment. It was good therapy, an "acceptable" release for my tension; its consistent record of both "good" and "bad" days enabled me to look for patterns of behavior (with classes and individuals); it helped me to maintain my objectivity, to step back and not take the students' behavior so personally, giving me a perspective I needed when I felt too close to a "problem"; it provided insights for my teaching, theories, intuitions, and a deeper understanding of what was happening in the classroom; and I noticed that whenever I wrote log entries in class, it had a calming influence on the students.
>
> Being a Teacher-Researcher made me more observant in the classroom and thus improved my teaching. It allowed me to offer support but simultaneously maintain a "distance." This turned out to be a good cure for my dedication, more popularly referred to as "burn-out." I still cared — very much so — but part of me was able to step back and look at what I was doing or what the students were doing. Keeping the log forced me to think about what was happening — every day. What is so unique about that revelation? The answer is simply, "Nothing." It is something I had to learn for myself by doing it. All the classes I've attended (and taught), all the curriculum guides I've followed, all the lesson plans I've written, and all the texts I've read, really didn't mean anything to ME PERSONALLY until I became a Teacher-Researcher.

For a teacher-researcher, the shift in stance is not a shift away from being a teacher toward being a researcher. It is more a shift away from being only a participant, even a thoughtful and conscientious one, toward being someone who has the distance to take a look at the participant role. That means being prepared to address the tensions and questions that characterize the experience of doing both at the same time. Addressing those tensions and questions is one source of the depth of understanding that results from being a teacher-researcher. We are not teachers *or* researchers, but both.

Involved distance, authority based on questioning authority, and multiple roles are challenges that exist for all researchers, not just for those who are teachers. Researchers, no matter what methodology they use or what research questions they pose, are coming to recognize that the role they play in their research is crucial, as is the need to be forthright about their own contexts, backgrounds, and beliefs. This recognition is a healthy change from the days of the researcher who intended to disappear from the research report and whose decisions along the way were often omitted in the research conclusions. Your stance as a teacher-researcher reflects this change and also offers you the opportunity to explore how being part of your own research works in the best possible way.

REFERENCES

Falcone, B. (1982). Why students won't write: A personal search. *Research in writing: Reports from a teacher-researcher seminar.* Fairfax, VA: Northern Virginia Writing Project, George Mason University.

Johnson, G. (1982). Facing the blank page. *Research in writing: Reports from a teacher-researcher seminar.* Fairfax, VA: Northern Virginia Writing Project, George Mason University.

Heath, S. B. (1993). The madness(es) of reading and writing ethnography. *Anthropology and Education Quarterly, 24,* 256-268.

Spence, L. (1986). Gaining control through commentary. *English Journal, 75,* (3) 58-62.

Spence, L. (1997). When students teach — everybody learns. *Falls Church High School Teacher Research Project.* Fairfax County, VA: Fairfax County Public Schools.

WHAT MAKES YOUR RESEARCH
VALID AND RELIABLE?

At the end of her first research study, Randi Adleberg, searching for the right words, added the following note to comments that MacLean had asked teacher-researchers in the group to write:

> *Marion, I want to add one thing. Throughout my own re-search process, and while listening to the final reports, one question has gnawed.* ~~*Do we find real things in a natural way*~~ *Are our con-clusions pure and accurate — or does the fact that we are research-ing/focusing/highlighting something* taint *the research & make us find things that aren't really there — or that* aren't valid*? — Randi*

All researchers wonder at times whether they are finding or seeing things that aren't really there. Teacher-researchers, like Adleberg, often wonder whether — and how — the research they conduct in their own classrooms can be trustworthy since they, as involved participants, are also the researchers. How can their own findings about their particular students be considered dependable in a different time or place either for themselves or others? If these questions concern you, you are not alone, even among experienced teacher-researchers.

The terms most often used to discuss these questions are validity and reliability. Quantitative research methodology uses set measures for deciding whether a research study is valid and reliable. The scientific value of qualitative research studies, which include most teacher research, does not depend on clear-cut or numerical indicators. Some researchers even question the value of the terms in reference to qualitative research.

Elliot Eisner and Alan Peshkin's book, *Qualitative Inquiry in Educa-tion: The Continuing Debate,* includes a lively exchange among Madeleine Grumet, Harry Wolcott, and Philip Jackson about how these terms are or are not useful to qualitative researchers. In a discussion of differences between experimental and qualitative research, Eliot Mishler makes the following comments about judging inquiry-guided research by quanti-tative standards:

These studies… are not designed as experiments, and do not "test" hypotheses, "measure" variation on quantitative dimensions, or "test" the significance of findings with statistical procedures. Criteria and procedures based on the dominant experimental/quantitative prototype are irrelevant to these studies in the literal sense that there is nothing to which to apply them. When the standard model is misapplied, as it often is, inquiry-guided studies fail the test and are denied scientific legitimacy (1990, pp. 434-35).

Yvonna Lincoln and Egon Guba make similar distinctions when they discuss "trustworthiness" as an alternative standard to validity and reliability in naturalistic research (1985, pp. 289-331). They also use the terms "applicability" and "transferability" to describe how naturalistic researchers determine the trustworthiness of findings from one context to another (1985, pp. 296-297). In their discussions of meta-ethnography, George Noblit and Dwight Hare suggest using the term "translation" to describe the process of establishing reliability in qualitative research (1988, p. 25).

Discussions like these are now occurring in relation to teacher research. In a 1999 *Educational Researcher* article, Gary Anderson and Kathryn Herr suggest criteria for validity in teacher research, placing it in the context of qualitative, naturalistic methodology. As these discussions of standards and terminology continue, it is important for teacher-researchers to inform themselves about these issues and debates. It is also important that they contribute to those discussions. Here we suggest some ways of defining validity and reliability in teacher research that have been useful to us and ways of making sure your research is a trustworthy addition to the field.

WHAT MAKES YOUR RESEARCH VALID?

Validity in research is the degree to which a study is honest and true to its intent, its context, and its reporting. It is the result of your integrity both as a teacher and as a researcher. It poses the question, "Does your data say what you say it says?" All of the research strategies you have been using — observing, writing, interviewing, documenting, analyzing — are ways to ensure validity. The following guidelines, for use alone and with your research group, are ways to achieve validity in your research:

- revisions of your research question to ensure a focus on your current teaching and students' learning
- choice of appropriate methods to yield results that have value to you and your students
- frequent, consistent writing of your own observations to discover what you think and to record what happens over time
- written reflections on and interpretations of data to determine your next steps
- collection of a broad database to provide grounding for the interpretations that emerge from the data
- ongoing examination of your work by other teacher-researchers to challenge your data analysis and interpretations
- collection of a variety of kinds of data from different perspectives to triangulate your findings
- reviews of your reading of the data by those who were your sources and informants to check on the accuracy of your interpretations
- readings from theoretical and methodological frameworks to seek different theories and methods that challenge and deepen your own

Teacher-researcher Randi Adleberg, whose question about validity opened this chapter, uses a number of these strategies during her research. Her work illustrates what the effort to achieve validity looks like. She had been teaching a required vocabulary curriculum to her eleventh grade English students but saw many problems with it. She decided to implement a team learning approach to see if it would help her students learn. After giving students their first "team test," she wrote:

> *I asked kids for reactions and feedback. Twenty-four students said they thought they had done better on this test than they would have if they had taken the test alone. And all twenty-seven students agreed that a team test was better than an individual test. "Why?" I asked.*
> *"If you weren't sure of an answer, you could discuss it with your group," "Everybody contributed," and "I studied harder because I*

*knew people were depending on me." Students in a bilingual group
(Two members speak Spanish and English and two speak only English) said, "Learning what the word meant in another language
helped us remember the English meaning."*

Adleberg continued recording the data from tests, from her questions to her students, and from her observations. As she analyzed the
data, she wondered about the overall efficacy of the method and what
she might reasonably conclude. She hoped that her hard work in establishing the groups had paid off in higher test scores. In her research
report, she wrote:

> *To corroborate my last hunch, I pulled out my grade books from
> the last two school years. I studied the test scores from eleven [unit]
> tests — the two we had before the student learning teams and the
> nine after implementation of the teams. I compared this year's grades
> with the grades from the 1987-88 and 1986-87 school years. To
> my chagrin, I found* no *change. "This can't be!" I thought. I figured
> out class averages for each test each year. Again, no difference!*
>
> *"O.K., forget class information. How about individual student
> grades?" I wondered. I went back through my grade books and looked
> at the quarterly vocabulary averages for individual students. I saw
> that this was the only year in which no student had a D or F aver-
> age in vocabulary.*

Adleberg had discovered that "F's" on individual tests had not disappeared, that she had received the same percentages of failures, but
that the failures were made by different students over the course of the
year. With the team approach, no lone student was left to fail consistently on individual tests. She discovered not that group work was *the*
answer, but *how* it assisted her students in learning vocabulary. Adleberg's
pursuit of data that would challenge her interpretations, her refusal to
dismiss disconfirming results, her periodic return to her students to
check her interpretations, and her examination of alternate interpretations helped her establish her study's validity and its usefulness both to
her and to others.

You control the validity of your study. The degree to which you achieve validity determines how useful your research will be to you. It also determines the degree to which your readers will understand and be able to trust your reporting of your research.

WHAT MAKES YOUR RESEARCH RELIABLE?

Reliability in research is the degree to which a study can be repeated by other researchers under the same conditions to yield the same results. It poses the question, "To what degree can I count on the results of this study?" In research of any kind, the answer is, "It depends."

When medical researchers test a new drug, they carry out experimental studies to determine precisely how patients will react to the drug. Even drugs deemed reliable in controlled trials create different reactions in individual patients. Educational research that depends on experimental design has led many teachers to be understandably suspicious of claims of reliability in classroom settings. For example, how "reliable" can research be when findings based on one specific classroom are generalized to apply to all? No study can ensure collections of 15-year-olds that are remotely similar, to say nothing of their teachers. The context of an educational research study matters, especially to teachers.

Context is information of a variety of kinds about the people, the settings, and the interactions basic to your study. It's information about you — your demeanor with your students, your beliefs and assumptions, your personality, your insights. It's information about your teaching choices and about your classroom — from how you teach vocabulary to how you set up groups. It's information about your students — what they say and do. And it's information about all of you as you teach and learn over a year's time. Context includes the multiple factors that contribute to the creation of the experiences that you and your students have.

Since settings and conditions are never the same in classrooms, teacher research derives its reliability from providing enough information for a reader to be able to make reasonable comparisons to other situations and contexts. To test reliability, you do not try to recreate the context of a study. Instead, you consider the methods and the findings and imagine how a similar effort might work in your classroom. You think through the similarities and differences of the two contexts. You ask questions. How does the context affect the findings in the study? What different variables are in your context? If the multicultural mix of students in your classroom was substituted for the more homogeneous one in the research study, for instance, how would that affect the findings?

After you have done your part as a teacher-researcher to create the reality of your research as fully as you can, reliability depends on your readers, on those who study your work and decide that it could be useful to them. Through the specific nature of your reports and the personal nature of your interpretations, other teachers and readers see what can be reliably extracted for their own use and adaptation in their classrooms. We illustrate the process of working out reliability in the following narrative from Mohr's teaching.

At one time Mohr worked part-time as a high school teacher and part-time as a resource teacher in the elementary schools of her school district to help launch a new curriculum in the teaching of writing. Although she had studied research in writing and had done classroom research on the process of revision in her high school classroom, she had never taught in an elementary school and knew little about how the writing research she was familiar with would work in elementary school classrooms. She did, however, know some elementary school teacher-researchers and their work, as well as the work of qualitative researchers in the field such as Donald Graves's *Writing: Teachers and Children at Work.*

As she prepared to work with the elementary school students and their teachers, she planned lessons based on a combination of her own ideas and ideas from the research she had read. She practiced ways of talking to the children about their writing and designed assignments based on the research she was reading. From reading and rereading teacher-researchers' articles, she came to know some of their classrooms as well as her own and felt able to "see" what happened with their students as if she had experienced it herself. She "translated" or "transferred" from the research what seemed reliable for her use.

As she worked with the elementary teachers, she and they together worked out what was, in practice, reliable from the research she shared with them. Each time she and the students worked together, she talked with the teachers about the lesson. Slowly she learned the context of their classrooms. They compared their own experiences of teaching writing with those written about in the research. As a group they began to see that some of the research findings were truer to their experiences with the children than others. She and the teachers reminded themselves that the research they were using needed to be translated, transferred, and adapted to their own contexts; they understood that the results of this research were not to be treated as inflexible findings to be used with all students in precisely the same way.

At one of their after-school meetings, a teacher remarked that she agreed with one researcher's general findings about how to introduce spelling, but because many of her students were already readers when they came to first grade, they already knew that all words have their own spelling. They asked different questions and had different expectations from the students in the study, who had not yet learned to read. That meant, she thought, that she had to develop an approach to spelling for her first graders that took into account their different backgrounds. She added that five of her students who were just learning English had different spelling needs as well. Even though she saw distinct differences between her teaching context and that of the research under discussion, she extracted concepts that she found reliable from the research. She viewed it as her responsibility to adjust and develop some of the findings to fit her own experience of teaching.

You can ensure that your reporting of your research is accurate, rich with context, and fully documented. By doing so, you will make it possible for others to depend on your research as trustworthy.

What Are Valid and Reliable Assessments of the Work of Schools?

Up until now we have discussed validity and reliability in relation to your work as a teacher-researcher. We extend the discussion to include the assessment of the work of schools because, even when your research is valid and reliable, if assessments of your school do not include or value qualitative data, the usefulness of your research may not be understood.

Although qualitative research has gained currency in the field of educational research, school districts and most schools of education are still bound to quantitative studies and statistical reporting as the way of describing and assessing the work of schools. Educational policy makers who emphasize statistical measures over a mixture of qualitative and quantitative methods fail to recognize the *scientific* value of ethnography and other "inquiry-guided" research. They fail to make use of the qualitative data that helps educators and researchers understand and interpret accurately the meanings of quantitative data.

Standardized test scores, grade distributions, student enrollment by ethnic group, numbers of students who qualify for free and reduced lunch benefits, and other statistics about our school systems — all have the power to help us educate American school children. These kinds of data, however, are usually reported as if the scores alone — or even a collection of scores and statistics — are sufficient basis for meaningful conclusions. What we have found is that statistical data is often a sufficient basis for meaningful *questions*, and that reliance on statistics alone in educational research represents the unethical and irresponsible use of such data.

Conclusions can be too hastily reached from any single kind of data. Educational researchers who hope to produce meaningful studies must conduct research that leads to an understanding of the underlying issues and complexities that characterize educational situations. Educational leaders and policy makers must use research that represents the fullest possible array of data and methodology to ensure that the decisions they make are meaningful for schools. Wherever human relationships play a central role, as they do in schools, educational leaders and policy makers must also rely on research that acknowledges, documents, and attempts to understand those relationships. Only educational research that fully represents school realities can provide a sound basis for the valid and reliable assessment of the work of schools.

REFERENCES

Adleberg, R. (1989). Vocabulary teams: Let's talk about it. *Research in writing: Reports from a teacher-researcher seminar.* Fairfax, VA: Northern Virginia Writing Project, George Mason University.

Anderson, G. & Herr, K. (1999). The new paradigm wars: Is there room for rigorous practitioner knowledge in schools and universities? *Educational Researcher, 28* (5) 12-21, 40.

Anderson, G., Herr, K., & Nihlen, A. S. (1994). *Studying your own school: An educator's guide to qualitative practitioner research.* Thousand Oaks, CA: Corwin.

Eisner, E. W. & Peshkin, A. (Eds.). (1990). *Qualitative inquiry in education: The continuing debate.* New York: Teachers College Press.

Graves, D. (1981). *Writing: Teachers and children at work.* Westport, CT: Heinemann-Boynton/Cook.

Kirk, J. & Miller, M. (1986). Reliability and validity in qualitative research. *Qualitative Research Methods Series #1.* Newbury Park, CA: Sage.

Lincoln, Y. & Guba, E. (1985). *Naturalistic inquiry.* Newbury Park, CA: Sage.

Mishler, E. G. (1990). Validation in inquiry-guided research. *Harvard Educational Review, 60,* 415-442.

Noblit, G. & Hare, R. (1988). Meta-ethnography: Synthesizing qualitative studies. *Qualitative Research Methods Series #11.* Newbury Park, CA: Sage.

Oram, L. (1990). Using student input: How a second year teacher makes decisions. *Research in language and learning: Reports from a teacher-researcher seminar.* Fairfax, VA: Northern Virginia Writing Project, George Mason University.

WHAT ETHICAL PRINCIPLES GUIDE TEACHER RESEARCH?

As an ethical teacher-researcher, you are honest and tell the truth as you understand it. You do no harm to the students and colleagues with whom you are conducting the research, and you give respect and credit to students and colleagues whose work prepared the way for your current thinking. As you read the following principles, you'll be reminded that, in general, your ethical behavior as a teacher-researcher is the same as that of any researcher. Ethics in any field are never simple, however, and what we hope to do in answering this question is to establish a few general principles that you and your colleagues can use to help you evaluate the individual ethical situations that will arise as part of your research.

1. Treat your students and colleagues with respect and care. Present-day standards for research on human subjects, as discussed in Paul Anderson's 1998 article in *College Composition and Communication* on ethical issues in composition research, can be traced to the 1979 Belmont Report, the result of a U.S. congressional commission which itself derived from the Nuremberg Code drafted by the judges at the Nuremberg war crimes tribunal in 1946. This historical background shows the seriousness of the issues at stake.

As a teacher-researcher, your human subjects are your students, your colleagues, and yourself. Your students and colleagues are co-researchers who exchange information with you and sometimes are even your collaborators. When Lin McKay Spence's students worked with her to learn what would happen when they taught poetry to physically disabled students, their relationship evolved into a collaboration. When Barbara Falcone examined her students' reluctance to write, she was challenged to develop a relationship that allowed for both teaching and research without the direct collaboration of her students. You and your students work out your understandings and disagreements together, with recognition of and mutual respect for your differences. Your advantage as a teacher-researcher in difficult classroom situations is that your emphasis on asking your students questions about their learning, listening to what they say, and placing a value on their answers engenders respect between you even if you disagree on classroom behavior or curriculum.

2. Give credit. The sources you credit in your research will be those whose comments and ideas have become important to you in conducting your research. Like most teacher-researchers, you will probably not conduct a full and systematic literature search. Your credits will mention readings that have come your way through colleagues' recommendations and sometimes non-research-related reading which has set you thinking. You may give credit to:

- a colleague who has helped you work out your research
- a particular group of students whose thinking influenced you
- an article which delineated a problem to solve or gave you an idea for your question

You may write the part of your research report that discusses influences as a history of the development of your question — the story of your search — rather than as an argument for your hypothesis. If you are doing a study of some aspect of a writers' workshop approach in teaching your twelfth graders, for example, you may cite not only Nancie Atwell's work with middle school students, but also a workshop you attended given by a fellow teacher who gave you the ideas on which you based your own classroom program.

There are many different ways to give credit to your students for their contributions to your research. Some teachers list all their students by name. Others quote the words and work of those who appear in the research report, protecting their identities with names made up for the occasion. We often refer teacher-researchers to "The Work of Others," a two-page guide by Joseph Harris with suggestions for citing students' and colleagues' work. He asks researchers for "a responsiveness to the ideas and phrasings of others." "Responsiveness" is a good term to describe the kind of ethical behavior you strive for as a teacher-researcher.

3. Disclose your plans, your methods, your results. Teachers conduct their research openly with their colleagues, their students, and their students' parents. They typically prepare a letter or statement early in the year explaining the focus of their research and why they are interested in the topic, asking for suggestions and assistance. Julia Lindquist's research report in Part III shows a teacher-researcher in communication with her students' parents in this way.

The information may also be in a letter which offers an overview of the year's work. The teacher-researchers of Lemon Road Elementary School sent the letter below. The parents already knew about the research group from their previous year's work and from various parent-teacher meetings and conferences throughout the year. The letter was a reminder and a request for permission to quote a child or refer to a work sample.

You could write a similar letter about your individual research, describing your work as an effort to better understand teaching and learn-

---

Dear Parents,

This past year marked the second year of the Lemon Road Teacher-Researcher Project. The project members have been investigating the learning of their students by collecting and analyzing classroom data. As teacher-researchers, we write about our research as a way to share what we have learned with our colleagues. This year our research questions have included:

- *What happens as ESL students learn to write in a second language?*
- *What happens as students work collaboratively?*
- *How do second and third graders use webs to pre-write?*
- *What happens when LD students are given choices about how to study for tests?*
- *How do first graders learn number facts?*
- *What happens in a small group guidance setting?*

In order to write about our research, we often find it necessary to quote students or include excerpts from their work. Before we include any student's comments or work, however, we obtain written permission from parents. In addition, we change students' names and sometimes change details about them in order to protect their privacy.

Because your child was involved in one of the research studies, we would like your permission to quote your child or refer to a work sample. Please sign and return the form at the bottom of the page if you agree to this.

Thanks, in advance, for your support of the Lemon Road Teacher-Researcher Project!

(The teachers signed their names here.)

_____

_____

_____

Please sign and return this form.

I hereby give permission for (teacher's name) to refer to the work of my child, (child's name), in his or her research report. I understand that she will use a pseudonym in place of my child's real name.

Signed_____Date_____

ing in your classroom and, ultimately, to improve your teaching and your students' learning.

In our experience, parents recognize and support the professional nature of teacher research. A small group of teacher-researchers in our school district had asked to be invited to give an informational program to parent association representatives. The teacher-researchers' apprehensions about parental responses were allayed when, immediately after the presentation, they were asked two questions:

1. How can I get my child into a teacher-researcher's classroom?
2. How can I talk the principal of my child's school into starting a teacher research group?

As the parents had listened to the teacher-researchers talk about their classroom studies, they realized that teacher research is highly professional behavior and that the teacher-researchers were vitally interested in the learning of their children.

We know of districts where parents have challenged the idea of teacher research, however, and sometimes the politics of a school system and its relationship to the community get in the way. These difficult situations are yet another reason to talk calmly and repeatedly with anyone who will listen about the relationship between your teaching and your research.

When you are a pioneer teacher-researcher in your area, you need to establish an encouraging atmosphere for your work, not just with parents and school administrators, but also among your colleagues. If you are willing to share your uncertainties about your teaching with your colleagues — often the basis for your research question — you will be off to a good start. If your treatment of them is ethical and professional, and if you are also willing to talk with them about what you find out, they will support you. Your colleagues will recognize, given the chance, that teacher research is not telling them what they are doing wrong, but respecting their thinking and practice at its best. Basically, teacher research ethics among colleagues is respect for each other's professionalism.

Secrecy and disguise are not a feature of teacher research. Your openness and disclosure, by showing others your respect for their thoughts and ideas, helps them to act in the same way with you. All through the research process, you take advantage of opportunities to discuss your research openly with others, from the forming of your original question to the final revisions on your report.

4. Acknowledge your beliefs and assumptions. Rather than attempt to present yourself as having no "bias," as researchers have sometimes tried to do in the past, you identify your attitudes and assumptions on a regular basis, reminding yourself that you are an integral and intimate part of your classroom and your research. Examples of the kinds of assumptions that can affect your research are:

◆ beliefs you may hold about certain teaching methods — "Students should not be stopped in the middle of a first draft to correct a spelling error."

- ideas about classroom management — "Talking to another student while I am explaining the proof is off-task behavior."
- generalizations about groups of students — "Thank goodness this class has a high percentage of girls — I'll have fewer behavior problems."
- reactions to school policies or programs — "How does the administration — or whoever dreamed up this new schedule — expect me to fill 90 minutes of class time with squirrelly ninth graders?"

Your beliefs may be proven correct by your research, but it is important to acknowledge the assumptions you carry along with you.

If your beliefs and assumptions change during your research, describe your changed viewpoints as well as any changes in the way you teach. Acknowledgment of your beliefs and assumptions at intervals during the research process and in reports and presentations of the research are ethical behavior for teacher-researchers because *not* to describe your role is to misrepresent yourself and your research. Who you are and what you believe will always be present in your research, as they are in your teaching. The closer you get to an honest explanation of your beliefs and how they affect your research, the more credible you and your research will be.

5. Discuss ethical issues with your colleagues. At some point in the progress of teacher research in your district, you will hold discussions about teacher research ethics with colleagues who are interested and need to be informed. We suggest you present some ethical dilemmas to the group and discuss them together. The discussion will involve the group in redefining teaching and research as well as looking at your particular situation. We say to the group: "Each of the following brief descriptions presents a situation that might occur as a teacher conducts research with students and colleagues. Consider the related ethical issues. What are they and how might they be handled?"

- In a parent conference on another matter, a parent says, "I hear you're doing research on the children in your class."

- A student asks, "May I read your research paper?"
- During an interview for your research, a student says, "I appreciate talking with you like this. I've been feeling depressed lately and have had thoughts about suicide."
- As you listen to the audiotape of a class discussion, you suspect that you are not getting the truth from the students.
- A teacher in your research group gives you an idea that becomes a key concept in your study.
- You are invited to a Parent-Teacher Association meeting to present your research on mathematics. The parents have criticized the math program at the school.
- You talk to your students about your research. One says, "Are we your guinea pigs?"

You can think of other situations relevant to your school and community to add to the list. This kind of discussion is a good preliminary step toward drafting an ethics statement.

As an individual, you need to be clear about your ethical standards, writing them down for yourself. As your teacher research community grows, you may need to draft or adopt a statement of ethics representing the group, one that you can make available to others, showing how your research is part of your day-to-day work and how it is a way to improve your teaching and increase and improve the learning of your students.

Mohr assisted in drafting a statement of teacher research ethics in collaboration with a group of high school teacher-researchers, an assistant principal, and an assistant superintendent in the Frederick County Public Schools near Winchester, Virginia. Their statement was geared toward explaining teacher research to a community audience and establishing guidelines for teachers and principals.

A group of teacher-researchers working with Jane Zeni at the University of Missouri in St. Louis put together a booklet entitled *Guide to Ethical Issues and Action Research*. Their statement brings together the university's traditional ethical guidelines and the particular situation of teacher research. Zeni is editing a collection of articles about ethical issues in teacher research, written by both K-12 and university teacher-researchers that includes the guides mentioned above and brings together current thinking on the subject.

We recommend that you follow and participate in the professional discussions of teacher research ethics in general and draft what you think is appropriate for your purposes and for your community. Ethical behavior is a highly individual matter, but as a teacher-researcher you represent your students, your colleagues, and your profession as well as yourself. Your ethics matter to us all.

REFERENCES

Anderson, Paul V. (1998). Simple gifts: Ethical issues in the conduct of person-based composition research. *College Composition and Communication, 49* (1), 63-89.

Harris, J. (1994). The work of others. *College Composition and Communication, 45* (4), 439-440.

Zeni, J., Ed. (In press). *Ethical issues in practitioner inquiry.* New York: Teachers College Press.

When Do You Find Time to Do Teacher Research?

Near the end of almost every one of our presentations about teacher research, as the participants begin to see the possibilities for research in their professional lives, a buzz of questions and ideas fills the room. Then, someone raises a voice to ask, "Teacher research sounds great, but when are you supposed to *do* this?"

In the context of most teachers' professional lives, when scheduling a bathroom break requires effort and cunning, no time is set aside for teachers to reflect on their work, let alone write or research. Even when teachers want to make time for research, they worry about slighting other important parts of their lives. But as long as teachers don't conduct research and don't take an active part in professional life, they are not viewed as people who need the time to think, reflect, and research. They continue to be seen as knowledge users, not knowledge makers. How do we get beyond this double bind?

The double bind exists at least partly because we work in school systems that structure teacher assignments and responsibilities in ways that make professional development such as teacher research difficult, especially because it is teacher-initiated and homegrown. This whole book, however, is an argument that teacher research is a worthwhile use of your time, and we know that many teachers, including the two of us, have budgeted professional and personal hours to make our teacher research possible. The decisions you make about how to use your time are personal and dependent on many factors. Even though we cannot create more time for you, we can offer you some observations about the use of time during a research project.

We see the use of professional time to do teacher research as a series of choices. To begin with, the choice to do teacher research should always be your own. You do it for yourself and your students, for your professional growth and development, and for your sense of efficacy — you are doing something of importance for the profession. *You* make the choices about when and how much to do. Consequently, there is no such thing as getting behind in your research — you are where you are. You may need to reschedule or replan, but you are not remiss.

Once you have started, you can choose to exploit the opportunities that teacher research offers you so as to make the most of the time you spend on it. You can also choose to integrate your research and your teaching to take advantage of researching as a way of teaching. Another choice, a qualitatively different one, is to speak out to those who make decisions about the use of teachers' time.

1. MAKE THE MOST OF THE TIME YOU SPEND ON TEACHER RESEARCH.

Teacher research is done with colleagues. Your research group meetings give you support, helpful talk, and listening, colleague-to-colleague, that make the rest of your teaching life easier and better. You learn a lot about teaching from your group and can discuss without fear what is and is not working in your classroom and develop more successful ways of teaching. The times when a few teachers are able to get together and talk meaningfully about teaching are rare. The time spent in a teacher research group is worth every minute.

If you are new to teaching or even to a particular school, you might choose to join the research group in order to learn from your more experienced colleagues in addition to learning about your teaching. In a teacher research group in our school district, one participant was a classroom aide wanting to learn more about teaching and another was a first-year teacher. Within the teacher research group they found nonjudgmental talk about the problems of teaching, ideas for ways to make their teaching more effective, and a sympathetic as well as professional outlook on their day-to-day lives as teachers. These novice teachers were not evaluated by the group but treated as fellow professionals who could solve their own problems, given the time to reflect and analyze. Even to these beginning teachers, participation in a research group was time well spent.

If you are faced with an ever-expanding curriculum, new statewide standards, and tests to match, you have an opportunity to conduct research that will benefit you and your students greatly. You could choose a research focus that will help you answer your questions about the new curriculum and test mandates. You are in a good position to ask fundamental questions about how these new programs work in real classrooms.

If it is your year to be evaluated as a teacher, you might choose to incorporate your teacher research into your goals for that evaluation. You will need to explain to your evaluator that as a researcher, what you discover when you change your teaching is not always a move to a new and higher plane of excellence. Show both the positive and negative findings you discover as you conduct your research and add data you have collected to the administrator's classroom observation data to get a more balanced picture of your teaching. Show your evaluator the benefit of teacher research.

2. INTEGRATE YOUR TEACHING AND RESEARCHING.

Teacher research can give focus to a fragmented professional life. You decide what to focus on during a given year, choose what you want to work on, and develop some skills in depth, instead of trying to do everything at once and in a hurry. Lisa Gruenhagen, a music teacher-researcher, designed a fugue project with her elementary students, transforming Bach and the fugue into history, mathematics, art, and writing in addition to music. It became the year of the fugue. A research focus like Gruenhagen's doesn't mean other things are neglected. Integrating, combining, and compromising are always part of classroom planning, and you are always making teaching decisions about what you can and can't do. Your research provides a focus for your studies in the year ahead. You have a research lens through which to view your teaching, "to see into your teaching" as teacher-researcher Shannon McClain put it during a discussion about doing teacher research.

Your research is not an addition to an already overloaded schedule, because a lot of what you do already serves research purposes. You collect data whenever you gather together a group of your students' papers. You use observing skills whenever you check to see how students are responding to a lesson. You analyze classroom context whenever you plan an assignment or a bulletin board. You analyze data when you look at patterns in your students' grades. When you have a stack of assignments to grade, looking at them also as data gives you a different perspective on the work and may even make grading easier by helping you decide what kind of feedback will benefit the students most. As you write comments to your students, you are also writing a research log entry — your summary of the data yielded by the papers.

You can use your research notes and log writings as a place to think through your lesson plans. If you are trying to design a plan to help students with a difficult lesson, look back through your research log to help you decide what to do next.

You can use your developing research habits to solve classroom problems. If something is rippling across the classroom that you know deserves your attention, get out your log and take notes. If a lesson has been a triumph, ask students to write about what contributed to their learning. They will get a chance to do some metacognitive thinking and you will have new data for your research.

3. ASSERT YOURSELF ABOUT THE IMPORTANCE OF YOUR TIME TO DO RESEARCH AND TO WORK WITH COLLEAGUES.

Trust your own judgment about your need for meaningful professional development. Unlike the many innovations that come your way through professional development programs such as cooperative learning, writing process, reading recovery, or technology, research requires time for you to reflect, think, and write. New teaching techniques, curriculum, or management schemes require you to learn what others believe is important for you to learn and often ask that you practice strategies exactly as they were conceived by others. Many are useful additions to your teaching, but they do not ask for your reflection, thinking, or writing. Teacher research is not an innovation of this kind. It is a way of looking at your teaching as a whole. It is a constantly renewable resource for helping you make sense of your students' learning and your teaching, including the teaching strategies that you are given in staff development programs.

Ask for time to write and give presentations about your research. Your articles and presentations inform the profession and give voice to teacher knowledge, but both require time outside of school. Even schools and districts that proudly recognize the work of teacher-researchers do not routinely budget time for such professional activities. By asking, you put the issue in front of them.

Whenever you have the opportunity, speak to the issue of time for teacher research. Could a teacher-researcher have a reduced teaching load for one year or an in-school fellowship from your local university? Can a research project be done during an in-house sabbatical? Can a grant be written to support one or two teacher-researchers a year? Can the office of staff development in your school district — even if it's just one person — keep a cache of leave available for teacher-researchers? One day of leave during the writing of a final report helps; a couple of days to attend a conference to report on research promotes the professional nature of teaching.

Teacher-researcher colleague Marty Swaim and her husband Stephen have written a book called *Teacher Time*. They discuss current practices and suggest actions to take to bring about changes. Their discussion will be helpful to anyone working to reform the way teachers' time is used in schools.

Nothing here suggests you buy a special kind of planner or get up an hour or two earlier in order to fit teacher research into your life. We know of only a few places where real time has, on occasion, been made available to teacher-researchers, so we write mostly with hope for future opportunities. You cannot wait for such reforms, of course, but once you have made the extra effort to learn to do teacher research, once you have completed a study, once you have worked within a research group — once you have done all that — then observing, documenting, writing, and analyzing will become a valued and integral part of the way you teach. Even during years when you are not doing a formal study, you will find yourself teaching as a researcher, assuming the authority of a thinker about teaching and learning, and doing it based on what you see happening in your classroom. It's a choice, it takes time, and it's worth it.

REFERENCE

Swaim, M. S. and Swaim, S. C. (1999). *Teacher time*. Arlington, VA: Redbud Books.

How Do You Lead
a Teacher Research Group?

The two most important qualifications for leading a teacher research group are experience conducting research in your own classroom and willingness to conduct research along with the group of teacher-researchers you lead. The past experience gives you knowledge of what's coming — the revising of questions, the shifting of roles, the struggle with analysis and writing, and other experiences typical of teacher research. Conducting research along with the other teachers in the group gives you the opportunity to be a full participant in the group, to talk about current research experiences, and to model the reactions of a teacher-researcher.

Since 1980, one or the other of us has been involved in leading a teacher research group. We have, as time and our jobs permitted, informed ourselves about educational research and, at the same time, developed theories and methods for teacher research through our experience in the field. Because of our backgrounds, we believe that teacher research groups can be led by people without every academic credential, although not without study and experience. Leaders of teacher research groups are not trainers or developers but colleagues with different information and a mutual interest — to conduct research about teaching and learning, and to do it well.

Because of our experience working together, we recommend that you lead the group with a partner, if possible. Many of our seminars have been led by two K-12 teacher-researchers. Leading a group with a partner allows you not only to share the workload but also to discuss, plan, and evaluate the group's work together. Pairing university and K-12 teacher-researchers makes a good combination since each can add to the other's field of experience. The university teacher will provide background in current research and methodology while the K-12 teacher will have practical knowledge of the workings of K-12 classrooms and schools. But whatever the combination, we think it is helpful to have someone to talk things over with as you learn to lead among your peers.

Once you accept the responsibility of leading a teacher research group there are some ways of working that we think you will find helpful. There are also some essential tasks that will be yours. You will organize the meetings and keep to an agreed-upon schedule, provide information about teacher research process and methods, respond to the work that the teachers are doing, and model a teacher-researcher at work. Although not every leader's experience will be the same, here are some ideas that have helped us to accomplish the essential tasks.

Organizing and planning the meetings. As group leaders, you take care of logistics — planning and getting on yearlong calendars (the school calendar, if possible, as well as the teachers' calendars), finding a convenient meeting place, making a list for people to sign up to bring refreshments, setting the meeting time and making a calendar of the research group's activities, reminding people of upcoming meetings, copying handouts and articles for distribution, and securing substitute leave time if possible. These tasks can sometimes be shared among group members, but they are essential to the group's functioning.

You might expect any group leader to do these things, but we list them because they are often difficult for teachers to manage during the school day with its tightly controlled schedule and little or no access to a phone, a convenient computer, or a functioning copier. It will be helpful if one of the group leaders has a more flexible schedule or has access to a phone or photocopier. Teachers appreciate knowing that when they come to research meetings at the end of a school day, the meetings will be well organized. But as in research itself, sometimes things will not work out as planned, so be ready to laugh and move on.

Providing background information on research process and methods. As a teacher research leader, you need time to reflect, read, and study, apart from the act of conducting research. You need a background in educational research that less experienced teacher-researchers may not have acquired. You also need to be able to select readings that will be useful to teacher-researchers in your group. This requires knowledge of the field of teacher research, including books, articles, and other available resources. You will benefit from your writing and reflection during times when you have done teacher research previously, as well as from the writing and reflection you do about the leadership of your current research group.

In Part IV you will find links to the many resources that are now available to support teacher research, along with suggested readings to supplement the references following each chapter of this book.

Responding to teacher-researchers' work. Your responses reflect your support and respect for the teacher-researcher's ultimate authority. You listen carefully, give advice while allowing for other options, and speak your mind when necessary. You base your comments on an intense interest in your colleagues' work. Specifically, you respond in group discussions, on the phone or through e-mail, in individual conferences with teacher-researchers after a group meeting, and in written responses to log entries, selected data, and drafts of research reports.

In responding to teacher-researchers we often use questions to describe the possibilities. "What other sources of data do you have available in your classroom that could help you answer that question?" instead of "You should videotape the lesson." Using questions as a way of explaining is a kind of teaching and leading that emerges from respect for the knowledge and thinking of the teacher-researcher. If you reread the questions we ask in Part I when you are preparing to lead a group, you will see them as a way of teaching as well as a way of learning about your research.

In addition to questions, you will need to

◆ **Restate what you understand a teacher-researcher to be saying or writing.**

" It sounds like you've come up with a way to help yourself look at that data. You've got a way to display it, at least — right? Be sure to let the rest of us know how it turns out."

◆ **Ask about a finding or a direction you see that the teacher-researcher has not mentioned.**

"I keep wondering what this finding would lead you to think about the student's underachievement or about how he feels about his learning or about school in general. You have rich interview data to mine!"

◆ **Connect a finding with the data or with an implication.**

"When I heard you say that you found students could not evaluate their internet research sources and were confused about how to tell what was reliable and what was not, it made me think that some lessons need to be developed to do that as well as to deal with the problem of internet plagiarism. Didn't you start to develop something along those lines once? The need for such learning is an implication of your finding, I think."

◆ **Request that a connection be clarified.**

"When you mentioned the second finding, I did not get the connection you were making to the first one. Are you saying that project learning in math works as well as if not better than test taking as an assessment? Wow! How? I think that could be true, but I don't see how the two connect. Would you give this another try?"

◆ **List on a separate sheet of paper what seems to be the important stuff.**

"You have so many important points to make it's hard to see which ones matter the most. As I reread your draft, I listed what seemed to me to be the main ones. I may be off base, but it may help you to see what one (very involved!) reader saw. Good luck with your next draft."

◆ **Number paragraphs to show a way of reordering them.**

"When I read your draft, I could see this order for your argument. Would it distort what you want to say to move this paragraph to the end?"

◆ **List problems in a draft that you think have yet to be resolved.**

"Your study is very complex! I'm sure it's hard to keep track of all the connections you're finding. Anyway, I kept a list on

this (very small) Post-it of the problems I think you have yet to solve. If you want to talk further, let me know."

Responding and commenting on each other's research is a responsibility group members share with the leaders. Uncertainty (deliberate or not) on your part as leader is often an invitation to others in the group to make meaningful comments. The difficulty with giving general advice about how to comment is that the exchange is always highly specific to the work and individuals involved. Mohr was once asked why she tended to end her spoken and written responses with, "Good luck." What did that mean? The process of talking about what needs to be done next lends itself to this kind of hopeful hesitancy.

Modeling a teacher-researcher at work. As teacher-researcher and group leader, you question your own assumptions and suspend judgment, thereby modeling a research stance for others. You are informed and inquiring about the broad range of educational research. You publish, attend conferences, and speak of your work in public and professional forums. The most important way you serve as a model, however, is when you work with a group of teacher-researchers and conduct your own research along with them.

Our colleagues Bernadette Glaze, Mary Ann Nocerino, and Courtney Rogers conducted a study of a teacher research seminar led by MacLean to try to find out how the group was led. All three were interested in becoming leaders of teacher research groups, but neither they nor we had ever systematically looked at what happened between the leaders and the other teacher-researchers in a group. In their article "Learning to Lead Among Peers," Glaze, Nocerino, and Rogers saw the leadership effort as directed toward encouraging the teachers to achieve certain goals for themselves. Here are their findings:

   ◆ **Teachers were researchers from the beginning.** The leader structured assignments which guided the participants through the research process.

   ◆ **Teachers participated as members of a community of researchers.** The leader arranged the chairs in circles, large and small. She facilitated teacher-researchers' talking to one another and looking to each other for support, information, and guidance.

- **Teachers examined their own classroom teaching and learning.** The leader's questions and comments led teacher-researchers to observe and reflect on what happened in the classroom as they worked with their students.

- **Teachers spoke with authority** on issues and topics related to their classrooms. The leader acknowledged and validated the participants' own questions, speculations, and findings.

- **Teachers contributed to the larger research community.** The leader facilitated class publication of the research articles and encouraged publication in other professional journals.

Even if you agree that these are the goals of a teacher research leader, you still have not solved the problem of how to act so that these goals are achieved by the teachers in the group. Here are some more hints from Glaze, Nocerino, and Rogers:

> *The leader is a teacher-researcher who understands and has faith in the process of teacher research.... The leader models teacher-researcher behaviors as she (or he) leads the course. The leader understands and demonstrates a style of leadership which allows teacher-researchers to find their own ways and who is comfortable and skilled in a facilitator role. The leader is knowledgeable about qualitative and quantitative research methodology.*

Becoming a teacher research leader places you in a more public and possibly vulnerable position for assertions and questions about research in general (You can prove *anything* by research!), the ethics of teacher research (You can't teach and do research at the same time!), the quality of teaching (Would teacher research be a good thing to require our marginal teachers to do?) and the quality of research (How can you call this research? Where is its theoretical base? Where is your control group?). Prepare yourself by imagining possible answers.

You will also become a spokesperson for teacher research as professional development and as professional knowledge. You may be asked to serve on research committees and boards, representing teacher-researchers. Being a leader of teacher-researchers offers you a change in your career that doesn't require you to leave teaching. We recommend it!

REFERENCE

Glaze, B., Nocerino, M.A., & Rogers, C. (1989). Learning to lead among peers: The teacher-researcher seminar. *Language and learning: Reports from a teacher-researcher seminar.* Fairfax, VA: Northern Virginia Writing Project, George Mason University.

How Do You Explain Teacher Research to Others?

Most of the time when you are explaining teacher research you will not be giving a lecture. Rather you will be in a conversation or discussion where you want people to broaden their definitions of teaching and researching to include teacher research. We are concentrating on early conversations here, knowing that as you gain more experience with teacher research, the conversations will become more complex. We begin with two general suggestions followed by a series of conversations based on our experience explaining teacher research.

Suggestions

Don't tell too much at once. Start with the simplest explanation that will answer the question and wait for more questions so that you can see where the questioner is headed.

> [Two teachers standing in the hallway after the students have gone home.]
> *Teacher: Why are you doing research?*
> *Teacher-Researcher: To improve my teaching of writing.*
> *Teacher: My students keep making the same mistakes no matter how often I correct them. What is your research about?*
> *Teacher-Researcher: Revision.*
> *Teacher: Well, what do you think about grammar? Should we go back to the exercises in the grammar books?*
> *Teacher-Researcher: I'm not sure. What I'm finding out is…*

"I'm not sure" are the words of a teacher-researcher. Be ready to follow the direction of the questioner, but also to provide information that the questioner has not asked for but needs.

Use your knowledge of the people and the context. Successful explanations depend a lot on the relationship you already have with the people in the discussion and how well you understand their point of view.

[In the principal's office at a meeting the teacher-researcher has requested.]

Principal: You want sub leave days to analyze your research and write it up? I need to get people to the state baseball tournament, remember. We're going all the way this year!

Teacher-Researcher: I know you love baseball, but I have always found you interested in academics as well.

Principal: You have an inservice program in mind? Some teachers won't even come to mandatory meetings!

Teacher-Researcher: Teacher-researchers sort of provide their own inservice. How much did you pay for that last program we had? I bet it was more than the cost of our sub leave days.

Principal: You're right, of course. Well, what do I get in return?

Teacher-Researcher: We'll report what we find out to the faculty, if you promise not to make it a mandatory meeting.

Principal: Would you come to the Parent Teachers Association board meeting next Wednesday night and talk to them about your research?

Teacher-Researcher: In exchange for the sub leave?

Principal: Maybe we'll lose in the semi-finals.

Teacher-Researcher: It's a deal. By the way, could the teacher research group count as participation on a school committee or as the required staff development instead of being an add-on? Let me know what you think and thanks for the sub leave.

The teacher-researcher used knowledge about the principal's concerns in order to provide information about teacher research and to get the needed sub leave days. They negotiate rapidly and in a friendly, knowing way with respect for their differences and individual priorities.

As you read the following conversations, you will see the two principles in action as well as some additional strategies for talking to people who want and need to know more about teacher research.

CONVERSATIONS WITH STUDENTS

[A middle school social studies teacher describes a research project to a class.]

Teacher-Researcher: This year I'm planning to study our class discussions. I know that you learn from talking, but I'm not sure of the best ways to conduct class discussions. Do you learn more in small groups or with the whole class? Should everybody talk, or do people who don't talk still learn? Occasionally I'll ask you to write the answer to one of my questions on a 3x5 card. I'll collect them to use as data.

Student: What do you mean — data?

Teacher-Researcher: Data is the research name for what I analyze in order to answer my questions. What I am doing is called teacher research. It means that I teach and do research at the same time. If you have special insights on class discussion, I would like to add them to my data. Does anyone have an idea right now?

Student: I do! Last week when we had that discussion on censorship, I had so much to say and kept waving my hand around, but other people shouted out their comments and I never got to say my piece!

Teacher-Researcher: Hold on, I want to write this down in my log. So what did you do?...

[A high school science teacher interviews a student after school as part of a research project.]

Student: Why do you want to interview me? What did I do?

Teacher-Researcher: Remember when I told you I was doing classroom research to find out more about how students write lab reports? That's what I want to interview you about.

Student: I sort of remember. What's wrong with my lab reports?

Teacher-Researcher: When a teacher wants to talk to you, it's not always because you've messed up, you know.

Student: With me, it is.

Teacher-Researcher: Well, this may be a first, then. I am interested in how you are able to write so apparently easily—it's called fluency — and to get your whole group started when it comes time to write. Do you always draft your group's report?

Student: Yeah.

Teacher-Researcher: Tell me about it. I'll take some notes while you talk, but will check them with you later to make sure I've written things down accurately.
Student: Well,...

[An elementary school teacher talks with the whole class about how they learn math facts.]
Teacher-Researcher: Class, today you're going to help me figure something out. I'm trying to learn more about how you learn your math facts. Who can tell me what math facts are?
Student: Those are simple! Like 3 plus 5 is 8.
Teacher-Researcher: How did you know that?
Student: I just knew it. We did those a long time ago!
Teacher-Researcher: Can you remember what helped you learn math facts?
Student: Some are hard. Some are easy.
Teacher-Researcher: Thank you for that! I'm going to write it down on the chalkboard so we can look back at our ideas as we talk.... Now, which ones are hard and which ones are easy? I see some hands...

Talk to your students about your research at different times throughout the year. As they become more involved with your study, they will have more subtle understandings. They will learn that, when you do research, you need their thoughts on a variety of subjects. They will also see that researching is a way of learning.

CONVERSATIONS WITH ADMINISTRATORS

[The teacher-researcher has asked for a five-minute conference in the first quarter of the year to inform the principal about this year's research project.]
Teacher-Researcher: Thanks for the five minutes.
Principal: One of your students stopped me in the hall today, very excited, and asked for five minutes, too, for an interview. I assume you're going to tell me what's going on! When I asked

Kevin, he said about computers as learning tools. Learning tools? Where did this come from?

Teacher-Researcher: *"Learning tool" is the term we've been using in class to stay focused on computers in the learning process, not just as something to use for fun. This year I'm studying the ways students learn with computers and the students are helping in the research. I'm not experimenting, in that sense of research. At least not any more than I am when I try new methods or curriculum! I'm observing and documenting. I ask the kids questions and write down their answers, and I collect certain assignments and analyze them.*

Principal: *Sounds like extra work, but Kevin was really excited about it. Well, what are you finding out? Aren't computers supposed to be great "learning tools"? We're sure spending a lot of money to get more of them.*

Teacher-Researcher: *I think they do some things very well, others not so well. That's what my kids and I are trying to find out. Kevin wants to interview you to add to our data.*

Principal: *Your data! Sounds like research. Well, let me know what you find out. I could use the information in this budget crunch.*

Teacher-Researcher: *In a few months I'll get on your schedule again and have you come visit our class. I know you have a lot of evaluations to do, but I promise this will be fun. The students will feel very proud to be reporting on our research to the principal.*

Principal: *Sounds great. Speak to my secretary. Was that only five minutes?*

[A small group of teacher-researchers is giving a presentation to a group of school administrators about teacher research and how it can be a part of a school's improvement plans. They have defined teacher research and are now answering questions.]

Administrator #1: *What I like about what you said is that this seems to be focused directly on student learning. Do teachers do this voluntarily?*

Teacher-Researcher #2: Only voluntarily. Typically you might have a teacher research group of three to five in your school at any one time.

Administrator #2: Is this an inservice program? It seems like it would really improve teaching.

Teacher-Researcher #3: There is evidence that teachers change the way they teach as a result of their research. It also provides knowledge that can help other teachers and their students, especially in the same school. Teacher research is "context dependent." It doesn't rely on large numbers but on interactions within classrooms.

Administrator #2: Then is it worth anything as research beyond the benefit to the teachers and students involved?

Teacher-Researcher #3: That depends on what happens to the research when it is completed.

Administrator #2: I can see having the teacher-researchers talk to the faculty about their work, especially if it's on a subject everybody is thinking about. And I've got an inservice program to plan.

Teacher-Researcher #2: Here's a list of ways you can let the teachers know that you back their efforts. For example, read their reports and respond to them. Give them a substitute leave day to work on their research. Send out for pizza when they are meeting after school.

Administrator #3: Does teacher research raise test scores? That's what I need.

Teacher-Researcher #1: We think it might, but for now, why not consider reporting teacher research along with your test scores? Test scores don't tell us why things happen or what to do about them. Teacher research does.

Teacher-Researcher #2: Next, we'll hear from the principal and teacher-researchers from one elementary school talking about the effect of teacher research at their school...

Conversations with school administrators usually are connected to their priorities. They want to see teaching in their buildings improved and they want a way to show that the students are learning. These are also interests of teacher-researchers.

Conversations with Parents

[Late in the afternoon, a parent hurries into her son's science class, just as the teacher is getting ready to leave.]

Parent: I'm sorry to rush in, but I really need to talk to you about my son. My question is going to sound crazy, but I don't get why he's doing well in science, but not in other classes. Are you sure he's not cheating or something? I shouldn't say that, but frankly, I need some good news.

Teacher-Researcher: Let me get my grade book. I only have ten minutes because I have to pick up my daughter. If you need a longer conference, we'll schedule one.

Parent: Ten minutes is long enough for bad news. He said you kept him after school last week for an interview. Something about research. Is he in trouble?

Teacher-Researcher: No, at least not with me. He volunteered to be interviewed about his writing of the lab reports we do after an experiment. He often does the drafting of the report for his group and I think he is a good writer, at least in science. He knows how to draw conclusions from evidence.

Parent: He does?

Teacher-Researcher: We talked for about half an hour. He said he'd taken creative writing last year and learned to write drafts and write for different readers and purposes. Well, he certainly has put that learning to good use in science class.

Parent: I am so relieved. He almost sounds like a student when you describe him.

Teacher-Researcher: Well, I think he is in his own way. He certainly helped me with my research. I'm trying to improve my teaching of how to write lab reports, so I'm doing classroom research on what happens when they do the writing. I've talked to the whole class about the project and did also mention it at Back-to-School night in September.

Parent: We just moved here in January.

Teacher-Researcher: I know, and I should have kept up with my new parents. I'm sorry. Anyway, here's a letter that explains the research and asks permission for me to use your son's interview as part of my data when I write up the research.

Parent: *He's going to be in your write-up? Well, thanks so much. This is the best ten minutes I've spent in his school for a long time. Good luck with your research, and don't hesitate to call if he's any trouble.*

[The principal has asked a teacher-researcher to speak with a Parent-Teacher Association committee about teacher research.]

Teacher-Researcher: *The principal asked me to come tonight to discuss my research on goal setting with my ninth grade social studies students, but also to answer any questions you may have about teacher research in general. Do you have any questions to start with?*

Parent: *The first thing that popped into my mind when the principal mentioned research was that I didn't want my daughters to be used as guinea pigs for somebody's research.*

Teacher-Researcher: *As a parent as well as a teacher, I have the same reaction — not wanting experiments done on my children. Most of us have a picture of research as a laboratory with lots of equipment bubbling on the counters, but teacher research is descriptive, not experimental. It goes back to some of the original ideas of science — observing, documenting, analyzing. As I said, my research this year is on goal setting. For two or three years now I've asked my students to write goals for each quarter. This September, since I was researching, after they wrote down their goals, I categorized them. Then I told them what I noticed — that many were worried about taking essay tests. We talked, and I took notes on what they said. Before the next essay test I gave them tips on how to do well on the test, and the students who wanted to improve their essay tests gave a panel discussion about what they were doing to achieve higher grades. It was just great to listen to them, like a group of CEO's talking about the future of their companies! Well, I'm going on too long. It's so* *interesting to me that I'm sure you probably agree with my wife, who thinks I talk about goal setting a little more than is necessary.*

Parent: *It's a pleasure to hear a teacher so interested in his own teaching that he is willing to study to improve it. I think that's wonderful. And with ninth graders, too! I have one at home and, believe me, goal setting is not easy! Would you be willing to talk about this with our special committee for ninth grade parents or at the ninth grade parents' orientation in the spring?*

Teacher-Researcher: *Yes, I would.*

Parent (in charge of meeting): *We have a long agenda tonight so we have to move on, and you haven't really told us what teacher research is, although I'm beginning to get the idea.*

Teacher-Researcher: *It's research you do with your students. I try to find out how things work in my classes and why. I share my results with other teachers and with the principal — with anyone who will listen! Thank you for your interest.*

Discussing teacher research with parents enables them to see a professional teacher at work. You are not in a defensive position but in the position of talking about what you know. Nor are you showing disappointment in their children. Once they see that you are working to improve the way their children learn, they are usually on your side.

CONVERSATIONS WITH COLLEAGUES

Conversations with colleagues about your research are often brief, spontaneous, and informal like the one at the beginning of this discussion. You also need to be ready with the basic information a teacher needs before deciding to do classroom research.

[Several teachers collapse after school in the teachers' lounge and talk about one of the teacher's research class.]

Teacher #1: *I see you made those caramel brownies. Is your research class today? I saw it advertised in the professional development catalog, and somebody told me you were taking it. How is it?*

Teacher-Researcher: *I made them for class; you can have one. It's a group of teachers each studying something in his or her classroom. The leaders of the class are a high school and an elementary school teacher — that surprised me. They are doing classroom research, too.*

Teacher #1: *These are so good they're sinful! I never thought I'd want to be involved in research. Did you take that required course when you were being certified? It was awful. In my college they called it Statistics for Teachers — translate, dummies.*

Teacher-Researcher: *People in our group are mostly doing qualitative research, observing and documenting some aspect of their teaching. I'm looking at how my students work in small groups. I record the group discussions, let them listen to themselves, and they figure out what they're learning.*

Teacher #1: *Sounds like they're doing your project for you.*

Teacher-Researcher: *Well, in a way they are. One thing we discovered when we were analyzing the tapes right before we had a test was that it served as a great test review. Even groups whose discussion hadn't been so great learned from the other groups as they reported.*

Teacher #1: *I've got a test coming up, and I'm sick of those test review sessions. The kids don't pay attention even when they don't know what they need to know for the test. Hey, she made those for her class!*

Teacher #2: *Sorry. Can I have this recipe? What do you do when the class meets? It sounds like the work is all in your classroom.*

Teacher-Researcher: *Most of it is — my data is the tapes and the kids' analysis of them. We start writing our reports in another month or two.*

Teacher: *Reports?*

Teacher-Researcher: *We're going to write about what we found out and make a class publication. Some of the teachers are doing amazing things, and I'm so glad I'll have a chance to keep a copy of what they find out.*

Teacher: *How much time does it take?*

Teacher-Researcher: Well, it takes mostly thinking time — what I usually can't find time for in the first place. At least now I tell myself it's for a class assignment.

Teacher #1: Can you spare one more? Thanks. I missed lunch — yearbook meeting. If you are just doing this in your own classroom and you are the one doing it, aren't you contaminating your research? What good will it be to anybody else?

Teacher-Researcher: Remember when you just said you might try the tape analysis strategy for a test review? Well, you'll adapt what I did to fit your classes and it might work for you or it might not. If you were a teacher-researcher, you would collect more data, analyze it, and could then report to other teachers what you found out. Most of the research I've had thrown at me in inservice meetings had little to do with my kids. This does. Besides, we have great refreshments.

When you explain teacher research to others, it helps you clarify it for yourself. When you explain it with respect for the points of view of others, they will see you as a researcher, someone who reserves judgment, gathers evidence, and analyzes situations. Even if they don't want to do teacher research or worry about its value, they will see its usefulness for you.

OF WHAT USE IS TEACHER RESEARCH?

In *Mind and Nature* Gregory Bateson asks what is wrong with teachers that they do not teach "the pattern that connects." He describes a lesson that required students to closely examine over a period of time, a cooked crab. He displayed the crab to his class and assigned them to convince him that the crab had once been a living thing. The students were to imagine themselves as extraterrestrials — alive, but with no experience of crabs. What patterns could they see that would make the connection between the crab and life itself? (pp. 7-8)

If this book has a theme, it could be stated as "the pattern which connects." We have laid out before you "cooked" teacher research, asking you to see what makes it a living thing. The usefulness of teacher research is its liveliness, the fact that it emerges from a specific classroom context full of individual student and teacher voices teaching and learning, making connections, seeing patterns.

But teacher research is also useful because it moves beyond the classroom and has the potential to affect the teaching and learning lives of others. Like a spiral, it retains its characteristic structure even as it expands.

The following figure shows this outward growth and the usefulness of teacher research for each additional educational community. Teacher colleagues, the school, the school district, and the profession surround the classroom, but not as circles outside circles. Instead, each new ellipse returns to its classroom origin before expanding outward again. For instance, as the spiral grows to include the school's interest in identifying areas for school improvement, it still incorporates and depends on the use of teacher research by teacher-researchers, their students, and their teacher colleagues. The classroom is the dynamic core, the source.

To bring the spiral to life, we offer a series of reflections based on our own and our colleagues' experiences with the uses of teacher research.

OF WHAT USE IS YOUR RESEARCH TO YOU AND YOUR STUDENTS?

Your work as a teacher-researcher contributes first and most significantly to your work with your students in your classroom.

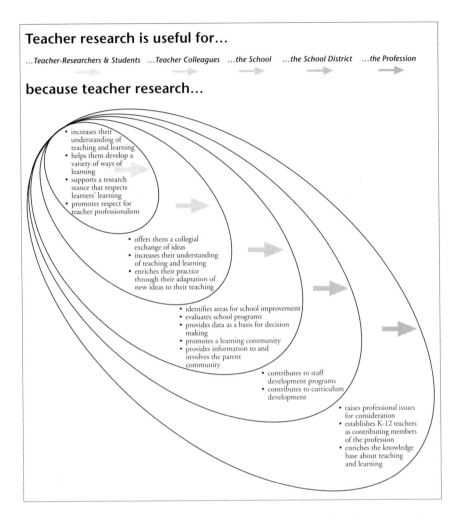

Teacher research is useful for...

...Teacher-Researchers & Students   ...Teacher Colleagues   ...the School   ...the School District   ...the Profession

because teacher research...

- increases their understanding of teaching and learning
- helps them develop a variety of ways of learning
- supports a research stance that respects learners' learning
- promotes respect for teacher professionalism

- offers them a collegial exchange of ideas
- increases their understanding of teaching and learning
- enriches their practice through their adaptation of new ideas to their teaching

- identifies areas for school improvement
- evaluates school programs
- provides data as a basis for decision making
- promotes a learning community
- provides information to and involves the parent community

- contributes to staff development programs
- contributes to curriculum development

- raises professional issues for consideration
- establishes K-12 teachers as contributing members of the profession
- enriches the knowledge base about teaching and learning

[A teacher stands in her classroom before school opens and reflects on whether or not to conduct research during the coming school year.]

Clean boards. Waxed floor. Supplies unpacked. Baskets out for sophomore notebooks. Folders for seniors. I have to decide whether to do Fahrenheit 451 *again this year. Maybe I'll wait 'til I know the kids a bit.*

Have to decide about research, too. Where'd I put that memo? "Teacher-researchers meet in room 243 at 10 a.m. Come before you decide whether or not you'll be part of the group!" If I decide not to, I'll regret it. If I do research, it will be for the same reasons that I always do it: for myself, my students, for my teaching and their learning — our learning. It's close to 10. Notebook, coffee, keys. I'll check Lisa's room to see if she wants to go.

[An English teacher reflects on the usefulness of her own research for investigating an identified instructional issue. She has just read — for a second time — her sophomores' drafts.]

Not what I expected. What's going on? Did they just ignore the instructions? The rubric? Why did we spend so long going over the purpose of this part of the paper? It's as if I was thinking one thing and they were off on a completely different train of thought.

Okay. What are the options here? I could just rate the drafts according to the rubric and give them back. No point, though, in just repeating myself if they didn't get it in the first place. But what didn't they get? Maybe I should take the papers back to the class. Set up a way for them to rate the papers according to the rubric. Or shift gears totally — figure out what they did do. I wonder what my research group would say. When do we meet again?

[A social studies teacher reflects at year's end on his research project with ninth graders.]

OK, I've cleared the bulletin boards, covered the bookcases, packed the closet. Oh, brother! Our list of goal-setting steps is still posted over the blackboard! Part of the woodwork. Cement-work, more accurately.

I think the research itself got the kids involved — feeling like they were important to my research project — and it was about their learning, their goals. The last time I had them write about their learning, a lot said they'd used strategies this year they'd only "known about" before. And some wrote what they wanted to re-member for next year. They knew world history, too — I loved their lists of favorite facts and cultures. Even during that last bit of data I collected, they were coming up with new insights — goals, learn-ing, social studies. Neat group of kids.

Some other teachers — not even in the social studies depart-ment — told me they want to try something like it next year. I never thought so many would read my research article. I hope some of them do join us in the fall. Let's see. Checkout form... where did I put that? OK. Keys? Yep. Lights out? Until next year!

Your students benefit from witnessing your work as a researcher. They see you learning not only about a particular question but learning from them something that you cannot understand without their help. Your modeling the roles of researcher and learner helps your students approach their own learning with receptive, inquisitive minds.

OF WHAT USE IS YOUR RESEARCH TO YOUR COLLEAGUES?

Beyond your classroom and the small group of teacher-researchers with whom you meet, your research is useful also to other teachers nearby.

[A third grade teacher is sitting at a table where two other teachers on his team are talking. He listens to the conversation.]
They sound pretty frustrated. So am I. Eleanor has worked hard with her kids on the math displays — and Jim on his students' "math in the real world" reports. Now they're talking about ditching great lessons they've developed to make room for new geometry requirements. I'm not ready to give up on what we've developed as a team. In fact, I'm going to focus on those new geometry standards in my research this year. My students and I can figure out what happens when we add geometry to the real-world math unit. I'll bet Jim and Eleanor would join me on that.

[The leader of the teacher research group at an elementary school reflects after the group reports to their colleagues about their research at a faculty meeting at the end of the year. Each teacher-researcher sat at a separate table and other faculty members chose three of these tables to visit for ten-minute sessions.]
Pretty amazing. Forty-five minutes. Faculty meeting, end of May. In the midst of statewide testing, difficult planning for next year, and the exhaustion that's started to hit.
We'd made a solemn vow to limit our talks to a few minutes and to do something to get the groups at our tables involved. We

brought bowls of snacks. The chocolate clusters in the little white cups disappeared fast, but so did the handouts.

At first, the teachers looked as if the effort to move was beyond them, but they got up, chose a table, and sat down to listen and talk. By the end of the first ten minutes, the energy level was noticeably higher. By the end of the second, I had to shout that it was time to move again, and by the end of the third, the conversation was darting around the room and hands were raised asking for more information — even a few requests to join the group next year.

Think like a researcher. What made them talk? Why did they see it as useful? This faculty is no pushover. First, they had a chance to talk about what matters most — not to be talked to or talked at, but to talk together. The talk was about our *students,* our *school — and the "experts" were home grown, teacher to teacher. The talk had breadth and depth, not administrative "memo" talk or teacher lounge gripes — the kind of talk that makes you think, the kind you learn from, the kind we all crave.*

Of What Use Is Your Research to Your School?

Although your group's plans for disseminating your research among others at your school will help your research become public, the informal lines of communication help establish findings and questions as part of the school community's thinking.

[The guidance director has been meeting with a cross-curriculum ninth grade team. They have been developing a program to promote success for students in their first year of high school.]

What a great group these ninth grade teachers are. Both the biology and the math teachers picked up on the goal-setting project Bob did with his world studies kids last year. It's a good thing I had a few copies of the teacher-researcher publication on hand.

They were talking about designing a goal-setting component for ninth graders across the curriculum and spending part of the opening inservice sessions getting the other teachers on board! I hope we can fit that in with all the other meetings. Well, we just will.

Is our teacher research team meeting at those opening sessions? They could help the group with data collection — or maybe some of the ninth grade teachers would want to be part of the research team. Bob could meet with the group, too. I'll catch him on my way to lunch duty.

OF WHAT USE IS YOUR RESEARCH TO YOUR SCHOOL DISTRICT?

Usually solutions to problems in education are developed by people outside classrooms in contexts removed from teachers, students, and classroom life. As a teacher-researcher, you are in a position to report on and develop interpretations about the contexts and situations where teaching and learning are occurring. You and your studies have the power to inform the understanding and the decisions of others at a distance.

[An administrator, stuck in traffic, thinks through how to support teachers as they implement a revised district curriculum and respond to new state-mandated achievement tests.]

I knew I was leaving too late! &$#%&! Now I'll just have to sit here, stalled, and worry about what I'm not getting done.

Those new tests! They've stuck new subject matter in completely new places in our curriculum. Teachers are scrambling enough to learn, much less teach it. Still, we want our kids to show up well on the tests, and our teachers will come through. How can I show them support and let the school board know that we're working on this?

What about that guy at the science teachers' convention last month? At the roundtable session where people gave reports on their recent research. He was funny and sounded like he'd been in a science classroom sometime recently. I wonder how much he charges.

Teachers keep asking for time to meet together and talk about how to approach this new stuff. I can't just give them time off to talk and call it curriculum or staff development! That's kind of what happened, though, at the roundtable sessions in that science conference. Hmm.

We could have our own roundtables. Research roundtables. Those middle school science teachers who've been researching how the kids learn some of the new material and trying out different ways of teaching it. I had a call from one of them just after I got back from the conference to tell me what she's finding out. The teacher-researchers could speak about what they found out. Other teachers would have time to talk, too, and ask questions — informally. Here's the plan. The university guy gives a short funny speech with some broad general ideas. Then the teachers talk about how it all works in their classrooms. Not bad.

The presence of teacher research in a school district can encourage those who are responsible for planning professional development to see the usefulness of teacher research as part of their plans. Working as a teacher-researcher puts you in a position that acknowledges you as a professional responsible for identifying your own instructional concerns, working with colleagues to pursue those concerns, and publishing your findings at least to them if not to a broader group of readers.

OF WHAT USE IS YOUR RESEARCH TO THE PROFESSION?

[A teacher-researcher is at a national educational research conference, thinking about an upcoming presentation on research ethics.]

How are we going to do this so that there's time for discussion of the ideas, not just explanations? I'm not sure how receptive this crowd is going to be to such a mixed panel. They're used to five or six speakers each reading a paper for twenty-five minutes to a numbing audience! And no K-12 teachers anywhere in sight.

Well, we've got an elementary teacher. He's talking about his efforts in several schools to try out the ideas that resulted from his research which were in conflict with some of his colleagues' ideas. There's the secondary school teacher who helped draft a statement of teacher research ethics for her district. A university professor who found her teacher-researcher students running into difficulties with the university's ethics policies. We have a school administrator who reviews research projects for the district and the editor of a research journal who sees connections between research quality and research ethics. Five. Quite a mix. I told them that even if no one came to our presentation, we'd still have fun talking to each other!

The hardest part of this was getting everyone to agree not to read papers and to limit their remarks to five minutes each. I brought my kitchen timer. I'll be happy if we end with everyone in the room talking excitedly at once.

Our studies give us and other educational researchers an increased understanding of the processes and the nature of teaching. This is no small accomplishment. As teacher-researchers, we have a responsibility to raise and address questions like the ones in this section of our book — and to do so openly among all of our professional colleagues.

REFERENCE

Bateson, G. (1979). *Mind and nature: A necessary unity*. New York: E. P. Dutton.

PART III

TEACHER-RESEARCHERS' ARTICLES

Introduction
Variety and Quality

Even teacher-researchers in the same research group, with a common experience of the research process, write a remarkable variety of articles about their research. We think this variety is a result of teachers' different purposes and the different audiences for whom they choose to write. That is why a discussion of quality in teacher research must also address purpose and audience.

When you choose to conduct research, your purposes may be both professional and personal. Some purposes are clear at the outset. Others are not, and some may change. Your original purpose may be to figure out whether short-answer quizzes can help prepare students for standardized science tests. In the process, your purpose may change to figuring out how students learn to think like scientists. You may start out with the purpose of changing your students' behavior and shift your purpose to changing something about your own. Your purposes could shift several times during a study, with corresponding adjustments to your research question.

It is not unusual, in the course of the research, to discover also that some of your theories contradict others, that you engage in some practices that belie your professed theories, or that one or two of your personal quirks have sneaked into your professional life. Your study may serve the purpose of introducing you to the research process and the benefits teacher research can have for your teaching. Because your purposes change according to your needs, teacher research has potential value for your growth as a person as well as a teacher, researcher, and theorist.

Different purposes result in different research journeys and in a variety of final products that speak to different kinds of audiences. Teachers' research sometimes appears in forms dictated by grant requirements, the expectations of a school's research group, or the criteria of a graduate course. For readers within a school's research group, for instance, you might write with an awareness of a shared knowledge about your school. For readers of a professional journal, however, you might include more description of context or a more conspicuous delineation of your research process.

This part of the book includes articles having different puposes and intended for various audiences. The articles include an end-of-the-year school report (Mohr), an in-house school publication (Lindquist, Sanford), a school district document (Ingalls), and a course collection (Manchey, Painter, Tendero). Teacher-researchers connect their research purpose with potential readers and report on their research accordingly.

Quality research has value to your students, to you, and to others in the educational community. Your research may be judged as valuable by your fellow teachers if it works its way into their thinking and teaching, and it may be valuable to your school if it becomes part of a school plan or program evaluation. Teachers beyond your school may value your work when they learn about it from a presentation you give or from your research article, and you may not even know of the influence your work eventually has.

Julia Lindquist, whose article is included here, spoke as a member of a panel at a teacher research conference to discuss her research on a reading program she had developed to include the participation of her middle school students' parents. Two teacher-researchers from another district who attended the panel judged her work as useful and wanted to adapt Lindquist's program for use in their own classrooms. They appreciated her understanding of the role teachers play in their students' lives, the relationship between the teachers' and the parents' roles, and the complexity of the interrelationships. Lindquist's research process and findings had value for them. As teacher-researchers themselves, they could observe and document the reading programs in their classrooms, comparing their findings with Lindquist's.

Lindquist went public by publishing her study and discussing it at the conference. It is, of course, up to you whether you publish your research beyond your local research group or school community. If you do so, you may discover that your research has findings and implications of value for others in your school system, your discipline, and the educational community as a whole. Your choice to publish also opens your work to many kinds of responses, interpretations, and critiques — responses from your students and their parents and responses from other teacher-researchers, teacher educators, and educational researchers. Such publication is always an opportunity for further professional growth and for you to influence the educational community's understanding of teacher research.

To summarize, the evaluation of your research derives from the following:

First, your own judgment of your work and its value for you and your students.

Second, your choice of purpose and audience, for they influence the usefulness of your research for others.

Third, your acceptance of the criteria for quality in research that have evolved in the research community:

* honesty and open-mindedness in the inquiry
* ethical treatment of students and colleagues
* productive use of methodology appropriate to the inquiry
* findings, discoveries, and interpretations well supported by appropriate documentation

These standards are both lofty and down-to-earth. You work in the best way you can, you offer to others what you find out, and you learn from how your work is judged.

The standards of value and quality for teacher research that we have been discussing helped in our selection of the articles for this book, as did other criteria. We selected articles that were written by fellow Northern Virginia teacher-researchers, that cover K-12 instruction, and that show the typical variety of purpose and audience. All were originally written for in-house publications.

When we were planning this book, we met with the authors individually after they had had a chance to reread their articles. We asked them to talk about their work and the role the article had played in their thinking since it was written. The introductions to each article include some of their reflections. In addition, they have, in collaboration with us, made some changes to edit and clarify their work for a general publication and to condense parts of their work in order to accommodate our space constraints.

As has been our practice for in-house publication of deadline drafts, we have arranged the articles alphabetically by author, without assessment, interpretation, or labeling. We wanted you to be able to read examples of what teacher-researchers have published for a limited local audience at the end of a year's research, because these drafts are similar to what you will write. They illustrate the rich understandings that only practitioners can give about the nature of teaching and learning.

Bob Ingalls

In the fall of 1987, department chair Bob Ingalls and the English department at Mt. Vernon High School began a four-year longitudinal study of students' writing at their school. The study focused on the portfolios of a targeted group of ninth grade students who would respond to writing prompts, participate in interviews, complete questionnaires, and contribute to a whole-group interview during each of the four years of the study, ending when they were seniors.

Ingalls wrote about different parts of the longitudinal study as it progressed. In 1989 he published a case study of one of the students. The following year he wrote "Getting It Right: A Story of Writing about Assessment," an article about the difficulty of serving as study coordinator, department chair, and English teacher at the same time. A later article, co-authored with Mt. Vernon H. S. English teacher Joyce Jones, first appeared in the National Writing Project *Quarterly* (1992) and was subsequently published as "Interviewing Students about Their Portfolios" in *Teachers' Voices: Portfolios in the Classroom* (1993).

In "Getting It Right," Ingalls describes the initial phases of the study:

> *After three years of a four-year comprehensive writing assessment study, I have reports of portfolio assessments, statistical records of writing tests, transcribed tapes of interviews, my personal logs, and notes of teacher discussions. The mere size of this ongoing project threatens me, and I am just beginning to analyze it....*
>
> *If I had more time, maybe I could standardize things better. But when bells ring, I am ready to teach, not to conduct assessments. Each year I have new classes to get ready for and my department duties to accomplish, e.g. textbooks to move and distribute and office supplies to sort through. In the first year of the study I was especially overwhelmed with rubber bands — I had accidentally ordered too many, and I had no closet to store them.... In addition, I had new teachers who needed me to show them the workings of the school and, most importantly, tell them what was taught in Mt. Vernon High School English classes. Instead of hand-*

ing them a detailed curriculum guide, I only had copies of our department's writing philosophy and our new assessment plan.

Each of Ingalls's articles reflects important information resulting from the study — implications for the writing program at Mt. Vernon, findings about students' learning about writing over the four years, implications for staff development, and effects and findings Ingalls had identified for himself as a teacher. Other members of the department and students at the high school had also reaped benefits from their work. Ingalls's research illustrates some of the many purposes that writing about research can serve. It also raises issues about the need for time to fulfill the responsibilities of a school leader and researcher and the importance of this work being done at the school level.

"Learning School/Learning to Write" was written during a summer with support from a county central office and is based on the only four-year longitudinal study of student writing that we know of that has been conducted by a department as teacher research.

Learning School/Learning to Write

by Bob Ingalls

As a teacher of writing I like to see students revise because it shows

+ they are concerned about their work,
+ they are concerned about their reader, and
+ they are concerned about learning more about their topic.

And when I don't see evidence of revision I am disappointed because I assume that students don't care about what they are doing in my class.

When I began studying student revision at our school, I expected to see more evidence of student revision in the increasing grade levels at our school because students would care and understand more about writing. I believed this evidence would increase when teachers emphasized the importance of revision in their classrooms. So when I examined student writing in our school where teachers were teaching more about revision, I was surprised to find little evidence of students revising their writing. In response to these circumstances, I decided to examine more closely what students were doing, what teachers were saying, and how I was teaching writing.

The issues of student revision unfolded over the last three years at Mount Vernon High School. At first there was promising evidence of student revision. In 1988 the results of our first writing test showed that our freshman class valued revision enough to surprise the evaluators. We examined revision by looking closely at changes made in second drafts of a targeted group of 30 students. Their writing tests showed that 93% of them had changed their writing from the first draft to the second. The majority of them were adding and deleting ideas. One of every four had changed her view of the topic. And this was without the help of student discussion groups, teacher guidance, or intervening weeks for the students to consider their ideas.

This baseline data for the sample group has never been duplicated in subsequent years; instead, evidence of revision decreased. When teacher-evaluators read the other tests, they did not compliment the students. They talked of what points needed development or clarification. This reversal in the evidence and quality of revision prompted me to search for a better understanding of what determined student revision in our school.

THE TWO-DAY WRITING TESTS

I examined the results of how students revised their writing over the three years. Compared to the 93% of papers that were revised in 1988, only 60% were revised in 1989 and only 78% in 1990. Then I looked at the following strategies used:

- when students substitute words or phrases,
- when students replaced the lead sentences of the first draft,
- when students changed the order of the paragraphs, and
- when students changed their views of their topic.

I saw only one area of increase — students were changing words more frequently in the 11th grade, certainly a more cosmetic change than what we had seen in the 9th grade when students were changing leads and the order of paragraphs. The results disappointed me as a teacher because, though these students were aware of various revision strategies, they were using them less as they advanced through school.

I considered several possible answers. I wondered if the papers were simply better in 1989 and 1990 and needed less revision. But such a direct comparison from year to year is not possible because we change the topic each year. The 9th grade prompt was a personal topic, the 10th grade prompt was a persuasive-letter prompt, and the 11th grade one was a literary analysis.

I speculated whether confidence was the key difference in these tests. Were students uncomfortable writing anything other than personal experience? I didn't think so for three reasons. One was the two years of classroom teaching which emphasized literary and persuasive essay writing. Second, the students were older and more experienced each time, better able to persuade and analyze (in fact, our targeted group had lost four of the lowest achieving students due to dropping out or transferring). And third, teachers were giving students more revision work in all different writing assignments since the department had set the goal to increase student revision after the disappointing results of these tests.

There was simply no evidence collected that students were applying what teachers had taught them about revision. I assumed the '89 and '90 prompts were more difficult tasks, and students had more reason to revise. This was especially true for the '90 prompt that asked students to analyze a difficult poem. For two years the students had been learning in their English classes to write learning logs when faced with difficult reading. Why didn't students jot down their thoughts and then begin to write a draft? I thought we'd see some application of these lessons. I expected to see at least the same amount of revision from these students as they had done in their first year of high school.

I considered what my colleagues had said when this issue was discussed in several department meetings. Joyce Jones suggested one answer when she wondered out loud about what the students were thinking, "Maybe they are trying to match an image, not so much discover what they know." We could not overlook that these were tests, and the students might feel they had to get a correct answer on a writing test. Test anxiety may have affected some of them or lack of interest in a school-wide test. Cindy Rufty thought the tests had measured student learning and the results of the 1990 writing test indicated that "revision is as much the knowledge of the topic as it is the caring about the topic." Her theory was that students revised more about a personal experience because they knew more than they did about poetry, literary analysis, and persuasive letter writing.

Though Cindy's theory made sense, I believed the students knew enough to revise in all the writing tests. Every year we worded the prompts in such a way that the students were to write their reactions, not guess the right answer. We were asking them to explain their opinions, nothing different from what we had been asking them to do for two years in their English classes. I expected students to be able to tap their own knowledge and use the first day of the writing test to reflect on what they knew, and on the second day make changes in their final draft.

The Interviews

Cindy's suggestion raised questions about student knowledge. Particularly interesting to me was what our students knew about writing. Each year we have interviewed these targeted students to better understand the impact of our writing instruction. I examined the pages of three years of transcribed interviews searching for answers to this question. In their freshman year we asked the targeted students about their writing processes, and they spoke with authority about how they wrote and what they needed to do to write more effectively. They didn't want to be graded on their first drafts because they wanted the chance to develop their ideas in another draft. Most of them enjoyed writing. But in 1988-89 we asked these same students about how they judged writing, and they did not sound so knowledgeable. They couldn't explain how they determined when they had written something good. They said such things as:

> *"It's comes back with an 'A' on top."*
> *"... the teacher told me that it was the best writing he has ever read that I wrote."*
> *"I don't know if I like it just because I wrote it..."*

The teachers who participated in this interview remarked later about how confused the students were about this issue. None of the students could adequately explain their criteria for judging their own writing.

I realized something more about what Cindy had said. The students were probably lacking the knowledge necessary to write and revise effectively. This wasn't just the facts or background of the topic, it included the knowledge of the writing form, standards of quality, and methods for measuring and evaluating the writing. This may not be true when they were writing personal experience pieces because even as small children they learned to identify a good story when they heard it, and writing stories relied so much on the sequence of events. I questioned how many of them knew the qualities of a good literary analysis or persuasive letter, but more importantly, I wondered how much practice students had evaluating their own writing.

I examined the 1990 interview. I rediscovered what had been a major issue in our session, teacher grading and its influence on what and how students wrote.

> St. #1: *"... when I write something for a teacher that she assigns I say the standard answers because it is expected and its easier."*

The students alongside him agreed and said they often did this.

> St. #2: *"You write superficially to get an A."*

> St. #3: *"It's hard to express yourself when you worry about your GPA."*

> St. #4: *Teachers don't credit students on "whether you took time to come up with your own thoughts... they just look at the paper and see if you did what they told you to do."*

This seemed to explain the reasons behind Cindy's theory. Students didn't feel they played a part in evaluating writing. In my own classes, I knew student evaluation was often sacrificed so I could cover another step in the curriculum. These interview results also shed light on what Joyce had said about students trying to match what was expected. According to our interviews, the students said they were not taking the time to reflect or rework their thoughts in the classroom; they were doing what their teachers told them to do and guessing what they wanted to hear. And if this was true for the writing tests, they saw no need to search for their meaning. The challenge of writing was simple: guess what the reader (teacher-evaluator) wanted to hear.

PORTFOLIO ASSESSMENT

I compared what I now believed about the writing tests to the portfolio assessments we had conducted over three years. These assessments showed a similar problem with student performance. Students seemed to be following directions more than struggling with what they had to express. Our results showed a disappointing lack of student responsibility for selecting topics and forms, making choices based on comments of readers, and independently revising and editing.

In 1988, teacher-evaluators said most of the revision appeared to be done at the direction of their teachers. Students changed words, paragraph order, etc., as teachers instructed and rarely went further. These freshman portfolios showed little revision; 65% of the students rarely if ever revised their work. Only 30% of the students revised half of their work.

After reviewing these results from 1988, the English department made student responsibility a major objective in writing instruction. We also set a goal for the department that 90% of the portfolios would show evidence of effective revision skills. In the next two years, the scores improved, but the problem of revision still persisted with as many as 22% of the portfolios showing little or no evidence. Then in 1990 the assessment returned to the results of 1988, only 3% of the portfolios showing revision in all or most of the writings, while nearly two thirds, 68% of the portfolios, showed revision in half of the work. The most surprising figure was that 26% of the portfolios showed little or no responsibility for revision. On the surface students did not seem to be revising their work. They were succeeding in following what teachers told them to do, using a certain form and organization, addressing a certain audience for a specified purpose and correcting certain mistakes. But there was no evidence of revision in response to reader feedback, student or teacher. In addition, students were not developing their initial ideas or adjusting the form for the writing.

During the portfolio assessments, teachers talked about students forgetting to include their rough drafts and other students who revised on word processors and only printed a final draft. But teachers agreed that students were not revising enough. In 1990 every one of the 11th-grade teachers of these students said they were disappointed with the lack of revision in their classes; they felt the students were "cranking out" their writing and not taking time to carefully express themselves. Teachers thought students seemed more concerned with turning in clean and correct drafts than in developing or discovering their ideas.

Joanne Marino explained the situation in a mass media analogy. "These students approach writing in a CNN [the Turner Broadcasting all-news cable channel] way — write it as fast as possible and don't take time to revise." Teachers felt the students only valued their immediate thoughts. I wondered what the students thought we valued. What had they discovered about us?

MY CLASSROOM

My analysis of one of the targeted students, named Kim, paralleled what I had seen in our department assessments. Kim rarely revised her work unless I told her what to change. Near the end of the school year she was writing a series of poems which were shallow rhymes — matching the poetic form but lacking meaning. She asked for my help, but I refused to give her words to change. Instead, I directed her to write reflectively about the poems in hopes of getting her to add more of her feelings. She tried and ultimately she did revise some of what she had written. Ultimately, it was my doing less work that forced Kim to do more. But doing less was difficult for me because I was concerned about her writing and the amount of revision she was doing.

Kim and I never had time to discuss the quality of her poetry. And when preparing her portfolio, she wrote in her self-evaluation about the only writing she disliked: "… I don't like… writing poems, only because I can never make one up." When we assessed portfolios, the evaluator said she was surprised by Kim's comment because the poetry was the strongest part of her work. I was pleased that another teacher liked Kim's work, but I was also disappointed because Kim had written something good and never learned of its quality from her readers. Her process of writing these poems was never completed; it never reached the evaluation stage when readers would judge her work. I saw how her inexperience with evaluating her writing was connected with her reluctance to revise. Why would she revise when she seemed unable to judge her writing?

REFLECTIONS

When I began this study, I thought I understood the relationship between learning and revision. I believed increasing the amount students revised was a worthwhile goal, and using statistics was a valid way to measure achievement of that goal. But rather than giving a valid measure of the quality of student writing, the statistical data only narrowed my interest to the number of changes students were making in their drafts, giving me a view of writing that equated it to simple labor measured like a worker's time card totaled with the number of revisions. The initial results of student revision were disturbing and prompted me to look more fully into student attitudes about writing and into my own teaching. By studying other aspects of student writing, through interviews with students and analyses of their portfolios, I saw revision in a broader context that clarified for me the difference between "learning school" and "learning to write." This distinction indicates what we need to examine in our teaching of writing at Mount Vernon High School.

If I want my students to learn to write better, I have to remember:

1. *Students revise* more effectively *when they are concerned about their work and their reader.*

This study showed that our students often revise by getting rid of what they believe and substituting what we want to hear. When I state how or imply what to write, students learn the easiest way to succeed is to follow my lead. I ought to emphasize the importance of peer feedback and evaluation, and decrease the importance of my opinion. Pushing students to revise as part of a departmental or school-wide goal also interferes with a student writer's genuine need to communicate with a reader. There is value in practicing and learning about revision, but the motivation to revise a piece of writing should come from within the writer.

2. *Students revise* more effectively *when they are concerned about learning more about their topic.*

As our students go through school they get wise to the system. They learn not to take risks. By junior year they are very task-minded, and they learn whose opinions matter — they figure out what to revise by discovering what teachers want. If I want their revisions to show what they have learned about their subjects, then I need to spend more time helping students to learn how to evaluate their own writing so they can revise with confidence. And I ought to continue to assign more writing that features and increases discovery as the primary concern. When I require students to search for their own answers, not just for facts, I teach students that writing is learning.

As teachers at Mount Vernon High School, we face a more complicated problem than a lack of student revision, and a greater challenge than getting students to work harder at their writing. Our greatest challenge is getting students to care more about what they write. More of our assignments should allow for student decisions that are respected, not penalized when they differ with teacher views. We need to allow students to care more about "getting it right" by their standards.

Julia Lindquist

When Julia Lindquist conducted this study, her own experiences as a reader, a student, a teacher, and a parent shaped her methods and understanding about her middle school students' independent reading. Although she had a firm conviction about what she wanted to accomplish, the situation seemed extremely complex. She commented, "When I was in the middle of it, I thought it was very confusing, but when I sat down and actually followed the process that I had gone through, it made more sense to me. Once I put it down on paper, it didn't look as disarrayed as when I did it."

About the study's effect on her use of independent reading and parents' involvement, Lindquist reflected, "It made me more confident with what I was doing… I really enjoyed the interaction between the parents and me — and the students and me. I learned so much from the parents, just from reading the comments they wrote, that let me know what was going on — a little glimpse into their home life. That always helps."

In addition, Lindquist's study about reading linked her back to her interests in the teaching of writing. "The response writings were real writing with a real purpose. I know that the project was about reading, but it actually had a lot of writing in it." Her experience with writing her report also affirmed the connections she had been studying. "I loved sitting down and writing this. Some [of the other teacher-researchers in the group] thought it was very painful, but it really cleared my head. There's always a lot of self-doubt when you're teaching, because you're in there alone. To see the thoughts on paper was validating."

Independent Reading: Just Do It!

by Julia Lindquist

Introduction

The Theban Mystery. That's what really sealed it for me. "When I become a teacher, I'm not going to force my students to read anything!" It was my senior year in high school, and I had trodden through world literature, but when it came time to read this boring mystery, I became more determined to "invite" students to read. Maybe it was the spring of my senior year when most students lose whatever drive they might have left after completing college applications, or maybe it was just a really bad book. I think I might read it again. Maybe distance might help. This is where the seed was planted: student choice is vital in reading.

So when I became a teacher, I wanted my students to choose what books they were reading. I was so afraid of "turning off" someone to reading because I was forcing them to read a book with which they couldn't connect. It helped assuage the guilt. "Well, if I force them to and they don't like it, at least they have their choice books."

What has become troubling through the years is what to do with independent reading. Endless reader responses were hard to keep up with. And dialog journals were just between teacher and student. I wanted responses to be shared with a broader audience, not just me. I came up with the idea of doing some teacher research to find out what activities can be done with students reading all different kinds of books.

I teach eighth grade English at Poe Middle School in Annandale, Virginia. Our students and teachers are divided into teams, and I teach on the Coyote team. I have 135 students in English this year. Our diverse classes are a mixture of learning Disabled (LD) resource, advanced (or gifted) and English as a second language (ESL) students.

Experiments

I. Home Involvement

My first concern was finding ways to get the students in the habit of reading. Most of their reading would be done at home. How could I assess this out-of-class activity? Knowing that parents wanted more involvement in their students' reading, I decided to have **parents** do the assessing. As a teacher and a parent, I know how much practicing must go on at home. I needed parent involvement. I wrote a letter home with a record-keeping sheet attached (Appendix A). I asked parents to "sign-off" on their students' record sheets and also give them an overall reading grade at the end of the quarter. Initially I asked parents to base their grades on record management, variety of books read, and difficulty level. I asked them to write comments or reasons why they gave the overall grade.

At the end of the quarter, I found that parent participation was overwhelming. Out of approximately 135 students, only 3 did not return their forms. I also found that most of the comments were favorable. The following are samples from the parent responses.

> *"Excellent way to make kids read. I'm giving W. an A because he read a book and started another one, and he enjoyed it."*
>
> *"My son read many books throughout this quarter. He read 18 hours in the spring break, so I give A+"*
>
> *"Wonderful! Great job, D.! I am very pleased with your reading progress, D. Your determination will help you reach any goal you set for yourself throughout your life. [signed] Mom"*
>
> *"M. gets an A because she did her reading every night and she followed her goal for the third term's reading. I'm very proud of her because she spent a lot of time reading over the holiday."*
>
> *"C. has begun to diversify the types of books she reads. I was pleased to see her read one of my favorites* A Tree Grows in Brooklyn *and look forward to her reading others like* Jane Eyre.*"*
>
> *"E. enjoys her reading! She is building her vocabulary and becoming a better writer."*
>
> *"K. has been reading every day, and even asks for books to read — I am excited! Yea K. — I would give her an A."*

Reflections. These comments helped me to realize three important points. First of all, parents were able to praise their children. Many times in the difficult teenage years, parents and children get bogged down in the child's struggle for independence. It was great to hear positive comments from parents. It was a change from the usual "Johnny isn't doing well in school. Why?"

Secondly, I realized many parents do not write in standard English. I have edited the above comments to reflect current usage. I knew I had numerous parents of ESL students who are not classified as ESL, and have lived in the United States all their lives, yet the primary language they speak outside of school is not English. The only practice they get using English is their experience in the school day.

From looking at parents' writing, I also learned that even some of the English-speaking parents, whom I expected to know standard English, could not use English properly. These writings gave me a whole new insight regarding the background of some of my students: their parents are very supportive of education, yet they are not highly educated. They are like cheerleaders: they cannot coach their children because these parents don't know the rules or how to play; all they can do is cheer. The situation reminded me of a poem in our literature anthology called "Women" by Alice Walker. The poem is about black women fighting for the right to send their children to school, even though they have never been to school. Walker catches the essence of the struggle when she says, "They knew what we needed to know without knowing it themselves."

II. SETTING GOALS

After my first experiment, I realized that parents and students may want to evaluate different aspects of independent reading. I decided that if this project were to be truly independent, students should set their own goals, and parents should evaluate children on these goals. I decided to add a twist to second quarter's independent reading. I asked the students to write letters to their parents (a good chance to review the friendly letter format!) about their reading goals and how they wanted to be evaluated.

I found that students had a wide range of goals. An ESL student said she would take time to look up the words she didn't know. Many GT students (gifted and talented students as labeled by the county) said their goal was to read more classics to prepare for high school. Some, whom I'll label as "reluctant readers," said their goal was to stick with a book from cover to cover. The students came up with so many more ideas than I'd thought of by myself. There are many ways to become a better reader.

One of the letters that particularly caught my eye was from a young girl who described herself as an "excellent" reader; there was nothing to improve about her reading. But, by the end of her letter, she decided, as she thought about it a little more, that there were some things she could improve. She decided to (1) read harder level books (classics); (2) not just guess at a word's meaning, but look it up; and (3) stick with the books she starts until she finishes them.

Reflections. This experiment had many implications for my teaching. I realized that setting goals is vital in today's increasingly diverse classroom. Independent reading personalizes education. Students were able to work on what THEY needed to improve. I felt like this activity met many students' needs.

III. Literature Circles

So, with all this reading going on at home (and some in class), now what? Students could write reader responses? Too much reading for me. Book reports? "Yuck!" my students would say. Summaries? Too boring.

I asked myself, "What do I like to do after I read a book?" I like to talk with a friend about it, recommend it, or — if my friend has read the book — ask her about the meaning of a scene. Could this experience be duplicated in the classroom? Could students discuss books they have read in the same way they talk about the movies they have seen? Maybe I was being too idealistic.

I decided to try a variation of literature circles as described in Harvey Daniels's book *Literature Circles: Voice and Choice in the Student-Centered Classroom* (1994). In this book, Daniels describes organizing students in small groups to discuss a common reading. To help students guide the discussion, he has developed roles: director, connector, literary luminary, illustrator and vocabulary enricher (there are more). The director comes to the circle meeting with questions about the reading. The connector, as the name implies, finds connections between the reading and events in the world, other literature, film, or personal experience. The literary luminary's job is to pick out funny, important, confusing, or otherwise memorable passages to read aloud to the group. I like to think of the literary luminary as a kind of "human highlighter." The illustrator creates a visual depicting something related to the book. The illustration could be a picture, cartoon, web, flow chart, or outline.

In Daniels's model, however, all students are reading the same book. Because my students were reading different books, I altered the directions and had each student do a small part of each role (Appendix B). As the students met in their groups, I visited each group and participated or wrote my observations. I recorded in my journal that students seemed to be animated and enjoyed talking about their books. This talk is important because it gave them a chance to share with peers instead of writing just for the teacher. Books were passed around and thumbed through. I actually heard, "Can I read that when you're done?"

I had a particularly shy student who had never participated in whole-class discussions. At the beginning of our third literature circle, I heard her excitedly say to her group, "Can I go first?" Students were becoming increasingly eager to meet in their groups.

Reflections. After a couple of literature circles, I decided to get some feedback from students during a whole-class discussion. In general, students liked participating in literature circles because they got to say what they thought of the book. Most students felt they understood the book more after going through the preparation process. Students also brought up the point that they could participate in a literature circle while they were still in the middle of the book. With book reports, readers can't write until they are finished with the book. Having a chance to discuss a book while they are reading it might motivate some students to keep reading a book until the end.

My more advanced students particularly liked making connections. Some of their connections were not "deep" enough, and when students recognized these shallow connections, they realized that either the book was too easy for them or too hard. In either situation they weren't able to make connections they valued.

One student said he liked reading passages from the book out loud (the literary luminary role) because he "noticed more things." Other students nodded in agreement.

My class with the lowest reading levels generally complained that literature circles were difficult and were too much work. Most students in this class said they liked writing summaries because it helped them understand the book and organize their thoughts. They wanted to do more kinesthetic activities such as "acting the book out" or developing skits. They thought literature circles would be better if they could choose one role. My fear was that they wouldn't see the bigger picture of the book. Maybe next year I will compromise and ask them to write summaries and then choose one additional role to prepare for the circles.

It was interesting to me that my higher-level readers enjoyed literature circles more than my lower-level readers. I believe that the roles mirror what the good readers do. They have assimilated each role and can synthesize them. Students who have difficulty reading may need more practice on each role before fusing them.

IV. Student Interviews

I started sensing that this "reading thing" might be catching on. I decided to interview some students about their reading habits. I was curious to find out if they could give me some new ideas about how to evaluate independent reading. I was particularly interested in comparing the responses of "eager readers" and "reluctant readers."

I asked my colleague to interview targeted students. The following questions were asked:

1. *What do you think is the importance of independent reading?*
2. *Should you be graded on independent reading? If so, how?*
3. *What do you like to do with the books you read: book reports, book talks, literature circles, etc?*
4. *What do you think about your parents grading you?*
5. *Would you be reading on your own if it wasn't a requirement for class?*
6. *Any thoughts or comments about independent reading?*

The Importance of Reading. My students always surprise me. The answers from both eager and reluctant readers were almost identical.

They thought independent reading was important because it improved their reading skills, and (I like this part) it was relaxing.

Grading. Again, most students were in agreement. Reading is "just for fun" and you shouldn't be graded on something fun. "It's your loss if you don't read." I was looking for new ways to grade/evaluate and learned instead that the students didn't want to be evaluated.

What to Do after Reading. Once again, most students were in agreement that they liked to talk about their books. Many identified literature circles as a good reading activity.

Parents Grading. Most students said parent grading was OK. One student pointed out that parents know if a student reads at home, the teacher doesn't. He also pointed out that he does more reading than his parents. Not all the comments were positive. One reader felt that parents grading students puts pressure on the students, and she felt that she was already getting enough pressure from teachers. She didn't need it from her parents, too. I thought she had a very good point.

Reading on Your Own. Their responses confirmed my belief. Those students whom I classify as eager readers would read anyway, even if they weren't being graded on it. But, students who were reluctant readers said they needed the structure of assigned independent reading.

Reflections. I began to wonder if this independent reading was a necessary assignment. I came to the conclusion that even though so many of my students say they would read whether they were being graded or not, independent reading was still a valuable assignment to them. It validated what many were already doing as important and worthwhile. For those not reading, it helped them get into the habit.

V. Reading With Parents

Students are a never-ending fount of ideas. In one student letter, a young man suggested that his parents read with him. I thought, "What a great idea!" I love reading with my son every night, and I wondered when my students had last read with their parents. Recognizing that many parents don't have the time to read with their children, I decided to make this shared reading an extra credit project.

I wrote a letter home (Appendix C). I suggested different methods for reading and discussing, and I encouraged students to read books in their parents' primary language since I have so many students who do not speak English at home. As a wrap-up they would write me a letter about their experience or tape record one of their discussions.

Usually when I offer extra credit, the response is minimal, but even though the kids whined and whined when they first heard about the opportunity, I had more positive responses to this extra credit than any other offer I have made. Most students and parents wrote letters telling me about the book and how they read it (sharing one copy, each reader with his/her own book, etc.). They said that being able to discuss the book while they were reading it helped them see different aspects of the book they might have missed if they were reading alone. Here are some excerpts from their writings. I have not edited these excerpts in order to show the variety of language backgrounds.

> *Every night when I went to bed, I would read for approximately 30 minutes. When my dad went to bed he would also read for about 30 minutes so we would be in about the same spot in the book (*Singularity *by Sleator). It was kind of like tag.... When the book got really intense, we would have to be careful not to tell too much so that we would not spoil it for each other when one of us was ahead of the other.... It was a very intense book and we had trouble putting it down.* (This student and father went on to read the sequel — even though it wasn't for extra credit this time.)

* * *

> *During reading this book, my sister (age 22) and I stopped every chapter and we discussed it together. It remind me of my own experiences. It remind me of the first day of school in a country where most often I didn't know the language, but now, I'm in a good shape.... It was fun and sad reading this book with my sister. The sad part was I saw something of myself in these true stories. Other than that, it was fun. I got to spended more time with my sister, because this was the first time we ever do something together like this. It was fun when she told me about dating. We didn't know anything about dating when we just live here about a year. After a*

long time, we suddenly realized what's dating all about, and I still got alots to know about dating from her.

* * *

I didn't ask my mom what book did she wanted to read with me, but I know that she needed an easy one because she don't un-derstand English that much. so I pick the book called The House on Mango Street. *It's easy for me, but I have to help Tina (mom) understand what the book is about. Tina and I take turns reading the book. If she don't know what the word is or don't know how to pronound it I help her.*

After reading each days I asked Tina did she understand what happened during those page while she was reading. She did point out some conflict that I didn't notic while I was reading.

Yes! my partner and I recommend this book. My partner said that it really help her learning English. I recommen because it help me how to tranlate English into Vietnamese, and not forget Vietnamese.

Reflections. I found that discussing books is a motivating learning process for adult and student. This activity seemed especially helpful for ESL students. The responses also emphasize an earlier point I made about the students' backgrounds. What they accomplish in academics, for many, is done independently.

Encouraging students to cross language barriers made parents feel included. One parent wrote two pages in Spanish to tell me about read-ing a book in Spanish with her child. Reading books from their coun-tries also gave families a chance to share their culture. Literature circles could be a place to learn about cultures different from our own.

VI. Parent Survey

I knew when I asked parents to become such an important part in this initiative that I would need to get feedback from them. I sent home a very quick survey which asked parents to rate statements as to whether they disagreed or agreed (1 being strongly disagree and 4 being strongly agree). I had parents rate five statements:

1. I am more aware of my student's reading habits.
2. Independent reading of choice books is important to education in middle school.
3. I saw progress in my student's reading.
4. My student kept me updated because he/she knew I would be evaluating him/her.
5. I appreciated the opportunity to evaluate my student's reading habits.

Out of 50 responses, 37 responded with a 3 or 4 to every statement. Of the 13 other responses, 11 of those rated only statement four with a 2 (disagreement) and the rest of the statements were rated 3 or 4. Most of the parents who disagreed with statement four noted that their children already kept them informed. I was very pleased with these results, and I'm especially pleased that so many parents are more aware of their students' reading habits and appreciated the opportunity to grade them.

There were only two negative responses to the evaluating. In both cases, it seemed the parent felt that the teachers were more qualified to judge reading.

Reflections. After seeing students set such wonderful goals for themselves earlier, I am beginning to wonder if the students themselves are the only ones qualified to judge whether or not they've met their reading goals. Next year might be a good time to develop more self-assessment strategies with my students.

Conclusion

FINDINGS

As a result of this year's research, I was able to see what happened with independent reading in three important areas. The first area is parent involvement. Parents appreciated a concrete, organized way to be involved in their children's education. They were willing to take on new endeavors, such as reading books with their children.

The second area is setting goals or assessment. Students were able to set personalized goals which individualized diverse classes. One way I would like to expand goal setting next year is take the next step of self-assessment. What can the students tell me about reaching (or not reaching) their goals?

The third important area in my study of independent reading revolves around the importance of talking about reading. Interaction with other readers, whether it be in small groups at school or with family members, is motivating and keeps readers reading.

The tie that binds these three areas is choice. Choice of books is the first step in achieving these outcomes.

IMPLICATIONS

The implications of these findings are scattered throughout my research. I try one experiment, then based on what I find, I add to my teaching. When I started the year, I didn't plan these experiments. As I made each change, I analyzed it and thought about what implications it could have for my teaching, and then I took another step. I definitely see my research as a staircase, one step leading to another. Not only did I learn about reading, but I also learned how the research process has a direct effect on my classroom and my teaching.

I learned (again) why I'm an English teacher, and more importantly, why I'm a reader. I have learned more about the background of my students and how it affects their education. My philosophy about the importance of choice books has been reinforced. I have learned from observing literature circles and parents reading with children, that recommending and sharing **good** books to emerging readers is motivating. If you care about someone, reading her favorite book helps you understand more about her.

So maybe there is something to *The Theban Mystery* if my teacher wanted so much for us to read it. I think I know what I want to read at the beach this summer.

REFERENCE

Daniels, H. (1994). *Literature circles: Voice and choice in the student-centered classroom.* York, ME: Stenhouse.

Appendix A
First Quarter Letter to Parents

"Practice Makes Perfect"

Dear Parents,

A major goal for your student this year is to become an excellent reader, and the best way to accomplish this goal is to read on a regular basis. Unless there is a writing assignment given for homework in English, I would like the students to read 20-30 minutes each night, Monday through Thursday. They may read books that they select with guidance from you and me. GT students should be reading higher level books to prepare them for high school, and they should expand their reading to 30 minutes, five to six times a week.

Parents, now is your chance to become involved in assessing your student's reading. On the back of this letter is a form for you to keep track of your student's reading progress. I will ask you to monitor on a daily basis and provide a grade at the end of the quarter. You should consider what they read (difficulty/variety), how consistent they have been, and their maintenance of this form.

Please send this form back to school after one week (Date: _____) so I can verify that you have seen this letter and are initialing your student's daily progress.

This form will need to be returned with the final grade indicated on November 1st, and please write comments so I will know why you gave your student that grade.

Thank you so much for participating in the reading program.

Sincerely,

J. Lindquist

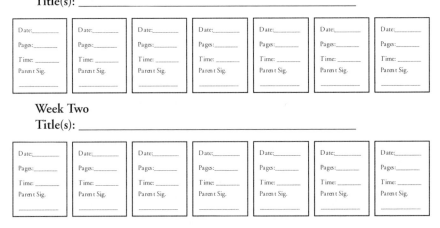

Week One
Title(s): _____

Date:___	Date:___	Date:___	Date:___	Date:___	Date:___	Date:___
Pages:___	Pages:___	Pages:___	Pages:___	Pages:___	Pages:___	Pages:___
Time: ___	Time: ___	Time: ___	Time: ___	Time: ___	Time: ___	Time: ___
Parent Sig.	Parent Sig.	Parent Sig.	Parent Sig.	Parent Sig.	Parent Sig.	Parent Sig.
_____	_____	_____	_____	_____	_____	_____

Week Two
Title(s): _____

Date:___	Date:___	Date:___	Date:___	Date:___	Date:___	Date:___
Pages:___	Pages:___	Pages:___	Pages:___	Pages:___	Pages:___	Pages:___
Time: ___	Time: ___	Time: ___	Time: ___	Time: ___	Time: ___	Time: ___
Parent Sig.	Parent Sig.	Parent Sig.	Parent Sig.	Parent Sig.	Parent Sig.	Parent Sig.
_____	_____	_____	_____	_____	_____	_____

[This letter includes forms for all 9 weeks of the grading period. The last page of the form includes **Final Grade:** _____ and a section for parents' **Comments**.]

Appendix B
Literature Circle Role Sheet

Literature Circles for Independent Reading Books

You will be preparing a presentation about a book that you are currently reading or have read this quarter. Instead of preparing one role sheet for the literature circle, you will do a little for each role. Hopefully you'll find out more about your book as you prepare this presentation, and I hope other readers might learn about a book they'd like to read in the future. Read below to find out your requirements, and write them out on your own paper. Check off each section when you have completed it.

Summarizer   Completed_____

You will need to provide a good summary first. Start with the title and the author and remember to include characters, setting, plot events, and conflicts. Don't give away the ending, in case someone in your group wants to read it next.

Literary Luminary   Completed_____

Pick out two to four passages to share. Mark them with your Post-it notes. Be ready to explain why you chose these sections. Some possible reasons might be: important, funny, surprising, informative, controversial, well written, thought-provoking, confusing.

Connector   Completed_____

Find two to three connections between your reading and the outside world. Connect your reading to something in your life, community, other similar events, or to other people/places.

Illustrator   Completed_____

Make some kind of picture related to the reading. It can be a drawing, sketch, cartoon, diagram, flow chart, or stick-figure scene. You should draw an idea or feeling you get from the reading, or a key point of the book. You'll need to explain what your drawing means.

Vocabulary Enricher   Completed_____

Find three vocabulary words (mark them with Post-it notes), and teach them to your group. Make sure to read them in their context and give dictionary definitions.

Your literature circle will be on _____. All parts must be completed and brought to class on _____.

Appendix C
Letter to Parents About Reading

Dear Parents,

Thank you for your involvement in your student's reading this year. As your student may have told you, I am experimenting this year with different ways to look at independent reading. I am part of a federal grant for teacher researchers at Poe and two other Fairfax County schools. There are two more aspects to my research this year. One item is a parent survey which will be distributed at the end of third quarter. The second item is an extra credit option to read a book with your student. It was actually suggested by one of the students in a letter to his parents. When was the last time you read a book with your child? Usually this activity ends when we stop "putting the kids to bed." One of the best things about reading is being able to share and discuss what you gain from the reading. That's what is fun about reading. The purpose of this letter is to outline some ideas on this extra credit option.

Step One: Choosing a book. I suggest you pick a young adult literature selection. This genre is really expanding, and you might be surprised at the quality of the writing and the variety of issues being explored. I particularly like historical fiction. You may use one book and take turns after chapters; buy one and check the other out from the library; buy two copies; or check out two copies from the library. There are lists of books in the classroom for students to check out when making a selection.

You may also share one of your favorite books with your child. Maybe they will learn something about you. It is all right if the book is in another language. Students could even compare English translations to the original language.

Step Two: Recording your experience. I hope you will discuss the book as you are reading it. Talk about decisions the characters are making, what you would do; talk about what you are noticing about the writing; make predictions.

Then, after you have finished your book, you can either write about the experience or tape record (video is ok, too) a discussion of the book. Tapes and videos will be returned. Please label them. Some possible items to discuss are:

1) How did you choose the book?
2) What process did you use to read it?
3) Did your partner point out anything you didn't notice in the reading?
4) Would you recommend this book? Why or why not?

I hope you have fun with this experiment. It is not required and extra credit will be given to those who participate. I thank you VERY much and your student will certainly be appreciative!

Sincerely,

Julia Lindquist

Theresa Manchey

Theresa Manchey teaches in Frederick County, Virginia, at James Wood High School, where she is English department chair. To initiate a teacher research program she garnered support from school administrators, educated herself and colleagues about teacher research, and responded to the interests and needs of fellow teachers. Manchey is a recognized leader in her school district, where she now leads teacher-researcher groups, but her teaching experiences are the grounding for her thinking and action.

The year of the research reported on here, Manchey became intrigued by the effects of an assignment she had used off and on during several years of teaching. She remembers when a class had studied first *Candide* and then *Billy Budd*, and she had first asked her students to draw a metaphor representing the life of Candide. The results were up on the bulletin board. When they finished reading *Billy Budd*, they repeated the assignment and placed those drawings on the bulletin board as well. At once the students began to see differences in the pictures and to discuss how those differences were related to the literature. They began to create their own literary theory, and Manchey never got to give her prepared lecture comparing the two books. Even though she is a "stick figure" type of artist, she says, she wanted to learn more about the effects of drawing and sketching to learn and understand literature.

DRAWING: ANOTHER PATH TO UNDERSTANDING

by Theresa Manchey

THE QUESTION

For several years I have included drawing in my English classes as a means to help students see big concepts and to provide an incentive for closer reading of a text. Recently my school chose to implement a block schedule. Longer class periods (90 minutes) allow more time to complete drawing activities, and I've found myself using them more frequently. This year a conversation with another teacher caused me to rethink this method. Talking about her feeling that students in her single period classes were doing better than students in her block class, she said, "In the single classes we just move right along." No one likes to believe they're asking kids to do useless "stuff"; so I began to wonder. What effect does the drawing have on students' learning? Is it really worth the time invested in it? I decided to investigate and began by asking my English 10 students to recall what they could of the topics we studied first semester.

GATHERING DATA

Our course was organized into units based upon the archetypes or story patterns found in one of our texts, *Man the Mythmaker*. When the students responded to the survey, they had completed the first two chapters of the text, "The Earth Belonged to Them All," a series of creation myths depicting the idea of a golden age and "The God-Teacher," stories such as the Prometheus myth in which humans received special knowledge from their gods. As a review of the second unit, the students were organized into small groups and asked to draw their concept of these mythical figures who taught humans important lessons. In looking at their responses to this preliminary survey, I noted several references to the drawings we did as well as other visual cues:

- We drew pictures of our ideal god-teacher.
- I remember the picture we drew [of the god-teacher].
- I remember when we made the god-teacher posters, too.
- There was a musical score on one page and a piano with things placed inside to alter its tones [a reference to a page in their text].

One student volunteered the following information about her learning:

I learn best when we do things besides read and log, read and log, for example: games, movies, filmstrips, drawing, etc.... Reading and logging is okay sometimes but the information just doesn't stick.

There was certainly some indication that the drawing played some role in the students' memories of units of study. I followed this initial investigation by closely observing students' reactions to other drawing activities through the year.

SOME DRAWING ASSIGNMENTS

Next, I assigned *A Separate Peace*, by John Knowles, and asked students to do a drawing for each chapter rather than the usual written response (log). My idea was to focus on symbolism in this book, and I hoped certain objects — the tree, the river, etc. — would surface in these drawings and help students see the relationship of these objects to the meaning of the story. On the day the drawings were due, I asked students to spread their drawings out and look for objects that occurred in more than one drawing. Not surprisingly, all the major symbols from the book surfaced in the ensuing discussion. Their drawings were very interesting: some included quotes from the book (Figure 1), some were completely visual (Figure 2), others relied heavily on words (Figure 3).

After a quick survey of which objects occurred in the drawings of most or all students, we looked at a few objects that were found in only one or two students' work (such as Anne's locker drawing mentioned below). I felt the assignment had been really successful since the objects

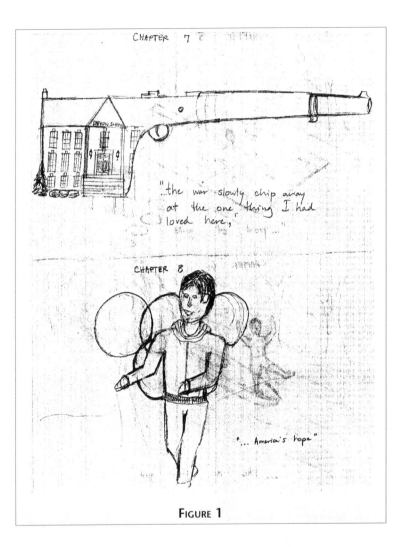

FIGURE 1

that occurred most frequently in the drawings were those most critics agree have symbolic value in the book, and the occurrence of personal symbols in some drawings helped us make some distinction between universal and personal symbolism. Because the students had already chosen these objects as significant by using them as representative of events in particular chapters, they found it easier to see how Knowles could use such objects symbolically. By the end of class, I felt we had achieved one of the objectives for study of this book as I had recorded it in my journal 1/3/95.

FIGURE 2

I'm thinking tonight there are 2 things I want to get from A Separate Peace: 1. How symbols occur and function in a novel and 2. Vocabulary building.

At the conclusion of that activity, I asked students to reflect on the merits of this drawing in contrast to the usual written responses to the reading. Almost all students said they enjoyed the break from writing, though several kept logs along with their drawings. Most indicated the drawings helped them focus on the main idea of each chapter, while

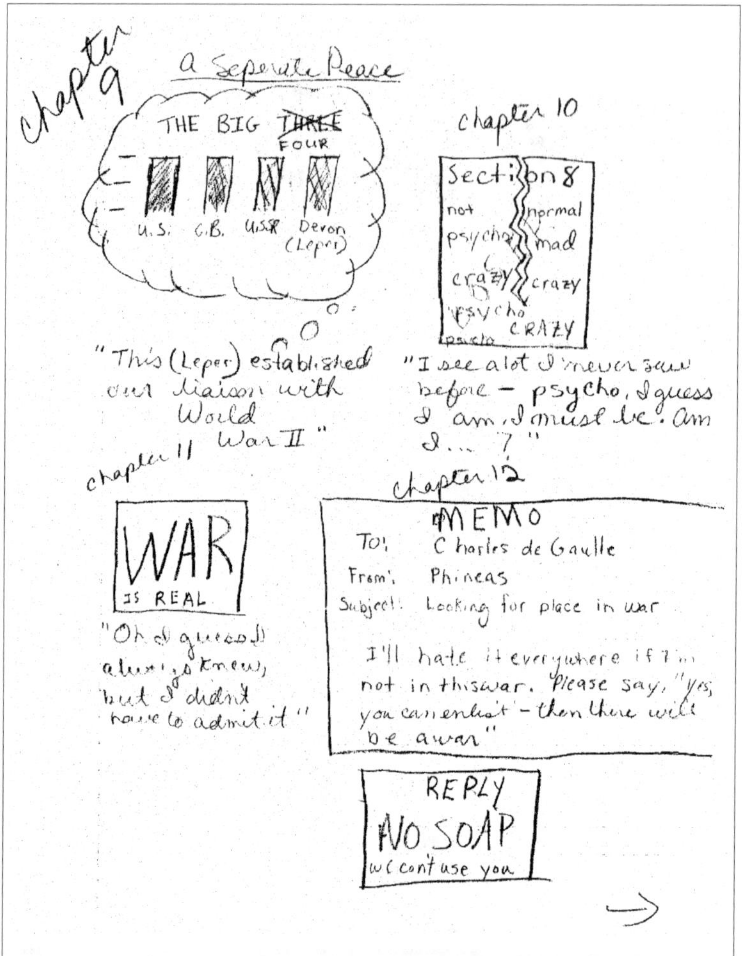

FIGURE 3

writing brought reactions to the smaller details. They found the drawings took less time than writing and were not as much of an interruption to their reading. Other interesting comments were:

- *Some things are hard to express in words.*
- *A picture captures an important moment in time.*
- *Sometimes a chapter gives me a picture in my head.*
- *Pictures give words actions.*
- *Using colors helps show emotions.*

A few students described the process they used in determining what to draw:

- *I run through pictures of events in the chapter and pick the main one.*
- *I weigh the importance of events.*

Others felt the pictures would benefit them later:

- *Seeing the pictures makes you remember the chapter.*
- *I'm able to visualize the story later.*

Colleen added a less positive comment about the picture logs on her midterm exam:

- *I think writing logs helped me understand more than the picture logs although they [the pictures] were easier.*

Colleen's comment alerted me to a pattern that seemed to be emerging — some students seem to rely more on the written word than others.

After our discussions of *A Separate Peace*, I assigned an essay demonstrating how one symbol was used in the book and a visual project presenting the main symbols. The paper was due about a week before the project. I wondered after looking at their comments on the drawings if perhaps I should have reversed those due dates. When I posed this question to the students, the responses were mixed, but they favored doing the visual first by about two to one. Some representative comments were:

- *I think the visual should have come first because when I was thinking about what to do for it, I gained a better understanding of how I actually looked at the different symbols of the book.... I could've used my thoughts from that to help me with my writing.*
- *I feel the visual was somewhat of a brainstorm for me and gave me more ideas.*

Interestingly, these two comments come from students with widely different degrees of artistic talent. Both show the feeling of the two-thirds of the class who saw the visual project as a means of pulling together their thoughts on the symbols.

The other third had equally clear statements of how the process worked for them:

- *The essay helped me think of ideas and things to do for the visual.*
- *Working on the essay first established the background and content of the visual.*

One student indicated a benefit from all these visuals that I had not anticipated — the ability to *see* and learn from other students' ideas:

- *I think the project could also have gone before the essay and that would have been helpful too because then everyone would have gotten more input and ideas to use in their essays.*

When asked if they used their picture logs to complete these two assignments, the students were almost evenly divided. Some representative comments follow. Some said the drawings were a kind of road map for them:

- *I did use my pictures occasionally. Mostly when I was trying to find a certain part of the book.*

Others systematically reviewed their work looking for patterns:

- *For my visual I looked at all the symbols I drew and carefully decided which one to draw. I also looked at how I drew them in my chapter drawings and decided if they had any special meaning.*
- *For my essay I used them to look at the different ways that I had previously looked at or thought about the water.*

Some who did not use the drawings cited the quality of the drawings as the reason:

- *I'm not very good at drawing and it would be hard for me to interpret them anyway.*

Others noted their preference for words over pictures:

- *... I looked back in the story. I don't believe the drawings were a good idea.*

The essays proved to be quite good and showed the understanding of symbolism that had been my original goal. Two students actually mentioned their drawings in their essays, even though they were not asked to do so.

> *While I was reading* A Separate Peace, *I didn't notice a lot of the water. Even when I drew my pictures, I didn't make the connection. It wasn't until we laid all of our drawings out that I noticed.... In my pictures I had drawn the lake, the ocean, the rain, and Gene and Finny swimming... it [water] plays an important role.*

This first excerpt is most interesting since Rose had indicated that she did not use her drawings to help with the essay.

The second excerpt shows how a personal symbol surfaced in the drawings:

> *The main reason I remembered this part [Gene's open locker] is because for my Chapter 13 picture I drew the locker left open. When asked about the symbolism in the book, this part came directly to my mind, and it stuck there. This part of the book was a powerful image to me so I analyzed what I felt the symbols were. By playing sports I know when I see an open locker that is empty it symbolizes the end of a season, clearing out and going on. Gene's locker represents the end of a season for him too.*

It seemed I had achieved my objective. The drawings had helped most students see the role of symbolism in this novel. While a few students claimed the drawings did not help them understand the novel, none really felt the drawings were a hindrance to their reading. In addition, I discovered that having those projects displayed in the room was helping students see more interpretations of the story and its symbols.

TAKING A LOOK BACK

In the midst of this study, a member of my research group, Vicki Pitcock, told me that drawings from my classes last year had been mentioned in her class. She had asked what they knew about the idea of the hero. Several students recalled that we spent considerable time on the hero archetype. Then Susan remembered a drawing they did showing a metaphor for the hero's journey. "She seemed kind of surprised like she thought the drawing hadn't meant anything until just then," Vicki said. Susan's memory of that drawing then set off a kind of "wave effect" in the class as others remembered their drawings and thus the pattern of those hero stories.

As a result of this experience, I decided to interview a student from last year's class to see what she could remember and if drawing had any role in those memories. An excerpt from that interview follows.

> *T: One of the things I'm interested in is the drawing activities we did. Can you remember any of those at all?*
>
> *M: Like in our projects?*
>
> *T: Uh huh. What you did for your projects and we did some group drawing in class.*
>
> *M: The charts and stuff we used to do. I don't know if it [drawing] helps a lot, but like looking at them [the group drawings] — it helps you remember. When you looked at them — when you come into class, you remember what you did last time.*

Once again the idea of the drawings as memory aids was surfacing. Mary went on to say that she didn't feel the group drawings were all that helpful for her but did say there were some small benefits.

M: I don't know… I think it was fun. They say that drawing is really a stress reliever and that… we did think about oh we could use this because that means symbolism and put that on there and let's do this… maybe more of a time limit.

Our conversation next turned to the value of art projects. Mary's attitude was quite different toward this type of visual.

T: What about your projects?

M: I loved drawing like projects. Remember the time I made that shirt from reading… um, uh, about the school.

T: A Separate Peace.

M: Yeah. I loved that and I like made that shirt. I really had fun doing that. I had like a lot of fun doing the drawing. I did one this year that really looked like a person. Yeah. The face looked real.

T: What do you think you get out of doing a project like that where you have to draw rather than write?

M: I don't know… you can… like with the shirt, I like thought of like a lot of different aspects that I could use in it… like different events or you can… I don't know… it kind of helps you pick out… if you want to draw a picture of an event or a person that you really thought was the best in the book or the most interesting… it kinda… I don't know… it's more fun actually than having to write if you don't like to write very much.

T: Is that selection process, uh, you know like you said you had to think about it and pick out what you were going to draw or decide what colors to put on the shirt and all that?

M: Uh huh.

T: Do you think that that makes you look at the book any differently?

M: Yeah, cuz I had like both sides of the shirt to fill up so… yeah, cuz I went through each thing and oh I can put this on here like this and the symbolism that we used… I think you can do a lot of that in your drawing… oh I used this for a symbol for… you know, you can put 'em in your drawings.

The last thing I did was to run through a list of the drawings we did last year and ask Mary to respond if she remembered them. The only response she had was to the drawing of a metaphor for the hero's journey:

> *M: We made a puzzle and all those obstacles that they went through. Oh yeah because they'd start out then they'd get sidetracked and hurt and then they'd find their way back home and finding their family or whatever and coming home to it. I remember that one.*

Mary's mixed response to the drawings seems to indicate that she found the individual projects more beneficial than the group drawings, but in both cases my objective of having students think more carefully about their reading and having them find a pattern in groups of stories was met. In addition, she showed me an unexpected value of the drawings, they reminded students of the previous day's lesson, a valuable benefit when classes met on alternate days.

ANOTHER ASSIGNMENT

At about the same time, I began a read-aloud with my English 9 students during which they were asked to do a drawing at the end of each chapter and to write a chapter summary. My purpose in this assignment was to encourage the students to visualize the events of the story as I read to them. On their semester exam, these students were asked to recall events from the story and later were asked which activity most helped them to complete that question—the summaries or the drawings Some said that neither helped; they had not considered looking through their folders to help them answer the question. Several, however, did indicate that the pictures were most helpful.

To follow up on this information, I decided to interview one of those students. An excerpt from that interview follows:

> *T: When you read, do you visualize, in other words get pictures of what you're reading?*
> *E: Yeah.*

T: *Do you do that almost all the time or ...*

E: *Not really. Sometimes....*

T: *Okay. Let's talk a little about the* Deathwatch *thing where we did the drawings. Um. When I was reading out loud to you, could you picture what Ben was doing?*

E: *Yeah. Sometimes. When he was in the sand in the tubes. I could picture that...*

T: *Do you remember any other parts?*

E: *When he was uh... shot Madec... and what you read today.*

T: *The trial part.*

E: *Uh huh. I could picture that....*

T: *Now, I wonder, you may not be able to answer this, but when you knew you were going to have to draw a picture... did that have any effect on how you listened to the story or...*

E: *What do you mean?*

T: *Well, I guess I mean were you more likely to try to get a picture in your head because you knew you were going to have to draw a picture?*

E: *Yeah, kinda... yeah, I guess so.*

T: *Don't say it if it's not true... That's one of the reasons I was having you draw the pictures was to see if I can help you make those pictures in your head all the time when you read. So if it didn't do that, I want to know.*

E: *It did. It'd make you, you know, really think what they look like and what's going on.*

Ellen seems to be undecided herself about the extent to which she visualizes while reading and extent to which my assignment helped her. There is some indication that this kind of "forced" visualizing may be helpful. I think that at least the area deserves further exploration.

One More Assignment

All the talk we have done about drawing this year led me to try one more idea that I picked up at an Association of Supervision and Curriculum Development conference last year. The presenter suggested using drawings to help students learn vocabulary words. During our study of *A Separate Peace*, I asked students to list any unfamiliar words they found. At the conclusion of their reading, I had them select ten of those words and make flash cards on which they drew a picture showing the meaning of the word on one side and wrote the definition on the other (Figure 4).

FIGURE 4

About two months later, I had students take out their cards and we did a series of activities to determine how many of the words they still remembered and the extent to which the drawings aided their memory. Only three students indicated that their memory was unaffected by the drawings. Some representative comments follow:

- *I believe the drawing is a very good way to help. If you can get a mental picture of what it is then you can put the definition into words.*
- *When I was taking the quiz the only way I was remembering the words was by remembering the pictures.*
- *I missed five, but the other five I remembered because the picture would come to mind.*

- *Before I have never really pictured what strange words meant, but having pictures really helps!*
- *When my partner read just the words, I remembered some pictures. For example, I remembered the picture for languid, portliness, inebriate, and cogitation. But when we used the pictures it helped me a great deal. I think by visualizing the pictures I can remember these words more easily and for a longer time period.*
- *I forget things I cram for very easily. I remembered these words because I enjoyed making the pictures and could remember making them.*
- *Drawing helps a lot. You have something to place with them kind of like a reasoning behind them, the answer to why?*

One student really spelled out what others had hinted at as the key to their success with these particular words and the role of the drawings:

- *I think the pictures helped because I drew them and I knew what they were supposed to be. I think if I was looking at someone else's drawing I wouldn't have know the words by the pictures.*

This activity seems to have helped the most students and to have elicited the most enthusiastic response of any drawings I've tried. Such a response makes me trust my original belief that all this drawing in English class functions as a memory aid for students.

I CAN'T DRAW

In several instances throughout this research, the students expressed dissatisfaction with the quality of their drawings. Such statements are common when students talk about these assignments, and I'm most sympathetic to the feeling. My own drawing "talent" is limited to stick figures and smiley faces. As I have discussed this research with adults, most have asked if the students resist drawing. In fact, I have met with no such resistance over the years. I'm not sure why that is in light of the fact that many students apologize for the quality of their drawings. Maybe it's because crayons and markers on the table are an indication that today we'll be doing something different. Not "just" reading and writing. When students say, as they often do in response to a drawing assignment, "I can't draw," I just respond, "That's okay, this isn't an art class, just do the best you can." That simple response has worked so far. Another key may be that students' drawings are prominently displayed in my classroom all the time. Most of these are group drawings done within a class period. Perhaps the presence of these single draft works encourages others to give the drawing a try. Perhaps I should have asked my students why they don't seem to mind the drawing. Maybe next time I will.

Conclusions

My investigation has raised more questions than it has answered so far. There are a few things I believe can be said at this point.

- Drawing has more power for some of my students than for others, but occasional drawing activities do not seem to hinder anyone's learning.
- Drawing seems to be useful when used to pull together large concepts or to help students see a broad pattern.
- Drawing may also have value for readers who do not naturally visualize as they read to help them make that visual connection to the words of a story.
- Drawing can serve as a memory aid for large concepts as well as small bits of information such as vocabulary words.
- Having students' drawings and projects displayed in the classroom allows students to learn from each other and helps set the tone for each day's class.

Some big questions remain:

- *Are students' responses to assignments that involve drawing directly related to their learning styles?*

* *How useful can drawing be for students who do not normally visualize as they read?*
* *What role does talk about the drawings play in learning? Is it helpful to have to "defend" one's drawing before class?*
* *What type of talk goes on as groups work together on a drawing? What role does such talk play in learning?*

The answer to that initial question raised by my conversation with my colleague seems somewhat clearer now. In the future, I will continue to use drawings and I will not feel they are a "filler." Still, I will continue to observe my students' responses to these assignments, and I will heed Mary's caution to impose more of a time limit on such activities, but I will also remember Jane's needs:

* *The poster or project lets you put all your ideas and feelings into one. They all come together. I think the visual helps me understand the story a little better.*

I believe school offers little opportunity for students like Jane to exercise their strengths. Maybe further studies in this area will help to change the current balance of time in our classrooms.

REFERENCES

Jewkes, W.T., Ed. (1981). *Man the mythmaker*, 2nd Edition. New York: Harcourt Brace Jovanovich. Part of series *Literature: Uses of Imagination*, Northrop Frye, Ed.

Knowles, J. (1983). *A separate peace*. Englewood Cliffs, NJ: Prentice Hall Literature Series. Originally published in 1959.

White, R. (1972). *Deathwatch*. New York: Dell.

Marian Mohr

I think that it is very important for schools to go beyond numerical measures of achievement if they are ever to understand how teaching and learning in classrooms can be improved. This research report was my first attempt to contribute to that change.

I conducted the study with the reading specialist in 1989-90 as part of Hayfield High School's effort to improve the achievement of "targeted students," especially "underachieving minorities" as they were called in the school's improvement plan. The research report was a small part of Hayfield's huge end-of-the-year document, a required comprehensive report to our superintendent showing how we had met our improvement objectives for the year.

As a whole, the school's report was full of statistics to match the numerically phrased objectives and outcomes. Included were the scores of our students on tests like "The Degrees of Reading Power" (DRP) or the numbers of our students making D's and F's. I thought that the statistical reports were not representative of good research practice. The DRP was not intended for use as a measure of reading accomplishment, for example, and the so-called "D-F ratio," at least mine, changed dramatically from quarter to quarter, and sometimes indicated which classes had been assigned to me rather than a lack of effort on my part to improve my teaching.

I wanted to illustrate the statistics of the report with contributions by the students themselves and to include teacher research to show what the numbers might mean. The students agreed to participate. Since I was also interested in how our achieving minority students managed, I asked the teachers to recommend a few to participate in the interviews along with the underachieving students already identified. This gave us 50 participants total whom we fondly referred to as "The Fifty Kids." I have no evidence that anyone ever read the research report, although I found it so interesting that I often shared it with colleagues who were concerned with ninth-grade achievement and will always be grateful to those students for their insights.

Targeted Students: The Fifty Kids

by Marian M. Mohr

Fifty ninth-grade students were identified for study, several kinds of data were collected on their achievement, and they were interviewed to gather additional data on how Hayfield's programs to assist underachievers work or don't work and why.

Identification and Procedures

The fifty students were identified after the first quarter interim grades came out in October. Ten of them are high-achieving minority students recommended by their teachers. Forty are underachievers meeting most or all of the following criteria:

- Bottom quartile on Degrees of Reading Power (DPR) test
- Recommendation by teacher as underachieving
- D or F interim grade in either English or math or both

Thirty of the fifty are minority students. Seventeen are female. Seventeen scored 54 or higher on the DRP. Teachers frequently recommended students for the study who had already been identified by a combination of DRP scores and interims. By the end of the year, seven of the students had left the school.

After the students were identified, their English teachers reported anecdotal classroom data about them to the members of the ninth grade English team and the researchers. A database on grades and interims was set up to look for patterns in the students' grades. Finally, each student was interviewed with others who had English during his or her period, groups of about eight each.

Findings

Grades

From the interim and final grades in English and math, we could not discern a common pattern. For some, receiving an interim D or F or bringing the grade up to passing by the end of the quarter was a repeated pattern. Others seemed to be steady "D" students; a few failed steadily. We did not notice any students who broke out of the grade pattern established in the early quarters. This was true, also, of the achieving students. The implication of this analysis is that teachers must look beyond the "D-F" rate to understand at least these underachievers.

INTERVIEWS

All fifty students were interviewed for a class period near the end of the semester and asked to discuss their answers to our questions and, generally, to comment on how to succeed in the ninth grade at Hayfield. Peggy Ford and Marian Mohr conducted the interviews held during the students' English classes, approximately 50 minutes long.

The students seemed pleased to be asked to participate. We told them that the ninth grade English teachers were not happy that so many students in the ninth grade received low grades and wanted to find out why. We also told them that research done in 1988-89 had indicated that ninth grade was a crucial year for students at Hayfield. We did not make a point of how they were chosen, and they seemed to accept our interest in them as justified.

The interviews were taped and the interviewers also took notes. The students' comments were transcribed, compiled, and analyzed.

The interview included several questions about reading which are discussed in the first section of this report. The rest of the interview consisted of two questions:

1. *What makes ninth grade such a crucial year? Why is it difficult?*
2. *What helps students to succeed in high school? Which causes success in high school — hard work or being smart?*

The final part of question #2 was a follow-up to a study we had read about comparing attitudes of American and Japanese parents toward school success. This study indicated that Japanese parents believed that success in school was related to hard work and studying, in contrast to American parents, who believed that school success was related to the intelligence of students.

Our ninth graders agreed with the Japanese parents. Forty-five of them thought that the key to success was studying hard. Twenty-three of the forty-five believed that you needed both hard work and intelligence. The following comments are typical:

- *"You become smart by studying."*
- *"You have to study, but you also have to have common sense."*
- *"There's a difference between studying hard and studying smart."*

Only one student stated that being smart was the only way to achieve.

As we analyzed the rest of the interview data, six themes appeared repeatedly. To our surprise there was no appreciable difference between the comments of the achieving students and those identified as underachievers. They knew the same information. The themes and some typical comments follow:

1. To succeed in high school you need friends, even though the wrong friends "can get you in trouble." Friends "make you or break you."

By friends they meant not only peers, but also older brothers and sisters and, in some cases, parents. They indicated that their friends were of specific help ("It's easier to learn from a student." "Ask a student first.") and also generally supported them. Social life in high school is very important, they believed. You can make friends, they said, by participating in school activities, especially sports, but not everybody can be successful at sports. They saw success as expressed in popularity, that is, being known and liked.

2. In ninth grade a student must set standards and have goals. "You have to pass more classes." "Grades are more serious."

One scenario they proposed was that when a student fails, he or she blames the teacher, and then the teacher doesn't like the student. Students who fail "don't realize the future." Many of these students had been to summer school and mentioned that summer school is less pressured, more fun. "My friends are there," said one. Ninth grade is harder because you have to pass more classes, there is more writing, and "it counts." They weren't sure whether their ideas that standards were higher in the ninth grade meant that students or teachers had higher standards.

3. It's important to go to class, pay attention, do your homework, and study for tests. Go after school because "one on one with the teacher helps the most."

They agreed that you have to "be willing to learn." Their descriptions of good study habits could have come from a book on the subject by educators! They said a student needs to develop "good habits," review, take notes, and ask for help. They included good attendance in this overview of study habits. "It's harder to make up work." "When you fall behind, do your makeup work right away."

They admitted (achievers and underachievers alike) they found it difficult to discipline themselves to do homework. "I'm tired at the end of the day and I don't want to do boring work again."

4. You have to learn to use the greater freedom and independence of high school. "It's harder to learn if you don't like it." "There's more work and you have less time." "Assignments are due over time, not overnight."

They discussed their independence or lack of it at length. They said that some teachers treat them like "babies" and some like twelfth graders. High school is the real world, they said, where they don't usually baby you. "Teachers care less," said some. Most typical was the comment, "Teachers should concentrate on *you* more."

They were confused between "enjoying" learning and being responsible. They used the example that in English in the ninth grade they have to read boring adult English books that they don't enjoy. Therefore, being responsible is harder.

They felt that to be successful in ninth grade a student needs help to be organized. In intermediate school you had "more chances to make up work." "If they're behind at the end of the grading period, students give up."

They again discussed being bored, not just with English material, but with the routine of school and homework. At the same time, they felt rushed, forgot to take home the right books for their homework, didn't do the work, were bored with it anyway, and eventually failed.

5. High school is larger, bigger. "Books are larger." "There are more bigger people."

They repeatedly talked of how small they felt by stressing the reverse — how large everything seemed to them. They said that upperclassmen do not respect them and actively pick on them. "A lot of older kids underrate us," said one, to wide agreement.

One group spent several minutes on a nostalgic memory of their days in the sixth grade the last time many of them had felt that they were doing all right. "Sixth grade is your best year." In sixth grade you are more in charge, you're on top, you know what to do. Now being "on the bottom, you feel pressure." They remembered assignments they had completed to praise, leadership roles they had held, performances and responsibilities they had successfully accomplished, and even books they had read and liked.

6. Teachers respond differently to students in high school (as compared to intermediate school or elementary school.) "They don't stop; they just keep going and I'm afraid to ask."

Their perception of teachers' attitudes toward them (not just in English, and not everyone) was that they are busy people with a lot of things to do besides help them individually. It was acknowledgment of themselves as individual students they seemed to wish for. When a student would say that the teachers "don't care," almost every time another would respond by naming a teacher who, he or she believed, did care.

From earlier statements in this report, their concern about how they were treated by teachers can be elaborated. They stressed repeatedly how hard it was to keep up with long term assignments and how hard it was to catch up if you fell behind.

In summary, these students knew what their problems were and they knew what to do about them! Sometimes they talked as if they had prepared themselves for the interview by reading up on good study skills. The laughed often and sometimes joked about their own situations, but the overwhelming impression they gave was that they knew what they needed to do, but they had not managed to summon the interest, energy, and discipline to do it.

They were highly articulate and expressed themselves with force. They recognized that there were things which successful student do that make them successful; they simply had not yet decided to participate, or were doing so lethargically because they were "bored" as they put it. They seemed on the fringes of "school membership" as J. Howard Johnston said of "at-risk youth" at the Area II Principals' Forum, January 12, 1990.

They frequently mentioned being bored in class. Appeals to them based on the future or on the need for good grades were shrugged off. The interviewers were impressed with their humor, their apparent intelligence, and their keen psychological insight. As one student put it, "It's all technique." Being a successful student is behaving in a certain way, and behaving that way is a choice made by the student.

Implications

The implications of these findings for instruction are both simple and complex, They could be summarized in that favorite educator's term "motivation." These students need to be motivated. The complexity of motivating them, however, cannot be overestimated.

1. Motivation needs to be both sly and authentic, based on connections between what the students recognize *now* are their interests and needs and what the curriculum will allow.
2. Motivation needs to take advantage of their considerable pride. Although they may not have "self-esteem" as far as school is concerned, they have a great deal of pride in themselves and what they do. The pride existed even in the students who, we knew, were failing in many areas of their lives.
3. They need to learn how to plan work over a period of time and to have quickly accessible systems for making up work.
4. They need some sense that they are appreciated individuals in a large high school, perhaps by an upperclass student as a buddy or a teacher mentor. Long after the interview was over the students spoke to the interviewers about the issues raised in the interview and generally indicated that they felt pleased at being singled out and asked their opinions.
5. They do not need a course in "study skills."

Diane Painter

Diane Painter began this 1989 study to look at the use of computers by upper elementary students designated as having learning disabilities. She discovered instead that they were teaching her about the function of their conversations when they met at the computer. In her role as a learning disabilities resource teacher, she wrote frequent observations of her students at work. "I remember taking notes on what was happening as two students worked at the computers. An observer came in and started taking notes on my observing and taking notes on the students. She was so interested in what I was doing. I was totally absorbed and didn't realize she was there. When the two students finished, I talked with them, asked a few questions about what they had done, and took some more notes. The observer was fascinated with what they were learning from each other, by my learning from them, and by their reflecting on how they were learning from each other."

This study illustrates Painter's interests in special education, composing processes, and technology literacy — interests that have led her since to the completion of a Ph.D. in those areas. Currently a technology resource teacher at Deer Park Elementary School, Painter and several other teachers at the school have received a National Council of Teachers of English (NCTE) teacher-researcher grant to examine "how elementary students use language arts skills to work as teams researching topics to produce multimedia presentations."

What Happens When Students Engage in Peer Interaction During the Writing Process

by Diane Painter

In October I decided to try a brainstorming technique I had learned from a teacher of the gifted and talented. She uses an activity know as a "Dancing Box" to help children generate word associations and then write about how the words are related. I thought it might help two fifth-grade students, Brett and Zeb, generate ideas verbally, and this might help them begin to write.

"I want to try something new today," I began. I hoped they wouldn't notice I was slightly skeptical — not sure this would be very successful. "At the top of your paper I want you to put a word. Any word that comes to mind."

"My mind's blank." That sounded typical of Zeb.

"Mine, too," responded Brett.

"Relax," I coaxed. "Try not to think of anything and maybe a word will come to mind."

Brett pursed his lips and rubbed the tip of his nose. Sigh. Zeb went over to the pencil box and rummaged around in it. Brett sighed again, "Let's get this over with! Hey, what are you looking for?"

"A pencil."

"You have one."

"I know. I need an eraser."

When Zeb returned to his seat he looked down at his shirt. "I have paint on my shirt!" Then he leaned back and began to make clicking noises with his tongue. Two minutes passed. "I guess I'll do skateboards," he said rather softly.

Zeb wrote "skateboard" at the top of his paper.

"That's a good start," I said encouragingly. "Now, when you think of 'skateboard' what two words come to mind?" Zeb thumbed the table.

Brett kept pulling on his lower lip. He wrote "book" at the top of his paper. Zeb appeared interested in what Brett was doing. Brett wrote "pages" and "numbers" under the word book.

"That's good. Now what two words come to mind when you think of pages, and what two words come to mind when you think of numbers?" I was trying not to look at Zeb or to appear that I was aware that he had not written anything for five minutes. Brett continued to write. He wrote "thin" and "riting" (writing) under pages and "dark" and "boldface" under numbers.

"Now what word comes to mind when you think of thin and writing together?" I thought this was getting interesting. He wrote "tree." For "dark" and "boldface" he wrote "same."

"Let's now tie tree and same together. What one word do you think of?"

Brett wrote "leavs" (leaves).

"Let's see," I said trying to review what he had written. "You wrote that when you think of 'book' you think of pages and numbers. The word 'pages' makes you think of thin and writing. Numbers makes you think of dark and boldface. Thin and writing makes you think of 'tree' and dark and boldface makes you think of 'same.' When you think of tree and same, you think of 'leaves.'" I had this feeling that Brett was going to say, "Yeah, so what?" This was supposed to be an exercise to get them to write something "creative." How creative was he going to be with what he had just written?

Brett surprised me. He asked, "Oh, I have to write a story now, huh?" I nodded. He picked up his pencil and wrote for about two minutes. After he had stopped writing, Brett appeared to proof his work and then underlined some words in his paragraph. It read:

> One day I read a <u>book</u> that had <u>numbers</u> on the <u>pages</u> the <u>pages</u> were the <u>same</u> all <u>thin</u>. The pitchers were <u>dark</u> and <u>boldface</u> the <u>riting</u> was good at the end there was a <u>tree</u> with diffrant collor <u>leaves</u>

Zeb just sat and stared. It was now the end of the period. Brett asked to be dismissed. As soon as Brett walked out the door, Zeb picked up his pencil and wrote:

Skateboard
wheels ollie
fast round trick hard
Go complicated
tricky

It is hard to ride a skateboard. Its tricky and hard to do a ollie.
Itshard to go off a halfpipe.It takes a whille to lear all that stuff.

Zeb closed his writing folder and said good-bye and left.

This was a typical scene at the beginning of the school year. I was constantly trying to find a technique or approach that would stimulate Brett and Zeb's interest in writing. To them, it seemed, writing was a chore, something you do quickly and get "over with." I just couldn't quite get them to understand that once ideas are drafted, the real writing begins.

I wanted my Learning Disabilities (LD) students to understand that the writing process involves nonlinear, overlapping processes: planning, drafting, revising, and editing (Flower and Hayes, 1980). Research on the writing of exceptional children, particularly ones like Brett and Zeb who are learning disabled, suggests that exceptional children tend to have specific strategic deficits in idea generation, text organization and metacognitive control (Englert and Raphael, 1988). Englert and Raphael suggest that exceptional children are weak in these "knowledge-telling" strategies that would help them retrieve and organize their ideas and make decisions about overall presentation and ordering of their ideas in text.

In my program, an elementary resource program for mainstreamed learning-disabled children, a lack of "telling strategy" is only one of a variety of academic and learning deficits I face each day with my students. Brett needed to overcome writer's block, caused partly because of his poor spelling ability and feelings that his ideas were not worth writing. Brett seemed to be able to verbally generate ideas more quickly than Zeb. Zeb's problems were with oral language. I found that he had difficulty expressing himself verbally. Zeb would say his mind was blank. Perhaps he was just unsure of how to begin.

When planning writing sessions for these two fifth-graders, I knew I had a better chance of working with them if they became involved in their own learning. By involving them in identifying weak areas or identifying ways of learning that worked best for them, they would probably be more likely to develop and use the particular strategies that worked best for them as individuals.

In order to plan, I needed to identify the individual strategies and interests for each student. I also needed to know how they viewed writing in general and how they viewed themselves as writers. I devised a writer's attitude survey using many of the questions from the EMIG Writing Attitude Survey and adding a few of my own. Since I was using computers with my resource students, I included questions about using word processing and computer graphics.

I gave the survey to nineteen of my twenty-four students who had written language objectives on their individual education plans and who would be using computers to write. I discovered that six of the fourteen did not like to write at all. Ten expressed a definite interest in writing on a computer. Nine of the fourteen said they would prefer giving oral reports instead of written reports.

Zeb gave a definite "I do not like to write" response, was unsure about using the computer, and said he disliked giving oral reports. Brett said he liked to write "sometimes." He expressed a definite interest in using the computer to write and said he liked giving oral reports. Both boys said they completed their written assignments as fast as they could and only sometimes "re-read and revised" their work. It was hard to find much that interested them about writing. Brett said he sometimes liked to go to school; Zeb expressed a definite dislike for school. Zeb expressed more interest in writing with paper and pencil because he said he could write faster and "get it over with." Brett said he did not like writing with paper and pencil. Brett expressed a definite interest in participating in a "writing group." Zeb was unsure if he would like it.

The survey and interviews gave me information I thought I could use with Brett. Because of his interest in the computer and strengths with verbal skills, I felt that I could interest him in verbally planning and writing a name acrostic on the computer, using fancy font type print for the first letters of his name. Identifying Zeb's interests and strengths for learning was difficult. I was not sure that Zeb would "jump right into" the acrostic project because he seemed so withdrawn and he did not indicate a desire to use the computer.

Each boy worked individually on the project, demonstrating little interaction with each other. Brett seemed to like using the thesaurus option on Bank Street Writer III to brainstorm words that he felt described him. Zeb went through the motions rarely smiling and hardly ever speaking more than one or two words in a sentence. He seemed "stuck" when trying to brainstorm a word for "Z." He finally wrote "Zeb" for the Z and one-word adjectives for each of the other letters in his name.

Brett was very verbal and very responsive to my questions which were designed to help him expand his ideas. His name poem took time. He was determined to find creative words and phrases that described his personality and what he liked to do. When he completed his name acrostic, he asked to illustrate it and hang it on the computer lab's wall. Zeb shoved his name poem into his work folder, never to look at it again.

The next week Brett asked if he could write a mystery. He saw a picture from a story starter series I had placed along the chalkboard edge. The picture was a brick tunnel. Printed beneath this picture were the sentences, "You and a friend are playing ball. Your ball has rolled into a tunnel. You chase it. What happens next?" Brett studied the picture for a few moments then turned on his computer. He typed, "My friend and I were playing with a ball. We chased it to a dark place." I asked him, "Who is your friend?" Brett moved the cursor and typed, "My friend, Eric and I…"

"When does your story take place?" I inquired.

Brett moved the cursor to the beginning of the sentence and typed, "In 1760, my friend Eric and I were playing with a ball in a town in Spain." He was becoming more descriptive and was beginning to show evidence of writer's voice. "We flew out of the tunnel at top speed. We saw a wooden door and Eric and I thought it was our salvation."

As Brett's story became more involved, Zeb became increasingly fascinated. Up to this time he had only shown polite interest in Brett's work. Now he began to make suggestions, mostly regarding the spelling of a word or use of a punctuation mark. In terms of his own writing (a short description of skateboarding techniques), Zeb was being a very careful writer. He spent a lot of time making perfect, very short sentences. He spelled and punctuated correctly. He never asked, nor received, any "feedback" concerning his writing from Brett.

Brett worked on his story every day for three weeks. When the other fifth graders in his group came to the lab, he met with them to discuss his story and seemed to enjoy their comments. These students offered suggestions that seemed to help Brett revise the ideas and storyline. Zeb was more interested in helping Brett with the "editing," quick to point out spelling errors, need for capitals, and ending punctuation marks. Together Brett and Zeb used the spellchecker option on the Bank Street Writer III. I was beginning to discover Zeb's strengths and interests. Because he was a "better" speller and had a stronger knowledge of mechanics than Brett, Zeb was willing to "take a chance" and express himself during the *editing* process!

When Brett's final draft was the way he wanted it, he asked, "Can I have a copy for my teacher?"

"Brett, let's wait until it has gone through the final editing with me tomorrow. Don't you want to show her your final illustrated version?" I tried to sound convincing.

"Oooh. Do I have to? Well, all right. I want a copy now, though."

"Try to refrain from showing your teacher right now. Tomorrow it should be ready!"

Brett winced as he raced out the door. Soon after the last bell rang, Brett's teacher came into my room with several folded pieces of paper clenched in her hand. "Now what am I supposed to do with this? Brett put this under my nose when he came back from your class and told me it was his 'finished' story, but I am not allowed to look at it until tomorrow! I have never seen him as excited about anything before."

A lot of thoughts raced through my mind. I thought about how in the early fall both Brett and Zeb displayed avoidance of written work. I thought about how long it used to take Zeb to get started and how Brett used to say he couldn't write because he couldn't spell. Then I realized that Brett's "mystery" story was a result of peer interaction. Brett was the "idea" man and Zeb was the editor, and the other students in the fifth-grade resource class gave support and guidance. Writing became more than a linear series of steps; the students were engaging in recursive processes. They no longer demonstrated the thinking, "Now that I have something down on paper, I'm finished!" *Together* they were writing, revising, creating. Their working together seemed far more successful than their writing independently. I was beginning to discover an important element in my writing program: collaborative learning.

I decided to interview the boys to see what thoughts they had about writing "collaboratively" and using the computer to generate text. Brett was quite responsive to my questions. I discovered that he found revising easier on the word processor than writing with pen and paper:

> *I like writing on a computer because I can type faster than I write. I can do more on one and I can learn more. I like to write stories on it and I like to learn how to type.*

Brett described what happens when working with peers to revise his writing:

> *They helped (me) show more action and made it (my story) more interesting.*

When describing his interaction with Zeb, he said:

> *Together we reread it (the writing) and proof-look for misspellings and other things.*

I asked him what he thought about "getting help" from others. He smiled, laughed and said, "Oh, I don't mind!"

Zeb continued to say he would much rather generate text on paper. He said the computer slowed him down. It seemed to me that he took forever to just get started, no matter how he was writing — with paper or computer! It was so hard to get Zeb to generate ideas. As for interacting with Brett, Zeb had little to say, "Oh, it's all right."

I wanted Zeb to be interested in writing, not just going through the motions. I needed to find something that would *motivate* him to write.

Then one day Zeb asked if he could do his Black History report in my resource class. I thought this might be the answer to the motivation problem. The assignment was something he needed to complete for his classroom teacher and one that was required of every fifth-grade student, but it was also something Zeb seemed to want to do. Zeb was not restricted to any particular writing style, and he could choose any famous Black American to research. This seemed perfect — a writing assignment that *he* asked to do and one that gave him the choice of topic and style.

Zeb decided to use an I-Search format. Using this style of research allowed Zeb to first write what he thought he knew about his subject. Then he brainstormed what he wanted to know. Because he likes boxing, Zeb chose Larry Holmes. He used mostly secondary sources to gather information: magazine articles and a story from a fifth-grade supplemental reading series. Zeb balked when I encouraged a primary search, interviewing people who know about boxing. Interviews would require talking with people and asking questions, and for him, that was hard to do.

The first few questions Zeb generated were very basic: When and where was Larry Holmes born? What was his boxing record? Then he wrote, "Can he beat Mike Tyson?" It appeared that Zeb was willing to research facts and offer an opinion based on what he discovered.

As Zeb read his material, he began to verbalize questions: "What does 'accumulate' mean? It says here that Larry Holmes's bills began to accumulate."

He was asking the question out loud, but directing it to anyone who would listen. Brett responded with, "Why don't you use the thesaurus option on Bank Street Writer?"

Zeb typed the word "accumulate" on the screen and together they searched the list of synonyms for a word that they both understood. A few minutes later, Zeb asked, "Does this sound good?" He typed the sentence, "He dropped out of school." Zeb was asking for feedback!

Brett's response was positive, "Yeah. You know, why don't you boldface 'dropped out'? Make it look important!"

Zeb's report contained all the elements of who, what, when, where, and how. But as the report developed, Zeb incorporated elements of writing style. For example, in the second to last paragraph of his report he wrote:

> *In 1980 Larry fought and defeated his former boss, Muhammad Ali. People said that Larry lacked a champion's heart when he beat Ali. He felt pretty bad about people saying he didn't have a champion's heart.*

He tied this to the last paragraph when he wrote:

> *Larry and his wife, Diane, now live in an expensive home. He owns a restaurant, a sportswear building, bar, and an office building. Larry also works with several local handicapped children. This makes Larry a wealthy person with a BIG HEART!*

The writing group's reaction to this last paragraph appeared to be what Zeb needed. They told him they enjoyed reading his report, found it very interesting and really liked the ending. Zeb's reaction was a big, bright smile. He took his time to illustrate the report's cover. His teacher graded it an A.

I could see that Zeb's successful completion of this report had the same effect on Zeb as Brett's completion of his mystery; both boys began to display confidence in their writing ability. Their teacher and parents were pleased. Both boys were now completing all in-class writing assignments and homework assignments.

In many ways both boys have come a long way as writers. They are more willing to write, although Zeb appears to write more to meet a requirement than for pleasure. Brett initiates more writing for himself. He still does not pay much attention to spelling, capitalization or punctuation. However, he likes to verbally brainstorm and he generates text more quickly than Zeb. He also revises his ideas and text more often. Zeb is still the "careful" writer, making sure spelling and other mechanics are perfect. He does not revise his ideas as much as his sentences to make them more structurally accurate, although he does now ask for feedback from his peers.

I believe that involving my students in "peer interaction" during the writing process has been the most successful part of my program. In looking over my journal reactions, observations, and interviews with my students, I have discovered that it appears three recursive stages occur when my students engage in peer interaction: querying, declaring and planning. In the querying stage, students ask for assistance and seek approval. In the declaring stage, they express knowledge, engage in peer tutoring and express a desire to write. In the planning stage, they demonstrate a plan for writing and generate their ideas through brainstorming.

In the case of Zeb and Brett, these behaviors were distributed equally, but not each student exhibited all behaviors. Zeb was very interested in engaging in peer tutoring, demonstrating "knowledge," especially when helping Brett with the structure of his writing. Brett was far more overt in demonstrating brainstorming and generating ideas. Both engaged in querying, although Brett asked for more assistance than Zeb. Brett didn't seem to care who helped him, as long as he received guidance from time to time.

I also discovered that a student's feeling of "ownership" seemed to stimulate a motivation to write. In both cases when the boys completed their first "major" piece of writing that involved planning, generating, revising and editing, their attitudes toward writing changed. This was evident in their changed behaviors when completing writing assignments for their classroom teacher, as well as the responses they made on the second writer's attitude survey. The second attitude survey indicated that both boys, as well as the other members of their writing group, had more positive responses toward writing in general, working with a writing group, and believing that writing helps them learn new things.

I have realized that peer interaction and fostering a feeling of "ownership" in the learning process are important elements in teaching, which has helped me develop a more successful program. I am encouraging "collaboration" in all my classes. My students are writing more stories and reports then ever before. One sixth-grade student wrote,

Working with a partner is easier for me. I can tell him my ideas and if I forget what I say before I write it down, he reminds me. As

for using the computers to write, he added, "It is easier for me to change things. Sometimes I switch letters around. Now I can easily fix my mistakes. I like using spellchecker, too. Now I don't have to worry about spelling."

REFERENCES

Bos, C. S. (1988). Process-oriented writing: Instructional implications for mildly handicapped students. *Exceptional Children, 54,* 521-527.

Englert, C. & Raphael, T.E. (1988). Constructive well-formed prose: Process, structure, and metacognitive knowledge. *Exceptional Children, 54,* 513-519.

Flower, L., & Hayes, J.R. (1980). The cognition of discovery. *College Composition and Communication, 14,* 21-32.

Graham, S. & Harris, K.R. (1988). Instructional recommendations for teaching writing to exceptional students. *Exceptional Children, 54,* 506-512.

Lewis, M. & Lindaman, A.D. (1989). How do we evaluate student writing? One district's ANSWER. *Educational Leadership, 46,* 70-71.

Nodine, B.F. & Breiter, C. (1986). Research on written composition by learning disabled, reading disabled, and normal children. *Learning Disability Quarterly, 8,* 167-181.

Seeley, J. (1988). Peer editing: How to assign writing without multiplying your workload. *Journal of Virginia Education, 81,* 13-17.

Betsy Sanford

Betsy had just returned from a family vacation when we talked about publishing her essay on first graders as thinkers about mathematics. She remembered worrying that her discussion would sound too simplistic, but she was also determined to look at what conceptual learning of mathematics involved for her first graders.

Sanford did her first research study in 1984-85 on the revision processes of fourth graders. Teacher research showed her there were intellectually challenging things to learn about elementary school teaching. She went on to study discourse analysis in a masters degree program in rhetoric and composition, seeing it as an extension of her teacher research. Through it all, she kept wondering about her fourth graders' school lives. "I didn't just want to look at what was missing. I wondered what had happened before, where my fourth graders had come from." She decided to transfer to first grade.

In her first grade classroom she became interested in mathematical learning and thinking. She said about this article, "I always thought it was very valuable for me, but probably unintelligible to others. It was me pounding out my theory about learning. It's my shift from seeing teaching as managing content and managing children, to being a teacher whose primary responsibility is to create the circumstances that will make it possible for kids to learn, to ensure that they have what they need in order to do the learning they are going to do." In 1995-96, she conducted a study based on these concepts: "It All Adds Up: Learning Number Facts in First Grade."

BECOMING MEMBERS OF THE MATH CLUB: FIRST GRADERS AS EMERGENT MATHEMATICAL THINKERS

Betsy Sanford

> *We learn from other people, not so much through conscious emulations as by "joining the club" of people we see ourselves as being like, and by being helped to engage in their activities. Usually we are not even aware that we are learning.*
> — *Frank Smith,* Joining the Literacy Club

I. Introduction

In 1988, after nearly 20 years of experience teaching third and fourth grades, I accepted an assignment to teach first grade. Although I had several reasons for making the move, first among them was the desire to see what had "come before." I wanted to see the emergent stages of reading and writing in order to know what literacy groundwork students had laid before they got to the middle elementary grades.

At the time mathematics did not hold the same interest for me. Although I had always enjoyed teaching math in the middle grades, I did not have the same curiosity about it as I did about reading and writing.

Once I moved to first grade, the major pieces of the emergent literacy puzzle fell into place without too much difficulty. Before very long I could sense the significance of what my students were attempting and I learned ways to respond to and support them. Not so with math! That first year I dutifully followed the Program of Studies and the adopted text, too swamped by other things to examine mathematical instruction in depth. But by the second year, I was beginning to ask questions. What mathematical skills and concepts were most important to teach? What was the best way to teach them? Why did it so often seem that when I "taught" math, kids didn't "get" it? Questions like these have been my direction-finders ever since, and when we began planning the teacher research project, I knew I wanted to explore a mathematical research question.

II. The Research Question

When I began my research at the beginning of school year '94-'95, I thought that I might look at the use of manipulatives to learn math. I accepted the wisdom of using manipulatives, but I wondered what actually happened when students used concrete objects as they developed their understanding of abstract concepts. Which assumptions about the use of manipulatives might I need to revisit?

This first focus was simply a starting point, as I knew it might be. Watching my students as they used manipulatives to solve problems, explore ideas, and make crucial links in their mathematical understanding, I was forced to consider what it means to be an emergent mathematical thinker. In essence, my question has become, *"What do first graders need as they develop as mathematical thinkers?"*

III. Data Collection

One of my chief sources of data collection was my research log. I used my log as a place to write about class lessons and activities, record descriptions of individual students' responses (such as strategies I observed), and reflect as I attempted to understand what I saw. I also collected student work samples (learning log entries and writing and drawing students did during class activities). I conducted several class interviews, videotaping them in November, December, and March. In addition, I used my lesson plans (in which I often recorded my "research focus" for the week) as a record of the progress of my research and as a source of data about instructional decisions I made. Finally, I kept anecdotal student records, which provided a source of data about students' thinking.

IV. Research Findings

So what does it take for a first grader to develop as a mathematical thinker? My research this year tells me that **to become a mathematical thinker, one must learn to view the world mathematically.** Let me explain.

Math Happenings

Early in the fall of first grade is the time to begin work on addition and subtraction. This year, seeking a better way to link concrete, real-life experiences with mathematical concepts, I decided to use a "math happenings" approach to teaching the operations.

A math happening is an event in one's life that can be seen in terms of math. In school I ask students to share examples of math happenings that they have found. Using this approach helps students relate "school math" to real life. The eventual goal is that as students report their math happenings, they will relate them to the symbolic terms of mathematical equations. It is a strategy that strongly ties the concrete to the abstract and the real to the symbolic.

Often as we worked on addition and subtraction, I invited students to relate stories about math they had encountered. Aurora's math happening was typical of the ones that students offered:

> *My grandmother is visiting us right now. When she visits us there are three cars in our driveway: my dad's, my mom's, and hers. When she goes back to Towson there are two cars in the driveway.*

As students shared math happenings, I recorded them in an anecdotal record book. Doing this, I noticed that some students frequently offered to share math happenings, while others were attentive but never volunteered. I assumed that students who did not raise there hands simply lacked the confidence to share. Still, I wanted to know how those quieter students translated what they saw into math happenings. On October 28, I asked the class to write learning log entries in response to the prompt, "What happens when you look for math happenings?"

Some students had difficulty expressing their ideas clearly, while others wrote about their success finding math happenings. Here are some of their responses. (I have edited student writing for spelling and mechanics, and students have chosen pseudonyms for the purpose of confidentiality.)

> *Taylor: Why are math happenings much more important and I won't forget about math.*

Maryam: I come back from school. I go to places and I just look and I just know that it is a math happening and I found 2 math happenings.
Melissa: I learn a math happening right away, and I get excited. And the next day I tell it and the teacher thinks it's good.

At the same time, two students wrote about their difficulties finding math happenings:

Lisa: When I look for math happenings I get excited and usually do not find any and I like finding math happenings.
Dylan: I can't find them when I look for them.

I had assumed that our work looking for and discussing math happenings would be sufficient to show students how to recognize their own math happenings. I thought that what students needed was exposure to the *format* of math happenings. Once they had that, I thought they would begin to find math happenings everywhere. So what was I to make of Dylan and Lisa's difficulties? They were both among the most successful mathematical thinkers in the room — interested in activities, quick to accept a challenge, able to articulate their thinking and processes and strategies — and yet they were having trouble with math happenings. To paraphrase Dylan, they couldn't always *find* them when they looked.

Dylan's and Lisa's log entries surprised me, and I began to take special notice of their progress with this work. Notes I made about them in the few days after their log entries show that they gained ground quickly:

10/31: [Lisa] was able to find a 3+4=7 math happening when challenged.
11/1: [Dylan said], "I don't know if it's math, but there were 6 people and 5 had Popsicles and I didn't."

Before much longer, Dylan and Lisa became adept at "seeing" math around them, and they reported math happenings with frequency. Like them the rest of the students became more adept at this kind of math thinking, too. As we worked over the next several weeks, more students volunteered with math stories, and the frequency of spontaneous comments increased: "That's a math happening on the board!" one student might exclaim. "There was math in the cafeteria," another might report. To become good at math happenings, they had had to learn how to see the world around them in terms of the mathematical concepts they were learning.

This story about math happenings can stand on its own as one way to describe the process that first graders go through as they "learn" math. However, it has even more power when considered from the perspective of an article in neurologist Oliver Sacks's book, *An Anthropologist on Mars: Seven Paradoxical Tales.* The article, entitled "To See and Not See," is the account of Virgil, a middle-aged man who has been blind almost from birth. In his forties, he has the apparent good fortune of having his sight restored. Surprisingly, Virgil finds seeing a frustrating, confusing, even alienating experience, for he is unable to organize, comprehend, or give meaning to much of what he views. Only through a gradual process is he able to figure out what he might be seeing. For instance, Sacks writes about Virgil's difficulty recognizing trees:

> *Amy [Virgil's wife] had commented in her journal on how even the most "obvious" connections — visually and logically obvious — had to be learned. Thus, she told us, a few days after the operation "he said that trees didn't look like anything on earth," but in her entry for October 21, a month after the operation, she notes, "Virgil finally put a tree together — he now knows that the trunk and leaves go together to form a complete unit." (pp. 123-124)*

It seems hard to believe that recognizing a tree would be such a complex task for Virgil. And yet, it was. Sacks helps us understand this complexity by comparing Virgil's experience after his first operation to the experience of those who have always seen:

> *When we open our eyes each morning, it is upon a world we have spent a lifetime learning to see. We are not given the world; we make our world through incessant experience, categorization,*

memory, reconnection. But when Virgil opened his eye, after being blind for forty-five years… there were no visual memories to support a perception; there was no world of experience and meaning awaiting him. He saw, but what he saw had no coherence. (p. 114)

LOOKING VS. SEEING

What is significant and relevant about Virgil's story, as we consider first graders as mathematical thinkers, is the idea that we *learn* to see. That is, there is a difference between the physical act of looking and the interpretive act of seeing. In the same way, I suggest that there is a difference between looking at the world to find the math it represents (as Virgil looked, trying to find trees) and actually *seeing or interpreting* it in those terms. Of course, learning to *see* and learning to *see math* — learning to think like a mathematician — are not the same. Still, there are some important parallels. Could it be the case that, as adults, we make assumptions about the innate mathematical appearance of the world? And could it also be the case that emergent mathematical thinkers do not readily see those mathematical connections because they have not *learned how* to see them?

Certainly it's true that first graders come to us with some understanding of math. Most, if not all, have had exposure to some mathematical content — for example, counting, seriation, patterning, beginning operations. But being exposed to mathematical thinking is not the same as thinking mathematically. For emergent mathematical thinkers, seeing the world in terms of mathematical ideas requires organizing their observations in new ways. The mathematical ways that we organize our perceptions seem so apparent to us — for instance, that we see the cupcakes on the counter as a numbered set — but are not so obvious to them.

To further explore the learned aspect of mathematical thinking, consider Sacks' description of one of Virgil's accomplishments — the toddler activity of matching shapes to their corresponding holes:

He had at first been unable to recognize any shapes visually— even shapes as simple as a square or a circle, which he recognized instantly by touch…. For this reason Amy had bought, among other

things, a child's wooden formboard, with large, simple blocks —
square, triangle, circle, and rectangle — to be fitted into corre-
sponding holes and had got Virgil to practice with it every day.
Virgil found the task impossible at first, but quite easy now, after
practicing a month. *(pp.126-127; emphasis added)*

It took Virgil a month to see the connection between a cylinder's
appearance and the appearance of the corresponding circular hole, just
as it took Dylan several weeks before he even tentatively saw the math
content of his story about Popsicles and people. In each case, these tasks
seem simple and clear-cut to us, but they were neither simple nor clear-
cut to these novice learners.

Eleanor Duckworth, in *"The Having of Wonderful Ideas" and Other*
Essays on Teaching and Learning, describes 7-year-old Kevin who, with
no prompting, has the idea to arrange 10 different-sized drinking straws
in order from shortest to longest. He conceives of the arrangement and
then, with much effort, carries it out. As Duckworth tells it, "[H]e was
so pleased with himself when he accomplished his self-set task that when
I decided to offer them to him to keep (10 whole drinking straws!), he
glowed with joy…" (p. 1). Duckworth tells the story as an illustration
of what it means to have a "wonderful idea" — an idea not new to the
world, usually, but one that is new to the thinker and represents a step
forward in that person's thinking. To me, the story also seems to be
about learning a way to interpret one's perceptions, about having a new
lens through which to view the world. (And incidentally, in this story
about Kevin, it is a mathematical lens at that!)

Constructs and Conceptual Frameworks

If we agree, even tentatively, that emergent mathematical thinkers
are thinkers *learning* a mathematical view of the world, we must then
ask the question, "What does this learning involve?" After watching my
first graders this year, I have come to believe that when we talk about
concept development, we must consider the development of *constructs*
or *frameworks.* These constructs or conceptual frameworks are learned
ways that we impose mathematical meaning on a world we have learned

to see another way; they are like templates we use to organize what we see. For instance, although Virgil knew much about trees through non-visual ways, he was able to see trees only after he had a *visual* construct for trees, which he built through repeated experiences of how trees looked. As Sacks notes, "His vocabulary, his whole sensibility, his picture of the world, were couched in tactile — or, at least, nonvisual — terms" (p. 140). As a newly sighted person, he had to integrate his previous ways of knowing with this new way of knowing. In much the same way, first graders, as emergent mathematical thinkers, are learning a new way of knowing or seeing the world.

It is in their development of conceptual frameworks or constructs that we may be shortchanging our students. Consider how, as teachers or parents, we often go about teaching addition and substraction. We tell students that addition is "putting together," or that substraction is "taking away." At the same time, we show these concepts — for example, that addition is "putting together" by using unifix cubes, or toy cars, or groups of students. We probably also point out examples of these concepts in everyday life. Then, when we think students are ready, we move to symbolic representation — written number sentences: 2+3=5. After a while, most students become very good at "doing" addition and substraction. I wonder, though, whether we give them the time and opportunities for thorough concept development — for building constructs of addition and subtraction that they can use in interpreting their own worlds.

Let me explain with an example from my classroom this year. By December, we had been working on addition and subtraction for nearly two months and my students had done many activities to develop an understanding of these concepts. For instance, they had worked with math happenings, they had written stories to correspond to particular number sentences, and they had represented number sentences with a variety of concrete objects, from highly representational ones (e.g., toy cars) to more abstract ones (e.g., pattern blocks or tally marks). Students had begun to develop recall of basic facts, and they could do written addition or subtraction facts. They seemed well on their way to mastery of these operations.

But I felt there was another piece to the puzzle, and I approached it this way: I began to tell stories involving addition and subtraction, asking my students to determine which operation the stories involved. A typical story might be:

> *I went to the park near my house yesterday. There were some people sitting on a bench. I counted them, and there were five. Then I saw two people on another bench. I knew that there were seven people on the benches.*

One might expect, given how much exposure my students had had to addition and subtraction, they would select the operation easily. But that wasn't the case — not then, and not (for some students) for a very long time afterward. Rather, students were cautious in their responses, often seeming unsure of whether a particular story represented addition or subtraction. Many of these students were "doing" addition and subtraction quite capably, but most did not have an understanding of the operations that would allow them to interpret the world in terms of them.

To me, this indicates that students were still building their conceptualizations of these operations. They "knew" particulars about addition–for instance, that addition is "putting together," that three and three makes six, or that if you put one group with another you'll get a larger group — but they didn't necessarily know what addition "looked like." That is, they could do the computation and they had some understanding of the concepts, but they were not yet consistently able to use those learnings as tools to analyze or understand the world. They could **do** addition, but they couldn't quite *see* addition. Their "addition" and "subtraction" constructs were... under construction.

The next question must be, "How do we help students develop the conceptual understanding they need in order to view the world mathematically?"

V. Implications

What I am saying in all of this is that my first graders, as emergent mathematical thinkers, are learning to think like mathematicians about the world. This involves learning principles — in their case, the mathematics of first grade — in much the same way, for instance, that Virgil learned the visual qualities of a cylinder. It also involves learning how to see the world in terms of those principles, just as Virgil learned how to apply his "cylinder construct" to his field of visual perceptions in order to find the circular hole that the cylinder would fit.

When I consider how to help my students develop a mathematical view of the world, three issues stand out: experience, talk, and time.

First of all, first graders need to confront a mathematical idea many times before they begin to see the world in terms of that construct. They need to encounter mathematical content in varied contexts, applications, and situations if they are to build a foundation of understanding. They also need the math of real life isolated, highlighted, called attention to, so that they can see it and learn to interpret it in terms of the mathematics they are learning at school. They need these mathematical experiences so that they can forge crucial connections between the real world and the world of mathematical thinking.

Talk can be important in the development of mathematical thinking, too. The more students can articulate what they know and don't know, the more they begin to clarify their thinking. The more they are encouraged to talk about their thinking, the more they begin to notice that thinking. The more they hear the variety of ways that their classmates make connections between school math and the world, the more they see the value of their own connections.

And finally, it takes time for students to become adept at viewing the world mathematically. It is a gradual process, and most of the time we can't see the small shifts that students make as they add to their understanding. I caught Lisa and Dylan at the precise moment that they began to "see" math happenings; often, we miss moments like that in the jumble of daily classroom life. I have to remember to give students the time they need in order for concept building to occur, even when I can't see it occurring.

First graders come to us not yet ready to see a great deal, but able to build. We can't tell them how to interpret the world mathematically, but we can present the world so that its mathematical outlines are crisp. We can provide our students with opportunities to do the work of careful looking and to describe what they see. We can listen to those descriptions to understand at what stage our students' concept building may be and to determine what parts of the world may need more definition before students can interpret them as mathematics. We can assist students and cheer them on as they attempt to do what mathematicians do and think as mathematicians think.

First graders are fledgling members of the mathematics club. Working with them to develop their understanding, we provide the opportunities and guided experiences that will enable them to see the world through the same mathematical lens we have learned to use. For some it's a long process; for others, much briefer. No matter. We welcome each of these new mathematical thinkers, remembering that we were once novices, too.

REFERENCES

Duckworth, E. (1987). *"The having of wonderful ideas" and other essays on teaching and learning.* New York: Teachers College Press.

Sacks, O. (1995). *An anthropologist on Mars: Seven paradoxical tales.* New York: Alfred A. Knopf.

Smith, F. (1988). *Joining the literacy club: Further essays into education.* Westport, CT: Heinemann-Boynton/Cook.

Tony Tendero

Tony Tendero participated in a teacher research seminar in his second year of teaching, writing "The Gong Show" as a report of his research. For several years he led a teacher research group at the middle school where he taught and began thinking increasingly about disconnections between students' lives and their schools, particularly in the middle school years. Eventually his interests led him to enroll in the doctoral program at Teachers College of Columbia University, where he studied and worked with beginning teachers as they did their practice teaching. Through this opportunity to read and think with colleagues, he saw his research interests as including teacher research, collaborative teaching, beginning teaching, and the political and social role of the teacher in the classroom.

> *Identifying some of the gaps between then and now has been useful for me as I consider how I tell my research story. While I still look to share what I've come to know and practice, I now hope to avoid a singularly triumphant teacher success narrative. I am attempting to trouble my assumptions and sure understandings in the way that I tell the stories of my work. For example, in "The Gong Show," I see places where if I were writing today, I might interrogate assumptions through more data collection and narrative voices. One example might be the effects of and struggles over power in my classroom.*
>
> *Through my teacher research, I live the questions about my practice, learn from my students, reflect on my teaching moves, tell stories about my teaching, and all of this began with my performance on the Gong Show.*

Tendero, and other teacher-researchers like him, are searching for answers not just to classroom problems, but to how classrooms fit into schools and schools fit into society. As Tendero said, "It just keeps getting more and more complicated."

THE GONG SHOW: SOME THINGS I LEARNED ABOUT THE EVALUATION OF WRITING

Tony Tendero

Grades. There is something ominous about that word. It is like a huge gong, tolling doom to all those who can't quite cut it. The gong goes off and WHACK! Your ears are shattered but only if you aren't absolutely perfect. If you are, then you will have in your possession two of the finest earplugs ever made totally blotting out the sound of the gong. The only cost… assignment in on time, flawless, and you have to memorize everything the instructor said in a 576 hour time to get an A… Only then will you get this coveted pair of earplugs.

— George, grade 8

I hate these beep, beep grades, interims too, I wish they could just go to a far off land. I don't like to hear the word grade it brings great terror into my heart.

— Frank, grade 8

Confusion, Terror, Horror, Nightmares, Worse Nightmares, School, I forgot to do that assignment, I didn't know that's what we were supposed to do, Oh No, What page was that? Who me, No way, oops, I know I should have done it when it was assigned, I was absent, Give me a break, Oh please, I'll do it tomorrow, I guess I should have worked harder, and I always made good grades in elementary school.

— Sally, grade 8

Grades make me feel like it's that time again, it makes you look back on all the bad things you did in the past few weeks… and the concerts and parties that you get invited to this weekend but you can't go, the yelling you get from your parents and the pride you

have to get a better grade next time. That will probably go away next week.
   — Mary, grade 8

Gongs, Cursing, Excuses, and Apathy. With the help of these survey responses and others, I began to remember some of my experiences as a student writer, waiting for the gong. I also began to hear an echo of my experience as a second-year teacher attempting to evaluate writing. What if someone else were to grade my grading of student papers? I wonder what they would think if they looked at Ron's paper where I wrote, "I like what you've done so far with your thoughts on the time when you felt like you couldn't go on. Work more on revision. Try to have your character think on paper, too. Next time I'd like to see you use more details and dialogue in your story. Also work on punctuation and editing for spelling next time. C+." Would they agree with Ron that a "C+" did not make any sense?

I began with a question based on this wondering. *How can I become a better evaluator of writing?* With this question, I happened upon Betsy with a scrunched up face in writing workshop.

"How's it going?"

"I have a bunch of ideas, but they're all boring."

"Hmm… what could you do with this? How about start with your idea then make up an event to change the story? Or you could try and tell this in a poem…"

"I don't know… will I get a bad grade if it's boring?"

"Of course not. First just work on getting something down on paper."

Later that day, I wrote in my journal, "If a piece is boring, I won't want to read it or respond to it. And it would seem like the writer didn't put much into the piece. What role does interest play in the evaluation of writing? Who determines what is interesting? What is it in terms of style or content that makes a piece interesting? How will this be determined? What is the effect on evaluation if these criteria are unclear?"

With these additional questions, I decided to create a structure that might facilitate the inclusion of student voices in the evaluation process where some of these criteria were determined. I set up time for conferring on a finalized piece with each student. While other students were working on individual pieces, I met with each student over the course of two weeks. For my part of the evaluation, I discussed a couple of skills that they were using effectively and a couple of skills that I would like them to develop. After that, we looked over a goal sheet where each student had set goals for themselves in writing workshop. From this sheet we set goals together, negotiating things such as the number of exploratory drafts to be completed in the upcoming quarter.

These conferences began to nudge me in some particular ways. One example of this nudging was my conference with Betsy. I began in my journal:

> *My conference with Betsy was a pain in the butt. She whined to me that she wasn't a good reader or writer... that she was a slow reader. Each whine came in response to a goal that I tried to articulate based on our conversation. As we discussed her perfected piece, I said, 'One skill I'd like you to work on would be to tighten your focus. Instead of telling fifteen different stories of your trip, focus on one."*
>
> *"I've never been good at writing details. I either write too much or too little."*
>
> *She is so damn passive-resistant. Her only response in conference was that scrunched up face.*

But as I thought more about this difficult conference and this journal entry, I wondered whether she might actually be participating in this conference. Her whines were struggling to get into my definition of evaluation. She was definitely feeling underconfident and pushed beyond her ability with each goal. I needed to consider this and respond. This seemed to have something to do with evaluation.

I went back to my students for some more information in late November. In my second survey, I asked students to discuss their experience with the evaluation of writing:

◆   *I think the best thing would be for a teacher to get to know each of the students and be able to judge their work by knowing their goals and limits.*

- *The worst thing a teacher could do is to mark a paper down because they don't understand it.*

- *A good way to evaluate would be to watch people carefully, see if they were working hard and get to know the students.*

- *It sucks if your teacher doesn't know you and doesn't know what you are doing and unfairly judges you.*

- *One time I really tried on a project and I got a C. I was totally disappointed. I deserved better. I had trouble with it, but I really tried. She never knew how much I tried.*

The students named the action of "knowing" to be of particular importance. I started to wonder whether my struggles with Betsy were partly based on not "knowing." Furthermore, in this move of asking students to tell me about what they know about evaluation, I found their voices helping me to create some of the very structures that would generate the evaluation of their writing.

At this point, I wanted to attempt to negotiate with students over the criteria that comprised their evaluation. Building on a discussion in which I had participated during the Northern Virginia Writing Project's conference on evaluation, I assigned students a paper called a "book letter" in which I wrote my own version and presented it to the class. I said, "Okay. Based on my example of a book letter, what are some of the characteristics or criteria for a good book letter?"

"How long should we talk about it... should we give it away?"

"No... he did a brief summary."

"We need to make personal connections."

"Don't we got to talk about a quote or something?"

Later I asked, "Okay, is there anything missing or anything that you think we should add?"

"What about stuff like spelling and grammar?"

Ten students yelled, "NO!"

"Why'd you have to say that Erin? You're such a suckup.'

"It's important. People won't understand what you're saying if you don't do it right."

I intervened. "First of all, instead of looking at it in terms of using stuff you may have learned from the grammar book, let's use the term 'technique.' The technique of a writer. Writers are crafters. They need proper techniques to express their ideas fully. Think of it in terms of how your wonderful ideas might not be understood if you don't work on your technique. And remember, we still have to decide how important each one of these parts is." The discussion continued.

"Should it matter if it's on time?"

"I think that's really important."

"But what if it's a great letter and the person put a lot of time in on it and it was late?"

"Too bad."

I intervened again. "Anything else? Okay. Nominations for the least or most important?"

"Spelling should be down at the bottom."

"Grammar too?"

"Yeah, that technique thing should be last."

In looking back at this particular piece of data, I saw myself understanding a little bit more about the role of negotiation in evaluation. There would be times when the class would agree to things I valued such as turning work in on time. At other times, they might override things I thought were important such as the comparative importance of technique. Finally, I also came to realize that I was responsible for being part of this process and for making sure technique or revision are part of the criteria despite the move for elimination. I would not abdicate my role as teacher and final evaluator; however, I would listen and adjust based on conversation and persuasion.

In the second quarter, I decided to add another move to my evaluation repertoire. I wanted students to engage in a written self-evaluation which would inform my evaluation. Because of time constraints, I gave them the criteria which I had set for their final drafts. Their part of the negotiation would be in the final reading of the paper. Jill wrote the following about "6th Grade Camp":

It's about a lot of 6th graders going on a field trip for 3 days and having a lot of fun doing wild things and having a great time. I think I did the best with adding detail and putting information in it! It helps to understand and not confuse anyone who reads it. I noticed, when it was too late, that I need to put paragraphs in it. That's a bad habit I need to brake and hopefully I'll do better on my next piece.

I just need to use a blue pen but didn't have one so I just keep needing to boro one from someone and I keep drifting off in space (boys). I earned a 90. I have put in a lot of effort and time. I did it slowly so I could do it right so it could be my best. I have probably done the most work on this than any other.

Jill had entered into the negotiation. She saw detail and effort as her main criteria for success. She also helped me to know her, and the distractions boys were causing her. Finally, she shared with me her thoughts on her history as a writer. From her perspective, she had worked her hardest. I agreed.

Diane wrote about her poem "Jonathan and Me":

"Jonathan and Me" is about last summer when my friend and I were talking at the beach. I explained my situation well with the form of the poem, because even Mr. Tendero understood what I was trying to say and do. I would like to put all my mingled emotions on paper so the reader feels the heartbreak. I had difficulty trying to get all of my questions and strong feelings on paper.

98 in writing overall. I have improved but in these particular pieces, I have made them not as boring and "oh another Diane poem." In a way, I learned a lot about my feelings, by expressing and talking about them through my writing. I enjoyed "Jonathan and Me" because it made me feel free of confusion and helplessness when I wrote it.

Diane shared why the piece was of value to her as a writer and a person. She was able to come up with examples to support her evaluation. "Oh, another Diane poem" evokes such particularities for me, and I received fresh views of the writing. I also found the possibility for students to participate in the evaluation at a number of points from the structure, to the criteria, to the ending evaluation. And with each of these supports, I found myself as the evaluator becoming less and less fearful of the gong.

With some of these emerging ideas, I became convinced that I needed to return to students who had been informing my teaching at various points during the year. I chose three students who might provide me with some range of understanding — Karen, Matt and Bob.

I knew Karen was a good student and a good writer. Her parents' extensive experience in writing and editorial work had given her models of using reading and writing in real life situations. As we spoke, I became more aware of her sophistication. She had set up some unique ways to evaluate based on her past experiences with teachers.

> *Using good punctuation and seeing if they've followed the teacher's guidelines are the most important ways to evaluate… all of my teachers say, make sure you punctuate well… and of course if you follow the teacher's guidelines your piece will sound better.*

For Karen it seemed like her notions of evaluation began with the considerations of the teacher/reader. She also seemed to know a lot about the negotiations that evaluation involved.

> *Grades on writing seem to lose their meaning. It seems like you go to school just to get a good grade. And then I know a lot of my friends who try really hard and don't get an A or a B. Most teachers in this school don't grade on effort. They grade on what the final paper looks like. Styles, adjectives, etc. I mean what if they (the students) were never taught this?*
>
> *I think the teacher should try and understand what the person has gone through in order to get to this point, in order to try and get it to be a perfect paper. It may not be. It may be in their mind but not in the teacher's mind. So I think they (teachers) should consider what this person thinks a perfect paper is. Of course, the student needs to consider this (what the teacher thinks is a perfect paper) also.*

In this response, Karen started to help me see that there might be different ways of reading a text. The implications for evaluation seemed weighty.Later she bridged my interest in "boringness" to evaluation and negotiation.

> *Teachers should try and encourage the writers to make the writing interesting. But, most seventh, eighth and ninth graders aren't necessarily good enough writers to make their writing interesting. They haven't had enough experience. Plus there are so many different perceptions of what interesting is.*

This connection built upon one interest. My other interest in "knowing" was informed by Karen's experience with knowing and evaluation.

> *I'm an easy student to know. Teachers have known what I've liked as far as paper topics. They know what to expect from me. I like to stick to the facts. My 6th grade teacher knew this when she assigned me my research topic on Egypt. She gave me a large topic because she knew that I liked to go in depth. She also knew my personality and what to expect from me.*

With this interview with Karen, I found support for my emerging understandings about knowing and negotiations. However with Matt and Bob, I began to find some other dimensions to explore.

I was interested in talking to Matt because he significantly improved his grade from a D in the first quarter to a B+ in the second quarter. His interests in basketball and girls seemed to dominate his time. In talking about evaluation and writing, Matt had this story to tell about a time when he received what he felt was an unfair evaluation of his writing:

> *I thought it was good. Other kids thought it was good, but we didn't see the grammar mistakes that the teacher did. The kids didn't care about the grammar. I feel if the story's written and the grammar's not good, yet it's a good story, you can always go back and put it on the computer and spell check it. If they just turned in a rough draft then that's different. But if they tried… I mean went back and proofread it. I guess unless you are ready for a publishing stage I wouldn't bother with the grammar correction.*

Matt then broadened his observations.

> *Grades are based on memorization and homework, not learning. This is most every class. You never know why an answer is or how, it's just that it is. A lot of times you'll learn facts that won't do you any good until three years later. I think our schools aren't the best because they can't afford a more individualized system. I think the individualized goals we tried last quarter were important. Not everyone has the same skill or speed. But there's no way that financially they could do this... but this would be the best way. It's important because its coming from the fact that the teacher knows you... Not so much that you're friends... but it's not that easy to find a teacher that a student can relate to... sometimes teachers aren't exactly into normal things (or things we're into)... so when they can relate, they are able to set better goals and grade more effectively...*
>
> *And even if they didn't know them so personally, the teachers need to at least know what they've done in other places. Other teachers in the same grade level talking back and forth helps a teacher to know a student better... as far as portfolios from past years goes, they are all right, but people do change and improve...*
>
> *Conferencing was something that helped me... especially when I conference with a teacher.... Written comments are good too. It depends on the student. Some students like being with the teacher in conference, others think it's too personal and they're embarrassed. There are different ways of knowing and responding to students.*

Matt's different ways of knowing extended some of Karen's initial perspectives. After interviewing Bob, I began to see that the dimensions of evaluation had even more complexity than first imagined.

Out of all my students, Bob is the one student who can frustrate me at the drop of a hat. He is keenly aware of this. He is among my most skilled students, especially in reading, yet his grades have been extremely low. The grades are reflective of a lack of work. Lately, he has improved his grades under threat of no Christmas presents and the restriction of not being able to read at home.

I just try and do average. I don't want to be a fool or a genius. I work on getting C's, just to keep my dad off my case. If I come home with C's on the report card, he won't yell, he'll say, "Just do better."… He's a perfectionist for sure. He says a draft has to be perfect the first time. When he's writing he types, CLICK-CLICK-CLICK, then he makes a mistake and throws it out. One time I was working on "Wishful Thinking" [a recent piece about life as an inmate in the Miami State Penitentiary, which Bob sees as his best piece of writing]. I wanted to show him when I was on the eighth page, but he said, "No. I don't want to see it until it's perfect. I don't want to see any piece of junk writing."

… Overall, I can't say whether I'm a trashy writer or a skilled writer, or an average writer. A year ago I would say I was a trashy writer. I think it mostly depends on the topic and whether I like it. Sometimes I write trashy ones just as a joke. I'll write stuff that's trash when I'm in a bad mood or in trouble with the principal. I'll usually be sitting there, pissed off over what my mom said, or how my dad hugely favors my sister…

In kindergarten, all the teachers knew you. But you didn't get graded. Since then, I don't think any of the teachers have known me. I use a lot of different styles in my writing. Sometimes I'll show my sadistic hard side, and sometimes I'll show my soft caring style. No teachers really know me. Sometimes conferencing helps though. The teacher can see and hear my reactions while the conferencing gives me an idea of what the evaluation might be… but I still have time to work on the things to fix, if I feel like it. I would say that individualized goals are good also, if I can set them, because the writer knows best what they can do. If the teacher sets the goals without really knowing the students then I would think to myself, "Why do I want to give that to them? What are they going to give me?"… Having my Dad say he's proud of me that's the biggest motivation. I can't remember him saying that about one subject or piece of writing. If he could say, "That was good," about one thing, that would be good.

Through the interviews I had a much better take on how these three students think and write. I am more confident in how to evaluate them. Knowing them helps me to negotiate with them over criteria. I have seen some of this knowing and negotiation come into play with my I-Search papers. Karen choose the I-Search question, "Why are memories more important to some people?" It was a rather ambiguous topic, but I was able to discuss with her how she might pursue it and how I might evaluate her first draft. With the criteria set, she was able to feel comfortable about rambling on in her first draft without paralyzing herself with anxiety over whether she was doing it correctly. Karen knows the criteria which have been established, and the gong will not toll for her.

In talking with Matt, I was able to hear about how he was growing in confidence concerning his fluency and his editing skills. Thus as he writes (if he turns in his draft) I can push him. Currently he hasn't turned in his I-Search draft. Just when I thought he had seen some relevance in the process, he turns around and chooses not to do it. I guess a fairer evaluation isn't the sole determiner whether someone will see the writing and evaluation process as legitimate. His peers influence him a great deal as they did in the episode with the "unfairly" graded paper.

With Bob, I now see a boy who goes in and out of buying into the process of the classroom and writing. His father is now working in another city. Bob still hasn't turned in his I-Search draft. Evaluation seems to have lost its meaning for him. Perhaps he does not have something that he likes to write about for his paper. He might be writing something "trashy" again, for kicks. I do see him in need of support with his writing. He needs someone to balance out the critical judge sitting on his shoulder. And this is something that I will keep in mind in my evaluation, if his first draft ever comes in. Bob teaches me to step back and see some of the larger negotiations that might go on in and beyond the classroom. "What are they going to give me, if I give them this?" It's a question with some potentially unsettling responses.

It has been a little over six months now since I have taken up this subject of evaluation. As I typed my exploratory draft, I recalled my many struggles. Over this time, I have jumped from an inquiry into *What are the effects of self-evaluation on writing?* to *What is evaluation (can revision or conferring qualify as part of evaluation)?* to *How can I have students participate in the construction of an evaluation system?* to *What part does knowing and liking play in evaluation?* The whole time I was looking at my students and my classroom. But I was neglecting another person in the relationship. Me. Finally I asked, *How can I do a better job evaluating writing?*

This realization of myself as a subject of study leads me to now see my classroom in a new light. I see a number of parties in this evaluation process. Four of the principal parties are the student/writer, the teacher/reader, the text itself and the home reader. These relationships are negotiated. For me to be a better evaluator, I must be aware of these relationships.

With some of these research findings, I am beginning to see how theory can add some dimensions to my understandings. "Post-structuralism" is a word that I've run across in discussions and journals. As I consider it in the context of writing evaluation, I am starting to see some relevance for a word that I have disdained for its pretentiousness.

My beginning understandings indicate that readers and writers compose the text. The readers are writing the text by filling in the gaps with their personal interpretations. (Reading between the lines leaps to mind.) Depending on what Stanley Fish calls their "interpretive communitiy (e.g., teacher, student, boss, employee, academic, politician, etc.), they will fill in the gaps differently (Fish, 1980). Teachers are looking for a certain perfect paper, while students are looking to write a paper where different people (teachers, other students, parents, etc.) will have different interpretations. They straddle a number of different gaps.

What I have learned is that evaluation of writing is based in relationship. The process is messy. These relationships lead to inefficiency due to human variables. As we try and streamline evaluation processes with some cookie-cutter process for the nation, I see us sacrificing these relationships that are necessary for effective evaluation.

Knowing the writer is a key factor in evaluation. In-process and ending conferences along with student self-evaluation will give me a broader understanding of my students and their writing. This highlight on knowing will also have implications for the classroom. As I look at my five classrooms, it is in my smallest one, with twenty-one students, that I have the best possibility for knowing my students. While no stunning revelation, this means that as the need for more accurate evaluation is raised, the need for manageable classroom size is a must. How can we hope to evaluate in an accurate manner if we are doomed before we start? In my classes of twenty-seven students, the gong is dangerously close to striking me and my students and I haven't even started looking at papers.

In the day to day dealings of my classroom, I have used some terms which help. **Decision points**, as places where evaluation occurs, are very helpful. I start to imagine the specific times when these opportunities could occur. There will be evaluation in process as students write. These moves could include quick conferences, group shares, check-offs, writers' self-revisions, etc. **Reactions of the reader** are the basis for these evaluations as the reader gives personal responses about how the text affects the reader. **Ending evaluations** occur after students are (somewhat) satisfied with the work they have done. Here I will include self-evaluations, final teacher conferences, group evaluations and my own evaluation. These evaluations will be determined by criteria. These criteria will be negotiated by our different interpretive communities.

In addition to these practices, I will attempt to integrate a couple of other teaching moves based on my research findings.

- Work with the above terms in an effort to help students be more fluent in the language of evaluation and to improve their metacognitive ability to look at their writing.
- Work with students on how to improve their conferring skills in order to shift some of the response load for earlier drafts to students.
- Develop portfolios to enable students to get some sense of what is interesting in their writing and what they would like to abandon.
- Conduct ongoing surveys, interviews, and semester evaluations of my teaching to inform revisions of classroom practices.

- ◆ Find some practices which can integrate parents and the community into discussions of good writing.

If we look at the implications of these emerging understandings of evaluation for our larger society, the echoes could be far-reaching, authorities of the good and the true being called into question. Those who are usually voiceless and often evaluated could make themselves heard in the discourse of power. Three possible scenarios come to mind as a result of this din:

1. In struggles over evaluation and power, certain interests could emerge on top and install their particular hierarchies of evaluation.
2. The push for each person to simply evaluate herself with no connection to others could emerge.
3. As an interpretive community, we could slug it out over evaluation, in as civil and humble a manner as possible, to create something of value for each member.

For myself, this third idea holds the most hope in terms of writing, evaluation, and life together, yet its fragility requires contant care.

Each time I read over my paper and reach this point, I return to my opening four quotes. If we are to become better writers and evaluators of writing, those gongs, the cursing, the excuses and the apathy must be stopped for the evaluated and the evaluators. Then, maybe, we can start talking about what we value. We can start filling in the gaps together. We can finally turn off The Gong Show re-runs.

REFERENCE

Fish, S. (1980). *Is there a text in this class? The authority of interpretive communities*. Cambridge, MA: Harvard University Press.

PART IV

RESOURCES

In addition to explaining teacher research processes, we want this book to introduce you to the teacher research community and suggest resources that will support you as you become a part of it. We have divided the resources into four general categories as follows:

- ❏ **Networks**, both online and off, where other teacher-researchers offer discussion, response, and drafts of their work.
- ❏ **Grants** available to teacher-researchers and teacher research projects.
- ❏ **Courses and contexts** for conducting teacher research.
- ❏ A **bibliography** of suggested reading.

Networks

As soon as you form a teacher research group, you will be part of a network. As the number of teacher-researchers in your area grows, you will develop broader networks organized by the area of your research interest or the area where you work or live. In our experience, however, a separate teacher research network is hard to sustain because the people involved have many professional responsibilities already, so whenever you can, add a teacher research component to an already existing organization. For example, your writing project or your local professional organization might include teacher research as part of its overall program.

You might find that a computer listserv, conference, or an exchange of e-mail addresses is the most practical way to keep in touch with fellow teacher-researchers, and eventually many teacher research networks go online. Online networks enable you to be in touch with teacher-researchers with similar interests as well as experienced researchers who might serve as advisors and answer questions or give you suggestions.

The following list describes various networks that a teacher-researcher living in our area might be a participant in for different purposes:

1. **A SCHOOL DISTRICT WEBSITE, SUCH AS THAT OF THE FAIRFAX COUNTY PUBLIC SCHOOLS**

In our school district, this website is available as a Teacher as Researcher home page linked to the district website. It has a database of teacher-researchers and their work, the current newsletter of the Teacher-Researcher Network, "The Networker," and information about upcoming events and opportunities for local teacher-researchers.

2. **A LOCAL UNIVERSITY WEBSITE SUCH AS THAT OF THE NORTHERN VIRGINIA WRITING PROJECT AT GEORGE MASON UNIVERSITY**

Our writing project website has a teacher-researcher page where items related to the writing project and teacher research are posted. The teacher research page links to the National Writing Project on the internet.
http://www.gmu.edu/departments/nvwp/nvwp.htm

3. **THE NATIONAL WRITING PROJECT (NWP) AT THE UNIVERSITY OF CALIFORNIA AT BERKELEY**

The teacher research pages of the NWP have general information about teacher research including bibliographies. There are many links from this website to other writing projects with teacher research programs.

http://www-gse.berkeley.edu/research/nwp/tchrsrch.html

4. **THE TEACHER AS RESEARCHER SPECIAL INTEREST GROUP (SIG) OF THE AMERICAN EDUCATIONAL RESEARCH ASSOCIATION (AERA)**

This is a growing group of teacher-researchers who are members of AERA. They give presentations at AERA's annual conference and are organized into a special interest group which sponsors sessions and welcomes the ideas of teacher-researchers, K-university. Their pages on the AERA website keep SIG members and other interested people up to date on their activities.

Some members of the SIG attend the International Conference on Teacher Research which is held every year or so on two or three days before or after the AERA conference at a nearby location. Information about the conference and related activities can be found at the SIG's website.

http://aera.net (AERA website with link to Teacher as Researcher site)

http://www.ilstu.edu/depts/labschl/tar (Direct route to Teacher as Researcher SIG site)

We also include the Bread Loaf School of English, Middlebury College, Middlebury, VT 05753 (BLSE@breadnet.middlebury.edu) in our network resources since they have a longstanding degree program that includes teacher research networking both on- and off-line as a major component. Especially significant are their fellowships for rural teachers, which include Breadnet connections so that teachers and students in isolated rural areas from Alaska to Mississippi can connect with each other as they conduct research. They publish the *Bread Loaf Rural Teacher Network Magazine*, which is full of information about the program as well as reports from the research projects.

Finally, we include our own e-mail addresses in hopes that some of you will let us know how your research is coming along, and we will reply. That is how networks start.

marianmohr@aol.com   msmaclean@aol.com

Grants

Basically, teacher research is not an expensive enterprise, except for the one thing you need most — time in your daily schedule for reflection, writing, and meeting with colleagues. That time is very expensive, requiring more money than most grant programs now provide.

That said, however, quite a few sources of funding now support teacher research. They range from local sources such as Parent Teacher Associations to private national foundations such as the Spencer Foundation and the federal government's Department of Education. In our experience, difficulties in securing financial support for teacher research projects are related to finding time to write the grant proposal and figuring out how to spend the money.

Recognizing these difficulties, some organizations and foundations have adapted their grant processes to make them more compatible with a classroom teacher's experience of research. In such situations, your proposal might indicate, for example, that instead of hiring a graduate student as a research assistant as many university researchers do, you plan to hire another teacher to assist you as a member of your research group. Funding for some days of substitute leave time during writing and analysis might be a part of the grant request, or you might ask for support to attend a professional conference to present the findings of your study.

The suggested sources which follow all have an interest in teacher research and invite inquiries, especially from K-12 classroom teachers.

THE SPENCER FOUNDATION: PRACTITIONER RESEARCH COMMUNICATION AND MENTORING GRANTS

875 North Michigan Avenue, Suite 3930
Chicago, Illinois 60611-1803
Telephone: 312-337-7000

Fax: 312-337-0282

http://www.spencer.org

Spencer Foundation grants "seek to strengthen the effectiveness of teacher-researchers and to clarify the uses of teacher research."

OFFICE OF EDUCATIONAL RESEARCH AND IMPROVEMENT (OERI)

U.S. Department of Education

Field Initiated Studies Educational Research Grants

The application process for OERI grants is complicated, but it offers possibilities for groups of teacher-researchers in a school system or in collaboration with a university. We were part of an OERI-funded program from 1994-1997 which gave reassigned time to teacher research leaders in three schools to do their own research and to organize and support teacher research groups in their schools. OERI themes for their proposals change with different years (and different political administrations), and to apply successfully you need to know what they are. Large school systems and most colleges and universities have administrators in charge of grants, and if you are interested in a large, federally funded project, they are a logical source of information and help.

INTERNATIONAL READING ASSOCIATION (IRA) TEACHER AS RESEARCHER GRANTS

Division of Research

800 Barksdale Road, P.O. Box 8139

Newark, Delaware 19714-8139

You must be a member of IRA to be eligible for these grants. They currently go as high as $5,000. Studies must be focused on reading, writing, or literacy. Write to the above address for guidelines, application form, review procedures, and evaluation criteria.

NATIONAL COUNCIL OF TEACHERS OF ENGLISH (NCTE) RESEARCH FOUNDATION TEACHER-RESEARCHER GRANTS

Project Assistant, Researcher Program

NCTE Research Foundation

1111 W. Kenyon Road
Urbana, IL 61801-1096
Telephone: 217-328-3870

These grants also currently go up to $5,000. One of the earliest sources for teacher-researcher grants, the Research Foundation recently revised its application procedure to better accommodate teacher research proposals. The Foundation gives workshops at NCTE's national conference to answer questions about proposals.

THE VOICE

This newsletter of the National Writing Project publishes a regular boxed column called "Grant Opportunities," which is a rich source for exploration. Although the funding sources are not all knowledgeable about teacher research, they do support educational efforts that teachers initiate. The column also lists calls for proposals from various foundations and the government. Keep a file of these columns for future reference.

LOCAL POSSIBILITIES

Your own school system might support Impact II grants and include teacher-researchers as possible candidates. Local professional organizations are another possible source. In Virginia, where we live, both the local and state reading associations offer teacher research grants and publish teacher research articles and reports in their journals. Depending upon the amount of money you seek, other local sources that are interested in promoting education might consider offering a teacher research grant, sources such as the American Association of University Women or Phi Delta Kappa.

— ◆ —

Most grant funding agencies describe what they will not fund and give examples of funded projects. For example, the NCTE Research Foundation states:

> *Applicants must be members of NCTE. Projects or studies that do not focus on the teaching or learning of English/Language Arts are not eligible for funding. Grants are not intended to fund permanent equip-*

ment or commercial teaching materials, or to support research con-
ducted as part of a degree program below the doctoral dissertation level.

Funding agencies do not so often give suggestions for what can be funded. Here are some things to think about:

- Hire a colleague or two as research assistants to meet with you after school to read your work, help you code and categorize, and respond to your article drafts. Some teacher-researchers have also hired students (not from the class where the research is being conducted) as research assistants. They receive valuable learning in collecting and analyzing data and offer valuable insights to the teacher-researcher.

- Plan how many substitute leave days you can afford to take — we think four a year is the maximum and that is the limit for both the NCTE and IRA grants — and ask for money to pay a substitute for those days. You may even want to hire a substitute for a day you remain in school to observe and document, while your colleague teaches.

- Do you need a particular book to help you complete your research that is not available locally? Add that book to your proposal.

- Long distance telephone calls related to your research could be funded.

- If you want to use a consultant or mentor in your field, you can ask for funding to pay a stipend or honorarium.

- Most clerical costs can be paid for by grant money. You can buy audio and videotapes and pay to have them coded or transcribed, even though you will, of course, need to examine them closely yourself. If you use paper and copying machines at your school, reimburse the school. Or, if it is more convenient, copy commercially.

- Travel costs, especially to conferences, are usually *not* funded, but that varies.

Grant proposal writing is very difficult to do on a teacher's schedule, but it is also something that you can receive help with once you have conceived of the research project. See if there is someone experienced with grant writing — possibly your writing project director or someone in your school district — to look over your proposal and give you some response on its strengths and weaknesses. Most school districts have channels through which grant applications flow, and along the way there may be someone who can help you as well.

A last word on grant funding. If your proposal is turned down, don't give up on it. Be sure to read the criticism you received from the readers of your proposal. There are so many reasons a proposal may not be funded in a particular year that, when you have a proposal you believe in, you should revise it and resubmit to another source of funding. And still another if that one doesn't work out. Good luck.

Courses and Contexts

The most common initial experiences for most teacher-researchers are either graduate school courses or small groups in individual schools. We started out with a graduate course sponsored by our writing project and offered for graduate credit through a university and our school system. This was the original graduate seminar in teacher research that we have referred to often, the one which was the core of our previous book, *Working Together*.

What you will find here are descriptions of the courses, the school-based programs, and the university degree programs that we know the best, ones that developed over the years in Northern Virginia. We hope they are a useful starting point for your own planning.

Courses

The teacher-researcher seminar is offered for three graduate credits, spread out over a year's time and ending sometime in May, before the closing activities of the school year. The seminar meets bi-weekly, usually from 4:00-7:00 P.M., with a break for supper and talk. Members of the small research response groups within the seminar may hold additional meetings, talk on the phone, or e-mail each other, especially as the time nears for the deadline drafts to be completed.

Research in Language and Learning: A Teacher-Researcher Seminar

George Mason University English/Education 696

The purpose of this course is to assist teachers in conducting research with students in their classrooms to gain a better understanding of teaching, language, and learning. As they conduct their own studies, participants will become acquainted with the methods and findings of language and learning research. Class sessions will include discussions of readings, reports from guest researchers, and meetings of small research support and response groups. In the research response and support groups, participants will read, discuss, and offer suggestions about each other's research, also serving as sounding boards for developing ideas and theories.

In addition to research response and support group participation, assignments of the course include a research log of regular writing about the research process, reading of selected research articles and leading a class discussion of at least one, a research report based on the research study, and a final brief informal oral report of the individual research process in relation to the results. Teacher-researchers usually conclude the course with a publication dinner party.

Teachers sometimes took the course twice (once for English and once for education credit) and some went on to start research groups in their schools. The original participants were almost all teacher consultants with the Northern Virginia Writing Project. Eventually, however, more people became interested in doing classroom research who did not have a writing background and were uneasy about doing any writing at all.

To respond to the needs of these teachers, Betsy Sanford and Lynn Shafer, both elementary school teacher-researchers, designed a course to encourage teachers from many disciplines, including elementary school teachers, to write reflectively and to conduct research. Their two-part course is sponsored by the school district as a professional development activity and offers participants recertification points.

Introduction to Teacher Research and Reflective Practice

Part I. The first part of the course offers a brief overview of teacher research. Participants will hear from experienced teacher-researchers, read articles of and about teacher research, and be introduced to qualitative research methodologies.

Part II. The second part of the course is intended both to help classroom teachers, specialists, and administrators develop strategies for reflecting on their practice and to introduce them to some of the methods of teacher research. Participants will focus on areas of their practice related to teaching and learning. They will explore these areas for the length of the course using strategies of reflective practice and teacher research: in particular, observation, note-taking, interviewing, and reflective writing. A significant feature of this course will be the time spent in whole group and small group discussion, which will give participants the opportunity to deepen their understanding of reflective practice as they work collaboratively and individually to develop clarity and increased knowledge about particular aspects of teaching and learning.

The next course developed out of the increased number of school-based teacher research groups led by teacher-researchers in those schools. The leaders had begun meeting as a small informal network to discuss problems and strategies and to offer each other support. To respond to their needs, the teacher research leadership course was designed by Mohr and her colleague, Courtney Rogers, with suggestions from the original group of teacher leaders.

Leading Teacher Research Groups

Part I. This course provides experienced teacher-researchers with guided experience in leading a teacher research project in a school or across sites. Each monthly class meeting will focus on a topic, such as data analysis strategies, ethics in teacher research, or responding to colleagues' research drafts, appropriate to the time of year in a teacher research process. Class meetings will also provide problem solving and support systems for the participants as they work with their groups. An exchange and study of information and materials about teacher research and adult education and professional development will also be part of the course content.

Part II. This intensive two-week course will focus on one of the two topics (chosen by the participant):

- reading and studying background materials related to teacher research; or
- revising and preparing an article on teacher research for publication.

In either case participants will work on a previously identified project in one of the two categories above with the help of experienced colleagues. Each participant will belong to a small group for discussion of readings and writings.

Prerequisite: Experience in conducting teacher research.

Part I of the course runs during the school year, with ten 3- hour meetings once a month. Part II consists of 5 meetings of 3 hours each in the two weeks immediately after the end of school in late June. Participants are encouraged to take the course with a partner from the same school.

SCHOOL-BASED PROGRAMS

School-based teacher research groups as we know them have three to fifteen members and are made up of teachers from the same school or include some teachers from nearby schools where there are not enough researchers to make a full group. The participants may or may not receive credit, depending on how recertification and professional development are viewed in their district. The groups usually are started by one or more teachers in the school who have had previous experience with teacher research (perhaps in a graduate course) and wish to continue their work with the support of colleagues. Often these individuals agree to lead the group.

The calendar of a school-based group is similar to that of the graduate seminar. Groups meet about every three weeks, making adjustments for the school year (no meetings the week grades are due, for example), and they usually hold one meeting in August before school starts to get acquainted and make plans. On three or four occasions during the year the group takes substitute leave to work together for a day away from school or alone in a place conducive to writing and analysis.

Some of these groups have begun because of the original interest of an administrator either in or outside the school who may or may not attend the groups' meetings, but who offers support to them in the form of additional information and leave time. School administrators also offer support by making the activity of teacher research an important, recognized part of the school program. Their support can range from simply including the group on the school calendar (an important sign of legitimacy in most schools) to reading and helping to disseminate teacher research throughout the school. Some administrators have arranged for book distribution celebrations when the group publishes their research articles or school-wide inservice meetings where colleagues can learn about the teacher-researchers' work. Once school administrators recognize the value of teacher research in their schools, they may include teacher research as part of the school's planning and evaluation procedure as well as its professional development program.

School-based teacher research programs also begin as professional development programs within a school district. Such programs are sponsored by the school district and teachers receive recertification or salary credit for their participation. In Frederick County, Virginia, a small school district near Winchester, such a program was initiated by a teacher and an assistant superintendent in charge of professional development programs. In Arlington County, Virginia, another nearby district, teachers active in the National Education Association developed a plan for including teacher research as an option in a professional development cycle that was introduced as a way of evaluating teachers in the system. The staff development coordinator and the superintendent supported their efforts.

Large school systems such as Fairfax County, where we work, support research groups of teachers from neighboring schools as well as groups from the same school. Groups have also formed based on a common research interest, such as one which concentrated its efforts on parent participation in their children's education. These are year-long programs and may continue for several years as different teachers join and leave the group.

DEGREE PROGRAMS

In some universities, graduate programs are being redesigned to include teacher research. Teachers can enroll as a school team in a George Mason University masters degree program that includes an individual teacher research project the first year and a team project the second.

An increasing number of college teachers are themselves teacher-researchers and recognize its value to their own understanding of teaching and learning. Cathy Fleischer (1995) in *Composing Teacher-Research: A Prosaic History* and Janet Miller (1990) in *Creating Spaces and Finding Voices: Teachers Collaborating for Empowerment* have written about teacher research in both K-12 and college and university teaching. Both are university professors with a background in teacher research, both offer analyses of the experiences they have had as teacher-researchers and university teachers, and both agree, as Miller and her colleagues write in their introduction, "that teachers' voices, in all their similarities and differences, still are not heard in the clamor for educational reform and in agendas for research on teachers' knowledge."

The principles of teacher research are also working their way into undergraduate teacher preparation programs, and some beginning teachers come to their first jobs looking for a teacher research group to join. Many have kept journals of reflection during their student teaching experiences and some have worked on research projects with experienced teacher-researchers. Damali Pittman, working as an instructional assistant with the special education team at Lemon Road Elementary School during her first year, was familiar with the idea of reflective practice when she came to the school. She joined the teacher research group and did a study of the perceptions of gender roles by the elementary school children she worked with each day.

We have described the courses and contexts with which we are most familiar and briefly indicated how they were developed and supported.

There are other models in other areas of the country and we urge you to learn about as many as you can, adapting what you learn to your own school district's priorities. If you want to create and sustain a teacher research program, we think you need to be able to juggle four variables and answer three questions. The variables are *experience, time, support,* and *questions*; the questions themselves are:

- *What would you like to have for a teacher research program?*
- *What is in existence that supports teacher research?*
- *What stands in the way of a teacher research program?*

After you list the specific variables in your school community that fit into the four categories and write your specific answers to the three questions, you will have created a practical information sheet about your area. When you and your colleagues talk about what you have written down and compare notes, you will find yourself drawing arrows from one spot to another, underlining or highlighting important people or ideas and gradually, you will be on your way to starting and sustaining a teacher research group in your school community.

REFERENCES

Fleischer, C. (1995). *Composing teacher-research: A prosaic history.* Albany, NY: State University of New York Press.

Miller, J.L. (1990). *Creating spaces and finding voices: Teachers collaborating for empowerment.* Albany, NY: State University of New York Press.

Pittman, D. (1997). Seeing is Believing: Student Perceptions of Gender Roles. *Lemon Road Elementary School Teacher-Researcher Project.* Fairfax, County, VA: Fairfax County Public Schools.

Bibliography of Suggested Reading

Reading research and works about research are important to the work of teacher-researchers. Our own ideas have been cobbled together out of our experiences and our reading in various fields. What follows is a short bibliographic essay and a bibliography that acknowledge how readings from different fields have contributed to our ideas about teacher research.

Bibliographic Essay

In this essay we explain the impact of our reading in relation to eight ideas that have influenced our thinking about teachers as researchers. We are grateful to these writers and hope that in our discussion of their ideas we are true to their intentions.

1. CHALLENGING ASSUMPTIONS ABOUT HOW PEOPLE LEARN

Some researchers have served us as exemplars for challenging established, authoritative theories. Margaret Donaldson in *Children's Minds*, Carol Gilligan with *In a Different Voice*, and Mary Belenky, Blythe Clinchy, Nancy Goldberger, and Jill Tarule in *Women's Ways of Knowing* have demonstrated to us the value of assuming a questioning stance, particularly when research marginalizes specific populations or is conducted on marginalized populations.

Donaldson opens *Children's Minds* in this way: "In the course of this book I argue that the evidence now compels us to reject certain features of Jean Piaget's theory of intellectual development. It may seem odd, then, if my first acknowledgement of indebtedness is to a man whose work I criticize.... No theory in science is final; and no one is more fully aware of this than Piaget himself" (p. ix). Similarly, Carol Gilligan's *In a Different Voice* challenges the work of Lawrence Kohlberg by questioning the extent to which the stages of moral development for men are applicable in the moral development of women. Like Donaldson and Gilligan we learned to challenge existing authorities, question traditional assumptions, and rethink what was "known" in order to see what was actually happening and what might happen.

From these researchers and others we also learned to recognize the power differential between the researcher and the researched. We saw that researchers who work with marginalized populations are ethically bound to challenge their assumptions about the relationships between them as part of the study. These researchers served us doubly well when they themselves were, as teachers sometimes are, part of the marginalized populations.

As a teacher determined to understand the task before her, Mina Shaughnessey saw her students and their writing as the subject of her learning. Her work *Errors and Expectations* examines the logic behind the errors made by her freshman (basic) writing students when the City University of New York first implemented its open admissions policies in the 1970s. Instead of using their "deficiencies" and errors as ways to rate their writing as inadequate and failing to meet standards, Shaughnessey assumes the stance of a researcher — a teacher-researcher. By probing and understanding the principles of her students' learning and usage, she challenges her assumptions not only about the teaching of writing but also about her students' abilities and capacities for learning.

Both of us came to Mina Shaughnessey's work through the Northern Virginia Writing Project. Her work served as an important example of the basic principles of the Writing Project — not just about student learning but about how teachers learn. Observing students, writing about teaching, asking questions of students about their learning, and challenging assumptions were all part of our shared experiences as teachers in the writing project — a fertile place for the seeds of teacher research to grow.

2. Using Qualitative, Naturalistic, and Interpretive Research Methods

The concepts of qualitative, naturalistic, and interpretive research are basic to our ideas of teacher research. We both originally learned educational research against the backdrop of experimental and quantitative methodology. When we read Eliot Mishler's question, "Meaning in Context — Is There Any Other Kind?" we recognized a fundamental principle with which we could, as teacher-researchers, agree. When Eliot Eisner asked, "Can Educational Research Inform Educational Practice?" we understood him to mean that, really, there was no useful or meaningful educational research that did not come from the context of the classroom and the teachers and students within it.

The experimental and statistical educational research with which we had been familiar seemed far removed from classrooms. Our own research was grounded in the day-to-day interactions with our students. In the work of Barney Glaser and Anselm Strauss, we recognized the description of such groundedness in their theory-building methodology. Their explanation fit and articulated further our own theory-building methods. In addition to Glaser and Strauss, the work of Egon Guba and Yvonna Lincoln gave us a legitimate research vocabulary — terms like discovery, interpretation, and invited interference. Their work also helped us think about limits to a researcher's claims and approaches to our own involvement in our research.

Mishler, Eisner, Glaser, Strauss, Guba, Lincoln, and others challenged fundamental existing ideas about what research should be and what it should do. Their work helped us conceptualize the broad field of research as one that could include teacher research.

3. WORKING AMID POWER ISSUES AND POLITICS

We recognized that, as teacher-researchers, our work was complicated significantly because of the compulsory and hierarchical nature of public education. How could a teacher not know the answers to questions she asked her students? How could a school principal turn to classroom teachers to discover academic goals for the school? Who would own our research? Who would value it? These questions highlighted the fact that we were in the midst of political issues and that our power to affect those issues was limited. We saw educators and researchers like James Comer, Linda Darling-Hammond, Ann Lieberman, and others including ideas about the political nature of schools as they wrote about educational reform and change.

Other issues we faced as teacher-researchers were political by definition. Paulo Freire's *Pedagogy of the Oppressed* highlighted the political and often risky nature of teaching (and, by extension, teacher research) by describing education and society in terms of power relationships, construction of meaning, and self-determination. Teacher research calls into question the current structure of school systems and the hierarchical system of the profession, for in both of these the knowledge of teachers is not often rated highly either as knowledge or as a basis for decision-making.

4. Redefining Teaching

One of the early "redefiners" of teaching for both of us was Donald Graves, whose 1981 article "Where Have All the Teachers Gone?" expresses the need for teachers to conduct research in their own classrooms. He helped us see teacher interpretations as fundamental to any understanding of teaching and learning in a classroom.

We also found in the work of Lawrence Stenhouse explanations for a way of seeing connections between the processes of teaching and researching. He describes an educational system that is responsive first to the classroom, a radical shift in the relationships within the hierarchy of a school system and the profession in general, a shift that establishes learning and research as the fundamental purposes of education.

Other work that defined teaching and teacher knowledge helped us to conceive of teaching and research together, and also to clarify distinctions between teacher research and other descriptions of teacher knowledge — action research (Ernest Stringer), teacher lore (Stephen North), reflective teaching (Donald Schön) and critical pedagogy (Paulo Friere).

We turned also to occasional papers from the Institute for Research on Teaching (IRT) at the College of Education, Michigan State University. These papers provided us with the work of, among others, Magdalene Lampert, a public school teacher and a university researcher whose "How Do Teachers Manage to Teach? Perspectives on Problems in Practice" introduced us to another researcher reconceptualizing the nature of teaching.

5. Seeing the Classroom as a Field for Anthropology and Ethnography

Similarities exist between teacher research and the fields of anthropology and ethnography. Sometimes laughter ripples through a group of teachers who suddenly imagine themselves anthropologists trying to understand a strange and remote culture — that of their students. Another facet of this point of view, however, is the most important to us — respect for those being studied and their "culture." To understand that students have knowledge of value to the teacher and not just the other way around, that the context of the classroom is shared, is a change of profound importance.

From the work of cultural anthropologist Clifford Geertz we learned to think of "thick description" (*The Interpretation of Cultures*, pp. 3-30) as a way to build credibility for a context-dependent study of a place, like a classroom or a society, and reminded ourselves often to avoid "we-logical, you-confused provincialism" (*Local Knowledge*, p. 149) that applied very well to the world of teaching and schools. We found that much about James Spradley's strategies in *The Ethnographic Interview* made sense (with some adjusting) for teacher-researchers.

In the 1986 *Handbook of Research on Teaching* we discovered that Frederick Erickson had concluded his section on qualitative methods with a description of teacher research and the comment that "Real Women and Men who were school teachers, principals, parents, and students, as well as those who were university-based scholars, might find themselves doing ethnography… as a form of continuing education and institutional transformation in research on teaching" (p.158). We began to see that teacher research was not only redefining teaching, but also research on teaching.

The *Handbook of Research on Teaching* pointed us to other places where we could find other researchers engaged with similar issues — the *Anthropology and Education Quarterly* and the University of Pennsylvania Ethnography in Education Conference. We were developing both practical and theoretical ideas about research methodology that could be useful to teacher-researchers in classrooms.

6. Seeing the Classroom as a Society

Classrooms work as small social organizations as well as small cultures, and therefore another kind of reading that has been useful to us has been social science research. We read through basic introductions to social science research to glean methodological ideas we could adapt from authors like John and Lyn Lofland in *Analyzing Social Settings*. George J. McCall and J. L. Simmons's *Issues in Participant Observation* introduced us to "The Constant Comparative Method of Qualitative Analysis" by Barney Glaser. Ongoing analysis by constant comparison was a method we could use for managing and making use of a research context that we lived with daily for nine or ten months of the year. A teacher's class could be studied as a whole, we saw, as well as smaller groups and individuals within it.

7. CONNECTING TEACHING, PHILOSOPHY, AND LANGUAGE THEORY

Many theoretical works from different fields have contributed to our thinking. Lev Vygotsky's *Thought and Language* and *Mind in Society* have been important in terms of both seeing language as a tool and seeing research as a way of stepping back to reflect and know that we know. His books articulate the role of reflection and use of language in gaining insight and in making assessments about our teaching, but Vygotsky's work also helped us understand the roles of reflection, language, and play in our students' learning.

Michael Polanyi's *Meaning* and *Personal Knowledge* argue that the processes by which we create meaning are those that we implement ourselves, building on our prior knowledge and constructs, and creating a working knowledge that has meaning for us in our own contexts. As a fundamental principle of teacher and student learning, Polanyi's idea underscored for us the importance of having teacher-researchers identify their own questions and of supporting the individual nature of their research purposes.

Readings from the broader context of philosophy and theory — professional journals such as *Educational Researcher*, popular magazines such as *Scientific American*, and books in the fields of literature, science, history, and philosophy — also influenced our understanding of our work. We saw theories of teacher research in places where the authors had no intention of including such ideas. The connections we made resulted from our own questions about how teacher research fit into the larger field of educational research and its standing in theoretical debates like those about positivist thinking and constructivism. Often another teacher-reseacher would bring one of us an article from a totally different context and say, "Read this. It sounds just like teacher research."

8. Teaching and Researching

When they became available, we read books about teacher research itself, works written about the subject by colleagues from whom we have learned much. Dixie Goswami's *Reclaiming the Classroom*, Nancie Atwell's *In the Middle*, and *Inside/Outside* by Marilyn Cochran-Smith and Susan Lytle were especially influential in our thinking, as were responses to our own *Working Together*. We compared our work with that of others interested in teacher research to see how we were alike and different in continuing conversation.

We have advanced our own reading in the fields related to teacher research mostly by continually exchanging books, articles, tapes of speeches, and bibliographies. Mohr once received two books by Clifford Geertz as a birthday present from MacLean. MacLean once returned a book to Mohr that she had discovered on her shelves with "M. Mohr" plainly written on the flyleaf. Mohr discovered the same book on her shelves enscribed "M. MacLean." We have copies of articles that show each other's underlining and highlighting. And, of course, we have talked and talked. As we talked, we examined others' work in the light of our own experiences as teacher-researchers. Always, our practice was our grounding. This process continues, and our wish is that you will have similar opportunities to talk with colleagues about your ideas as you read further in the field.

Bibliography

This bibliography is divided into three sections, each labeled and with a short descriptor. We have included all the works referred to in our bibliographic essay as well as other books that are important to our thinking. We have also included works referenced in the individual chapters of this book unless they were published only in private, limited publications and are not readily available.

A Background for Teacher Research

The following are works about educational research in general which provide a background for understanding theory, research methodology, validity and reliability, writing about research, and adult learning. The emphasis is on qualitative, ethnographic, and naturalistic methods and on works we have found particularly helpful.

Anderson, P. V. (1998). Simple gifts: Ethical issues in the conduct of person-based composition research. *College Composition and Communication, 49* (1), 63-89.

Athanases, S. Z. & Heath, S. B. (1995). Ethnography in the study of the teaching and learning of English. *Research in the Teaching of English, 29*, 263-287.

Bateson, G. (1979). *Mind and nature: A necessary unity.* New York: E. P. Dutton.

Belenky, M. F., Clinchy, B., Goldberger, N. R., & Tarule, J. M. (1986). *Women's ways of knowing.* New York: Basic Books.

Bogdan, R. & Biklin, S. (1992). *Qualitative research for education: An introduction to theory and methods.* (2nd ed.). Boston, MA: Allyn and Bacon.

Comer, J. (1993). *School power: Implications of an intervention project* (2nd ed.). New York: The Free Press.

Darling-Hammond, L. (1996). The quiet revolution: Rethinking teacher development. *Educational Leadership, 53* (6), 4-10.

Delgado-Gaitan, C. (1993). Researching change and changing the researcher. *Harvard Educational Review, 63*, 389-411.

Donaldson, M. (1978). *Children's minds.* New York: Norton.

Duckworth, E. (1986). Teaching as research. *Harvard Educational Review, 56*, 481-495.

Eisner, E. (1984). Can educational research inform educational practice? *Phi Delta Kappan, 65*, 447-452.

Eisner, E. & Peshkin, A. (1990). *Qualitative inquiry in education: The continuing debate.* New York: Teachers College Press.

Ely, M., Vinz, R., Anzul, M., & Downing, M. (1997). *On writing qualitative research: Living by words.* London: Falmer.

Emig, J. (1983). *The web of meaning.* Westport, CT: Heinemann-Boynton/Cook.

Erickson, F. (1986). Qualitative methods. In M. Wittrock (Ed.) *Handbook of research on teaching* (3rd ed., pp. 119-161). New York: Macmillan.

Erickson, F. (1986). *Tasks in times: Objects of study in a natural history of teaching.* Occasional paper #95, Institute for Research on Teaching. East Lansing, MI: Michigan State University.

Freire, P. (1970). *Pedagogy of the oppressed.* M. Ramos (Trans.). New York: Seabury Press.

Geertz, C. (1973). *The interpretation of cultures: Selected essays by Clifford Geertz.* New York: Basic Books.

Geertz, C. (1983). *Local knowledge: Further essays in interpretive anthropology.* New York: Basic Books.

Gilligan, C. (1982). *In a different voice.* Cambridge, MA: Harvard University Press.

Glaser, B. & Strauss, A. (1967). *The discovery of grounded theory: Strategies for qualitative research.* Chicago, IL: Aldine.

Goetz, J., & LeCompte, M. (1984). *Ethnography and qualitative design in educational research.* Orlando, FL: Academic Press.

Graves, D. (1981). *Writing: Teachers and children at work.* Westport, CT: Heinemann-Boynton/Cook.

Guba, E. (1978). *Toward a methodology of naturalistic inquiry in educational evaluation.* Los Angeles, CA: Center for the study of evaluation, UCLA Graduate School of Education.

Harris, J. (1994). The work of others. *College Composition and Communication, 45* (4), 439-440.

Heath, S. B. (1993). The madness(es) of reading and writing ethnography. *Anthropology and Education Quarterly, 24,* 256-268.

Heath, S. B. (1983). *Ways with words: Language, life, and work in communities and classrooms.* New York: Cambridge University Press.

Jacob, E. (1982). Combining ethnographic and quantitative approaches: Suggestions and examples from a study in Puerto Rico. In P. Gilmore and A. Glatthorn (Eds.), *Children in and out of school: Ethnography and education* (pp. 124-147). Washington, DC: Center for Applied Linguistics.

Kirk, J. & Miller, M. (1986). Reliability and validity in qualitative research. *Qualitative Research Methods Series #1.* Newbury Park, CA: Sage.

LeCompte, M. (1987). Bias in biography: Bias and subjectivity in ethnographic research. *Anthropology and Education Quarterly, 18,* 43-52.

Lieberman, A. (1996). Creating intentional learning communities. *Educational Leadership, 54* (3), 51-55.

Lieberman, A. & Miller, L. (1984). *Teachers, their world and their work: Implications for school improvement.* Alexandria, VA: Association for Supervision and Curriculum Development.

Lincoln, Y. S. & Guba, E. G. (1985). *Naturalistic inquiry.* Newbury Park, CA: Sage.

Lofland, J. & Lofland, L. (1984). *Analyzing social settings: A guide to qualitative observation and analysis.* (2nd ed.). Belmont, CA: Wadsworth.

Macrorie, K. (1980). *Searching writing.* Westport, CT: Heinemann-Boynton/Cook.

McCall, G. & Simmons, J. (Eds.). (1969). *Issues in participant observation: A text and reader.* Reading, MA: Addison-Wesley.

Miles, M., & Huberman, A. M. (1994). *Qualitative data analysis: An expanded sourcebook.* (2nd ed.). Beverly Hills, CA: Sage.

Mishler, E. G. (1979). Meaning in context: Is there any other kind? *Harvard Educational Review, 19,* 1-19.

Mishler, E. G. (1990). Validation in inquiry-guided research: The role of exemplars in narrative studies. *Harvard Educational Review, 60,* 415-442.

Mortensen, P. & Kirsch, G. E. (1996). *Ethics and representation in qualitative studies of literacy.* Urbana, IL: National Council of Teachers of English.

Murray, D. (1982). Write research to be read. In *Learning by teaching* (pp. 103-112). Westport, CT: Heinemann-Boynton/Cook.

Noblit, G. & Hare, R. (1988). Meta-ethnography: Synthesizing qualitative studies. *Qualitative Research Methods Series #11.* Newbury Park, CA: Sage.

North, S. (1987). *The making of knowledge in composition: Portrait of an emerging field.* Westport, CT: Heinemann-Boynton/Cook.

Polanyi, M. (1962). *Personal knowledge: Toward a post-critical philosophy.* Chicago, IL: University of Chicago Press.

Polanyi, M. and Prosch, H. (1975). *Meaning.* Chicago, IL: University of Chicago Press.

Perl, S. (1979). Research as discovery. Talk given as National Council of Teachers of English Most Promising Researcher awardee. San Francisco, CA.

Ruddick, J. & Hopkins, D. (1985). *Research as a basis for teaching: Readings from the work of Lawrence Stenhouse.* Westport, CT: Heinemann-Boynton/Cook.

Schön, D. (1983). *The reflective practitioner: How professionals think in action.* New York: Basic Books.

Shulman, L. (1986). Paradigms and research programs in the study of teaching: A contemporary perspective. In M. Wittrock (Ed.) *Handbook of Research on Teaching* (3rd ed., pp. 3-36). New York: Macmillan.

Shulman, L. (1987). Knowledge and teaching: Foundations of the new reform. *Harvard Educational Review, 57,* 1-22.

Sockett, H. (1987). Has Shulman got the strategy right? *Harvard Educational Review, 57,* 208-219.

Spradley, J. (1979). *The ethnographic interview.* New York: Holt, Rinehart and Winston.

Stringer, E. (1996). *Action research: A handbook for practitioners.* Thousand Oaks, CA: Sage.

Vygotsky, L. S. (1962). *Thought and language.* Cambridge, MA: MIT Press.

Vygotsky, L. S. (1978). *Mind in society: The development of higher psychological processes.* Cambridge, MA: MIT Press.

Wittrock, M. (Ed.) (1986). *Handbook of research on teaching.* (3rd ed.). American Educational Research Association. New York: Macmillan.

Wolcott, H. F. (1990). Writing up qualitative research. *Qualitative Research Methods Series #20.* Newbury Park, CA: Sage.

ABOUT TEACHER RESEARCH

The following are written specifically about teachers as researchers. They describe teacher research and discuss its effects. Some also include examples of teacher research articles.

Anderson, G. L. & Herr, K. (1999). The new paradigm wars: Is there room for rigorous practitioner knowledge in schools and universities? *Educational Researcher, 28* (5) 12-21, 40.

Asher, C. (1987). Developing a pedagogy for a teacher-researcher program. *English Education, 19*, 211-219.

Atwell, N. (1990). Wonderings to pursue: The writing teacher as researcher. In B. M. Power & R. Hubbard (Eds.), *Literacy in process,* (pp. 315-331). Westport, CT: Heinemann-Boynton/Cook.

Berthoff, A. (1981). *The making of meaning.* Westport, CT: Heinemann-Boynton/Cook.

Bissex, G. & Bullock, R. (1987). *Seeing for ourselves: Case study research by teachers of writing.* Westport, CT: Heinemann-Boynton/Cook.

Burton, F. R.(1986). Research currents: A teacher's conception of the action research process. *Language Arts 63*, 718-723.

Christian, S. (1995). School reform and teacher research. *Bread Loaf Rural Teacher Network Magazine.* Middlebury, VT: Bread Loaf Rural Teacher Network.

Cochran-Smith, M. & Lytle, S. L. (1993). *Inside/outside: Teacher research and knowledge.* New York: Teachers College Press.

Fleischer, C. (1995). *Composing teacher research: A prosaic history.* Albany, NY: State University of New York.

Fleischer, C. (1998). Advocating for change: A new education for new teachers. *English Education 30*, 78-100.

Freedman, S. W. with E. R. Simons & New Orleans M-CLASS teachers K. Alford, R. Galley, S. Herring, D. W. Smith, E. Valenti, & P. Ward. (1994). Teacher researchers together: Delving into the teacher research process. *The Quarterly of the National Writing Project & the Center for the Study of Writing and Literacy, 16* (4), 8-17.

Gerow, S. (1997). Teacher researchers in school-based collaborative teams: One approach to school reform. Unpublished doctoral dissertation. Fairfax County, VA: Institute for Educational Transformation, George Mason University.

Glaze, B. (1987). A teacher speaks out about research. *Plain talk about learning and writing across the curriculum* (pp. 87-99). Richmond, VA: Virginia Department of Education.

Goswami, D. & Stillman, P. (Eds.). (1987). *Reclaiming the classroom: Teacher research as an agency for change.* Westport, CT: Heinemann-Boynton/Cook.

Graves, D. (1984). *A researcher learns to write: Selected articles and monographs*. Westport, CT: Heinemann-Boynton/Cook.

Graves, D. (1981). Where have all the teachers gone? *Language Arts, 58*, 492-497.

Hollingsworth, S. (1994). *Teacher research and urban literacy education: Lessons and conversations in a feminist key*. New York: Teachers College Press.

Hubbard, R. (1994). "A little too little and a lot too much": The data collection and analysis blues. *Teacher Research: The Journal of Classroom Inquiry, 2* (1), 132-140.

Hubbard, R. & Power, B. M. (1993). *The art of classroom inquiry: A handbook for teacher researchers*. Westport, CT: Heinemann-Boynton/Cook.

Huberman, M. (1996). Moving mainstream: Taking a closer look at teacher research. *Language Arts, 73*, 124-140.

Johnson, R. (1993). Where can teacher research lead? One teacher's daydream. *Educational Leadership, 51* (2), 66-68.

Kutz, E. (1992). Preservice teachers as researchers: Developing practice and creating theory in the English classroom. *English Education, 24*, 67-76.

Lampert, M. (1985). How do teachers manage to teach? Perspectives on problems in practice. *Harvard Educational Review, 55* (2), 178-194.

McCarthy, L. P. & Fishman, S. M. (1991). Boundary conversations: Conflicting ways of knowing in philosophy and interdisciplinary research. *Research in the Teaching of English, 25*, 419-468.

Mohr, M. M. (1980). The teacher as researcher. *Virginia English Bulletin, 30* (2), 61-64.

Mohr, M. M. & MacLean, M. S. (1987). *Working together: A guide for teacher researchers*. Urbana, IL: National Council of Teachers of English.

Mohr, M. M. (1989). The summer of the run-on sentence. *Kentucky English Bulletin, 39* (1), 7-11.

Mohr, M. M. (1996). Wild dreams and sober cautions: The future of teacher research. In Z. Donoahue, M. A. Van Tassell, & L. Patterson (Eds.), *Research in the classroom: Talk, texts, and inquiry* (pp.117-123). Newark, DE: International Reading Association.

Mohr, M. M. with J. Grumbacher, C. Hauser, G. Portwood, and K. Willoughby. (1989). Teacher-researchers: Their voices, their continued stories. *The Quarterly of the National Writing Project and the Center for the Study of Writing, 11* (2), 4-7,19.

Miller, J. (1990). *Creating spaces and finding voices: Teachers collaborating for empowerment.* Albany, NY: State University of New York Press.

Newkirk, T. (Ed.). (1992). *Workshop 4: Teachers as researchers.* Westport, CT: Heinemann-Boynton/Cook.

Patterson, L., Santa, C., Short, K. G., & Smith, K. (1993). *Teachers are researchers: Reflection and action.* Newark, DE; International Reading Association.

Pine, N. (1992). Three personal theories that suggest models for teacher research. *Teachers College Record 93*, 656-671.

Power, B. M. (1996). *Taking note: Improving your observational notetaking.* York, ME: Stenhouse.

Shannon, P. (1996). Teachers researching during troubling times. *Teacher Research: The Journal of Classroom Inquiry, 4* (1), 12-23.

Stock, P. L. (1995). *The dialogic curriculum: Teaching and learning in a multicultural society.* Westport, CT: Heinemann-Boynton/Cook.

Strickland, D. (1986). The teacher as researcher: Toward the extended professional. *Language Arts, 65*, 754-779.

Swaim, M. S. & Swaim, S. C. (1999). *Teacher time.* Arlington, VA: Redbud Books.

Wells, G., Bernard, L., Gianotti, M. A., Keating, C., Konjevic, C., Kowal, M., Maher, A., Mayer, C., Moscoe, T., Orzechowska, E., Smieja, A., & Swartz, L. (1994). *Changing schools from within: Creating communities of inquiry.* Toronto, Canada: OISE Press.

Zeni, J. (Ed.). (In press). *Ethical issues in practitioner inquiry.* New York: Teachers College Press.

WORKS BY TEACHER-RESEARCHERS

In addition to the articles in Part III, we want to suggest further reading of teacher research to show some of the history, depth, and richness of the field.

Alaska Teacher Researchers. (1991). *The far vision, the close look: A collection of writings by Alaska teacher researchers.* Juneau, AK: Alaska State Writing Consortium.

Anderson, G. L., Herr, K., & Nihlen, A. S. (1994). *Studying your own school: An educator's guide to qualitative practitioner research.* Thousand Oaks, CA: Corwin Press.

Atwell, N. (1987). *In the middle: Writing, reading, and learning with adolescents.* Westport, CT: Heinemann-Boynton/Cook.

Ballenger, C. (1992). Because you like us: The language of control. *Harvard Educational Review, 62,* 199-208.

Banford, H., Berkman, M., Chin, C., Cziko, C., Fecho, B., Jumpp, D., Miller, C., & Resnick, M. (1996). *Cityscapes: Eight views from the urban classroom.* Berkeley, CA: National Writing Project.

Bay Area Writing Project. (1990). *Research in writing: Working papers of teacher researchers.* Berkeley, CA: National Writing Project.

Burton, J. & Agor, B. (Eds.). (1994). Teacher research: A special issue. *TESOL Journal, 4.*

Carmichael, C. (1998). Mi voz suena asi (My voice sounds like this): Generative themes in second grade. *The Quarterly of the National Writing Project, 20* (4), 13-20.

Christian, S. (1997). *Exchanging lives.* Urbana, IL; National Council of Teachers of English.

Clawson, S. (1993). The impact of collaborative writing on the individual. *Teaching and Change, 1,* 55-69.

Cone, J. (1994). Appearing acts: Creating readers in a high school English class. *Harvard Educational Review, 64,* 450-473.

Crislip, A. & Mohr, M. M. (1994). Seniors' choice: To read deeply. *Reading in Virginia, 19,* 1-6.

Davala, V. (1987). Respecting opinions: Learning logs in middle school English. In T. Fulwiler (Ed.), *The Journal Book* (pp. 179-186). Westport, CT: Heinemann-Boynton/Cook.

Deardoff, R. (1996). Remaining a nonparticipant in a cooperative group setting. *Teaching and Change, 3,* 378-394.

Donoahue, Z., Van Tassell, M.A., & Patterson, L. (1996). *Research in the classroom: Talk, texts, and inquiry.* Newark, DE: International Reading Association.

Ellison, V. L. (1996). Having students select spelling words. *Teaching and Change, 4,* 77-89.

Franklin, J. (1997). The mitten is not a character: Dramatization in one kindergarten classroom. *Teacher Research: The Journal of Classroom Inquiry, 5* (1), 83-91.

Gallas, K. (1994). *The languages of learning.* New York: Teachers College Press.

Gardner, S. (1996). Giving social studies students greater decision-making autonomy. *Teaching and Change, 4,* 20-34.

Gautreux, W. (1995). Beginning students' perceptions: What is it like to learn French? *Teacher Research: The Journal of Classroom Inquiry, 3* (1), 36-54.

Giacobbe, M. E. (1981). Kids can write the first week of school. *Learning, 10* (2), 132-133.

Glaze, B. (1987). It's not just the writing. In T. Fulwiler (Ed.), *The Journal Book* (pp. 227-238). Westport, CT: Heinemann-Boynton/Cook.

Gray, L. (1987). "I think it has something to do with our minds": Using synectics to learn about history. In M. M. Mohr & M. S. MacLean, *Working together: A guide for teacher-researchers* (pp. 67-77). Urbana, IL: National Council of Teachers of English.

Grossman, A. (1987). What happens when Mickey writes? Reading between the lines. In M. M. Mohr & M. S. MacLean, *Working together: A guide for teacher-researchers* (pp. 77-94). Urbana, IL: National Council of Teachers of English.

Grumbacher, J. (1987). Writing to learn in physics. In T. Fulwiler (Ed.), *The Journal Book* (pp. 323-329). Westport, CT: Heinemann-Boynton/Cook.

Hankins, K. H. (1998). Cacophony to symphony: Memoirs in teacher research. *Harvard Educational Review 68,* 80-95.

Hauser, C. (1986). The writer's inside story. *Language Arts, 63,* 153-159.

Hermann, K., Carstarphen, N., & Coolidge, J. O. (1997). Meeting the challenges of diversity and conflict: The immigrant student experience. *Teaching and Change, 4,* 206-226.

Johnson, R. W. (1991). Using writing to learn with films. *Science Scope, 15* (2), 27-29.

MacLean, M. S. (1983). Voices within: The audience speaks. *English Journal, 72* (7), 62-66.

McGuire, B. S. (1990). Where does the teacher intervene with under-achieving writers? *English Journal, 79* (2), 14-21.

Milz, V. (1985). First graders' uses for writing. In A. Jaggar & M. T. Smith-Burke (Eds.), *Observing the language learner* (pp. 173-189). Newark, DE: International Reading Association.

Mohr, M. M. (1984). *Revision: The rhythm of meaning.* Westport, CT: Heinemann-Boynton/Cook.

Nelson, M. W. (1991). *At the point of need: Teaching basic and ESL writers.* Westport, CT: Heinemann-Boynton/Cook.

Northern Nevada Writing Project Teacher-Researcher Group. (1996). *Team teaching.* York, ME: Stenhouse.

O'Keefe, V. (1995). *Speaking to think, thinking to speak: The importance of talk in the learning process.* Westport, CT: Heinemann-Boynton/Cook.

Ozvold, L. A. (1996). Does teacher demeanor affect the behavior of students? *Teaching and Change, 3,* 159-172.

Paley, V. G. (1992). *You can't say you can't play.* Cambridge, MA: The Harvard University Press.

Parker, E. L. (1993). What do I teach next? Learning from the children. *Reading in Virginia, 18,* 4-7.

Peitzman, F. (Ed.). (1990). *The power of context: Studies by teacher-researchers.* (Vol. 2). Los Angeles, CA: UCLA Center for Academic Interinstitutional Programs, Graduate School of Education.

Portwood, G. (1990). It gives you the experience of what you think. In J. L. Collins (Ed.), *Vital signs I: Bringing together reading and writing* (pp. 96-109). Westport, CT: Heinemann- Boynton/Cook.

Rogers, C. (1987). A teacher-researcher writes about learning. In M. M. Mohr & M. S. MacLean, *Working together: A guide for teacher-researchers* (pp. 94-102). Urbana, IL: National Council of Teachers of English.

Sanford, B. (1987). Discovering revision. In M. M. Mohr & M. S. MacLean, *Working together: A guide for teacher-researchers* (pp. 102-111). Urbana, IL: National Council of Teachers of English.

Schaafsma, D., Tendero, A., & Tendero, J. (1999). Making it real: Girls' stories, social change, and moral struggle. *English Journal, 88* (5), 28-37.

Schulman, M. (1987). Reading for meaning: Trying to get past first basal. In M. M. Mohr & M. S. MacLean, *Working together: A guide for teacher-researchers* (pp. 111-120). Urbana, IL: National Council of Teachers of English.

Schwartz, J. (1990). On the move in Pittsburgh: When students and teacher share research. In D. Daiker & M. Morenberg (Eds.), *The writing teacher as researcher: Essays in the theory and practice of class-based research* (pp. 153-166). Westport, CT: Heinemann-Boynton/Cook.

Sevcik, A., Robbins, B., & Leonard, A. (1997). The deep structure of obscene language. *Journal of Curriculum Studies, 4,* 455-470.

Shafer, L. (1995). Anecdotal record keeping: Learning from Rosa, Ahmed, and Zhou. *Journal* (Greater Washington Reading Council)*, 19,* 16-23.

Shaffner, A. (1997). Rubrics in middle school: Rewarding or rueful. *Teaching and Change, 4.* 258-283.

Shaughnessy, M. (1977). *Errors and expectations: A guide for the teacher of basic writing.* New York: Oxford.

Spence, L. (1986). Gaining control through commentary. *English Journal, 75,* (3) 58-62.

Tendero, J. (1998). Worth waiting for: Girls writing for their lives in the Bronx. *Teacher Research: The Journal of Classroom Inquiry, 5* (2), 10-25.

Whitin, P. (1996). Exploring visual response to literature. *Research in the Teaching of English, 30,* 114-140.

Wilhelm, J. D. (1997). *"You gotta be the book": Teaching engaged and reflective reading with adolescents.* New York: Teachers College Press.

Womble, G. (1984). Process and processor. *English Journal, 73* (1), 34-37.

Wotring, A. M., & Tierney, R. (1981). *Two studies of writing in high school science.* Berkeley, CA: National Writing Project.